Beyond the Belt and Road: China's Expansion
Dr. Antonio Graceffo

Beyond the Belt and Road: China's Global Economic Expansion
by Antonio Graceffo
Published by Mary Labita Press, Long Island, New York
© 2019 Antonio Graceffo

For permissions contact: antonio_graceffo@hotmail.com
ISBN-13: 978-0-9998305-7-4

Contents

Foreword

China's US$1 trillion global infrastructure connectivity project, launched in 2013 and now involving more than 100 nations and organizations, [1] the Belt and Road Initiative (BRI) has become the backbone of Chinese foreign policy and the engine driving China's economic and political expansion abroad. The BRI truly went global when Chinese Foreign Minister Wang Yi, at a meeting in Chile, invited Latin America and the Caribbean to join. Plans have since been released for a "Polar Silk Road" which will provide China with a faster sea route to Europe, while giving Beijing an opportunity to exploit oil and gas reserves beneath the Arctic seabed. At present, the US, Canada, Japan, and India are the only major economies which have not joined. [2]

Concerns have been raised by both participating and abstaining countries, most notably the US. They cite such fears as mounting debts of countries which receive BRI-related loans, and the PRC's ever-increasing political influence in certain countries. A number of sovereignty issues have arisen in both BRI participant countries and their neighbors. PRC President Xi Jinping, at an economic forum held on Hainan Island, addressed these concerns by stating that the BRI "was not a Chinese 'conspiracy'" nor China's Marshall Plan. It was a new platform for international cooperation to benefit peoples along the routes. [3] He went on to say that the BRI offered the world a departure from Cold War rhetoric, and that China was a reliable friend and trading partner, while the US was not. [4]

In addition to asking if the BRI is good for the world, observers have also questioned whether China can actually fund and complete the largest project ever undertaken by any nation in human history.

Several contradictions surround the BRI. One is that Beijing, in order to fund the BRI, encourages outbound investment by Chinese firms, but on the other hand employs strict capital controls which hamper the flow of money out of the country. Another apparent contradiction is that one of the benefits of the BRI is supposed to be the exchange of information, yet censorship and media crackdowns in China have become increasingly more severe. [5] Beijing says that the BRI will provide greater connectivity for participating countries-so long as that connectivity is not through

Gmail, WhatsApp, Facebook, Twitter, or other blocked media such as such as *New York Times* . Perhaps with greater connectivity, Beijing was referring to a plan to cover the BRI, and then the entire world, with its BeiDou navigation system, which will eventually operate through 35 satellites, with 300 transponders, covering 30 countries. [6] This, of course, raises other concerns, Washington in particular seeing this as a potential security threat.

As a China economist, people often ask me how China's Belt and Road Initiative is going. I answer: "Extremely well." So, they ask: "How much money has it made?"

My answer is: "No one knows."

"How many projects have they undertaken?"

"No one knows."

"What percentage of the projects have been successful?"

"No one knows."

"How many more projects will be undertaken before the plan finishes?"

"No one knows."

"What will be the total value of Belt and Road projects?

"No one knows."

"When will it be completed?"

"No one knows?"

"Will it be a financial success?"

"We will never know."

There are other legitimate questions that people ask me, the answers to which are generally "no one knows." And the reason no one knows is that, as determined as China is to make the BRI the backbone of its foreign policy and outward economic expansion, Beijing has never properly defined the initiative nor listed the projects it includes. Critics in Europe have said that the BRI is actually a series of bilateral agreements rather than a single project . [7] Moreover, Beijing has never set a time frame in which the BRI needs to be completed. *The Diplomat* reported that the projects now included in the BRI are actually just a haphazard collection of projects, some of which are quite old projects. [8] A private Chinese company is trying to buy a Silicon Valley firm, and the government has claimed that this is part of the digital aspect of the BRI. Other activities which have been arbitrarily counted as successful BRI projects include: "establishing a new intergovernmental commission with Russia, financing a new road project in Tajikistan, signing an FTA with

3

Georgia, establishing a currency swap with Switzerland, and holding an annual beauty pageant in Sanya. " [9]

Alexander Gabuev has stated that, "The 'Belt and Road' concept has become so inflated, that it's no longer helpful to understanding anything about China's relationship with the outside world." [10] Having no fixed set of projects means that successful projects will be included in the BRI, even if they lay outside of the scope of the Belt and Road or were begun before the initiative's 2013 inauguration. Similarly, failed projects might be described as having never been part of the BRI. In fact, there need not be any failed projects; there is no time limit, so failed projects could be labelled as "in progress" indefinitely. Additionally, it is extremely unlikely that at some point in the future, Beijing will release a comprehensive list of projects, how much they cost, and how much revenue they generated. Therefore we will never know if the initiative was an economic success.

The reason I say that the BRI is doing extremely well is because, from both soft-power and strategic perspectives, all of this economic activity passing through developing countries has been good for China's clout, and plays well into the government narrative of China "restoring its rightful position" as a world leader.

While more or less presenting the BRI as a reaction to US hegemony, China has also admonished the US for not joining, suggesting that the US will somehow lose trade opportunities and be left behind, alone in the dust, while the rest of the world wisely signs up and moves on. The question of whether the US should or should not join the BRI is almost moot in that there is no clear definition of what it means to be part of the BRI. The initiative is not an organization like ASEAN or the EU. It is not even a free trade agreement, but rather a loosely defined set of projects which can sometimes be linked by lines on a map. Those who feel the US should join emphasize the projected GDP gains it would generate. But it is far from clear what Americans will miss out on; aside from the fact that most of the economic benefits generated by the BRI will go to Chinese companies, there has never been any promise that gains will be equally distributed among participating countries. The BRI is not even a blanket agreement, like the defunct Trans-Pacific Partnership. It is a series of bilateral agreements between China and other nations. Ostensibly, the gains generated will be split between China and the host countries. This means that if the US were to join, the projected GDP figures would bear no relation to any benefits the US might enjoy. The US would receive some extra GDP from BRI projects in the US, while China takes the rest. The US would not only be free to continue trading with member nations, but also to utilize the infrastructure and transportation lines built along the route, the only difference   being that the US would not be increasing its debt or its investment deficit with China. [11]

Through the BRI, China claims to be liberating the world from US domination. However, that liberation comes with crippling debts and a loss of sovereignty. Whether the BRI is good or bad, successful or unsuccessful, is almost academic. The initiative is going ahead. It currently comprises six global corridors, which may or may not include a Polar Silk Road through the Arctic. It looks nothing like The Silk Road Economic Belt and the 21st-century Maritime Silk Road that Xi unveiled in 2013. By 2020 or 2035, it will most likely look different again.

In 2035, regardless of whether BRI successes outnumbers failures, "the increase in China's external trade, military power, overseas investment and its imprint on various fields of global governance is undeniable." [12] This is coupled with, or because of a digitalized People's Liberation Army (PLA), the globalization of Chinese companies, "and a new generation of confident and sophisticated Chinese officials, officers and businesspeople." [13]

The question of whether a country should or should not join the BRI, or China's implied threats that countries which do not take part in the initiative will be left out of global trade, deserves very little discussion. The BRI is not an organization; membership does not grant a country access to certain markets or reduced import tariffs. For a country to participate in the initiative simply means allowing BRI projects to proceed within its borders. And as nearly any project undertaken by a Chinese company could be counted as part of the BRI, it is possible that some countries are participating without even knowing it. As one China journalist friend of this writer has said, "If you exist, you are part of the BRI."

Despite its unquantifiable nature and lack of transparency, the BRI is a vitally important concept which may actually change the global order, and which has undoubtedly already altered the future of the global economy. Ordinary citizens, academics, business people, and politicians around the world stand to benefit if they better understand the BRI.

This book will begin with a brief overview of the initiative, then proceed with chapters devoted to particular parts of the world. The final chapter will be an end-of-2018 status report, attempting to answer the question: How is the BRI doing up?

Even if you are not a China economist, this information is important to you, because, "if you exist, you are part of the BRI."

Chapter 1: The Belt and Road in 2019

"The world needs China, as all humans are living in a community with a shared future ... That creates broad strategic room for our efforts to uphold peace and development and gain an advantage." [1] — Communist Party "manifesto" on China's role in the world

This is how China sees its mission in creating the Belt and Road Initiative. The BRI now consists of six corridors: the China-Mongolia-Russia Economic Corridor; the New Eurasian Land Bridge; the China-Central and West Asia Economic Corridor; the China-Indochina Peninsula Economic Corridor; the China-Pakistan Economic Corridor (CPEC); and the Bangladesh-China-India-Myanmar Economic Corridor. [2] The 65 countries connected through the BRI account of approximately 30% of the world's GDP, 40% of global trade, and 62% of the world's population. [3]

Beijing's message to other countries sounds like something between an invitation and a threat. On occasion, PRC President Xi Jinping has announced that, via the BRI, he hoped to create " a big family of harmonious coexistence." [4] At the Belt and Road Forum in Beijing in May 2017, China was presenting the world with an alternative world order, but it was also implied that those countries who did not join would come to regret their decision. [5]

The addition in 2017 of Xi's political ideology, "Xi Jinping Thought on Socialism with Chinese Characteristics for a New Era," [6] to China's constitution was the first amendment of this kind since Mao. [7] Specifically added to the constitution was the phrase, "pursue the Belt and Road Initiative." [8] Now that Xi's words are part of the constitution, questioning or challenging him or his policies is impossible, as doing so would be tantamount to questioning the party. [9] In 2018, China removed the term limits that would otherwise restrict Xi to holding the presidency for no more than ten years. Theoretically, he could remain in power for the rest of his life. [10] This also suggests the BRI could be infinitely extended.

The PRC government derives much of its domestic legitimacy through continued economic growth. A successful BRI will help to keep the China's economy growing by soaking up excess industrial capacity, creating employment, and increasing exports. [11] Since Xi Jinping Thought and the BRI have been made part of the PRC's constitution, it will be very difficult for the Chinese public to evaluate its success or failure, since that would be seen as criticism. In the rest of the world, however, and possibly in private Chinese hearts, the success or failure of the Xi era will be determined by the BRI. [12]

China's economic engagement with countries along the BRI includes loans, investment, trade, and aid. While China is one of the world's largest sources of outbound direct investment, the overseas construction projects that are part of the BRI, should not be confused with investment. Overseas investment brings ownership. Overseas construction does not bring ownership, but does bring in money. Since 2005, China has signed construction projects worth at least US$100 million each in nearly 60 countries. The largest sector for Chinese overseas construction is transportation. [13] Building transportation infrastructure for developing countries is often masked as aid, as in the case of Cambodia, where 70% of all roads and bridges were built by China, financed through loans totaling about US$2 billion. [14]

BRI-related news reports often include statements such as Xi's pledge to provide US$100 billion to the project and his vow to fight poverty in the recipient countries. [15] One reason why the total value of the BRI is hard to calculate is because it is unclear if this type of aid should be counted, or if such promises of aid are actually kept. Further, when the West dubs a transfer as aid, it often takes the shape of a grant. When it comes from China, however, it generally takes the form of an interest-bearing loan, which drives the recipient country deeper into debt.

In addition to earning money through financing infrastructure development and then earning money from carrying out the actual construction, and selling raw materials to recipient countries, Chinese companies benefit in other ways. Jörg Wuttke, former president of the EU Chamber of Commerce in China said Chinese companies are using the BRI as an excuse to funnel money out of China, bypassing tight capital flight regulations. [16] All but one of the EU ambassadors to Beijing signed a document in which they criticized the BRI for hampering free trade and securing advantages for Chinese companies. One example would be Gwadar Port in Pakistan, a country very much in need of jobs; roughly 50% of the port's 1,000 employees are Chinese. [17] According to research by the Center for Strategic and International Studies, of companies involved in the BRI projects they have documented, 89% are Chinese, 7.6% are local, and 3.4% are from other countries. [18]

When China lends money, attached conditions typically stipulate that project contracts be given to Chinese companies and at least 50% of the materials, equipment, technology, or services to be sourced from the PRC. For example, loans extended by China's Exim Bank require that recipients use such funds to purchase Chinese products and services, and use Chinese labor and raw materials. [19] BRI-linked loans, such as those granted to Pakistan, carry interest rates as high as 8%, whereas international interest rates for similar projects would be about 1.6%. [20]

Other benefits China derives from the BRI, include: increasing exports; supporting "national champion" companies; credit; infrastructure; and trade agreements. PRC state-owned enterprises (SOEs) gain economies of scale, as well as government subsidies, and this has helped transform some of them into the largest firms in the world. The 2017 Fortune Global 500 included 107 Chinese firms, of which 75 were state-owned. [21] Infrastructure projects help boost China's exports in the form of construction-related materials. PRC exports to Pakistan, one of the most important countries in the BRI, increased 77% between 2012 and 2015. [22]

China also derives political and strategic advantages. Recipient countries such as Pakistan and former Soviet states in Central Asia have moved closer to China. Other countries, like the Philippines and Cambodia have reevaluated their military or diplomatic ties with the United States after receiving massive loans from China. [23]

When EU ambassadors to Beijing complained about the BRI's lack of transparency, they said that "the project flouts international transparency norms and is aimed at furthering Chinese interests." [24] China's state-run media has reported that a new court will be established to address legal concerns related to the BRI. This raises other questions, however. For example, why would these disputes not simply be handled by established international courts or the WTO? [25] It seems that China wants to control the very courts where disputes about the activities of PRC companies, carrying out a PRC initiative, are addressed.

During a 2018 visit to Beijing, UK Prime Minister Theresa May signed US $12.68 billion of deals with China, but declined to sign an MOU endorsing BRI trade strategy. Had she signed, the UK would have been the first Western country to do so. [26] Her refusal is consistent with a shift in the EU's attitude toward the BRI. European leaders once saw China as a counterbalance to US President Donald J. Trump, whom they distrust; more recently, however, many have become concerned that China may pose a threat to the EU. The repeal of PRC presidential term limits means that Xi's policies could theoretically continue, unabated for the next 30 years. This is disturbing, given that China appears to be moving away from openness to a more authoritarian society. Xi also seems to be playing a game of divide and conquer within the EU by trying to buy the support of poorer members states in Eastern Europe. Additionally, Beijing has formed the "16+1" group, which includes 11 EU member states. [27]

European leaders are also "wary of how China has become more aggressive militarily, in espionage, and in its investment strategy abroad." [28] Germany's foreign minister warned that the BRI is intended to expand China's power. Chinese acquisitions in Germany are beginning to raise suspicions, too. Chinese companies purchased a German machine-tool and robotics company, KUKA, then tried to purchase semiconductor company Aixtron. The latter bid was blocked after Washington raised security concerns. A small Chinese company also purchased 10% of German car manufacturer Daimler, raising the question of where the money actually came from. Germany and France have been pushing the European Commission to draft more strenuous screening laws, to block business acquisitions which could be harmful to the EU. [29]

The US, in addition to not joining the BRI, has cracked down on Chinese investment in the US, halting Chinese acquisition of technology firms among others. The US government's Committee on Foreign Investment in the US now pays particular attention to PRC investment, thereby slowing China's expansion into North America. [30]

In Southeast Asia, local workers are raising their own objections to the BRI. Chinese employers across Southeast Asia have been known to break local employment norms, refuse to recognize unions, and even to skirt or outright violate laws regarding worker rights. In Indonesia and other countries, these issues have resulted in large scale protests against Chinese employers. The Chinese have used these incidents to justify importing laborers from China, further exasperating local people who see their jobs going to Chinese. [31]

Many of the countries hosting BRI projects have complained that after an initial whirlwind of activity, projects often stall. One railway project in Indonesia, for instance, is seriously behind schedule and costs are escalating. Construction of what would be Indonesia's first high-speed railway began in 2016, but to date, the project is only 10% complete, although operations were due to start next year. Problems acquiring land and permits raised the price tag from US$5.5 billion to US$6 billion. Other delays are a result of CDB, which is handing 75% of the financing, refusing to disburse funds. This all raises questions about the future financial health of the Indonesian firms involved, and how, given the increased cost and the delay, the Indonesian government can repay the loans. [32]

Similar problems have arisen in Kazakhstan and Bangladesh. [33] There are complaints of loss of sovereignty in Sri Lanka, the Maldives, and Pakistan. India, which is not a member of the BRI, complains that Chinese projects in Pakistan threaten India. One example would be projects in the Gilgit-Baltistan, part of the disputed territory of Kashmir . [34]

Whether or not the BRI will benefit the world is a matter of opinion, but it seems that the initiative will not promote either democracy or improved governance in recipient countries. When Western governments grant aid, they often insist on internal governance standards, and push for improved human rights or democracy. Aid from the PRC, particularly projects associated with the BRI, comes with no such requirements. Consequently, the BRI has been well-received in certain low-income countries with poor human rights and democracy records. [35] Cambodian Prime Minister Hun Sen has stated publicly that he prefers Chinese aid to Western aid because the West tried to meddle in Cambodia's internal affairs. [36] US Treasury Secretary Steven Mnuchin has expressed his concern about China's BRI-related lending. [37] China's indiscriminate granting of loans has raised a number of questions in Washington and other Western capitals, first about the danger of overburdening poor countries with more debt; and second, for undermining Western efforts to improve democracy and human rights in those countries.

Some recipient countries are also beginning to push back, at least a little. Nepal's government has canceled a deal with China Gezhouba Group, an SOE, to build the Budhi Gandaki Hydroelectric Project. The ambiguity of benefits and consideration given to host countries has been a cause for cancellations. [38] For similar reasons, Pakistan has canceled at least one major Chinese project. The terms of the Gwadar Port project are such that 91% of the revenue will go to China for the next 40 years. Such onerous financing terms prompted Pakistan to cancel the US$14 billion Diamer-Bhasha Dam project, which was part of CPEC. [39]

Western observers have wondered if it is even possible for China to provide the US$1 trillion needed to complete all of the project now identified as being part of the BRI. A report by the American Enterprise Institute stated that, "the extreme dollar figures some associate with Belt and Road are currently unreasonable." [40] Li Ruogu, former president of

China's Exim Bank, has said that most of the countries along the BRI cannot repay their loans, with many having already reached liability and debt ratios of 35% and 126%, well above the standard warning levels of 20% and 100% respectively. [41] If these countries cannot repay their loans, China could eventually run out of money. As it is, China may already be finding it hard to finance the initiative. Wang Yiming, deputy head of the Development Research Center of China's State Council, said that, in spite of funding from the Asian Infrastructure Investment Bank, New Development Bank, CDB, the Exim Bank of China, and the Silk Road Fund, a tremendous funding gap of US$500 billion per year still exists. [42]

To close the funding gap, Beijing has called for greater private-sector participation, but private companies need to earn profits and many BRI investments look risky. First off, many of the debtor countries pose a credit risk. Next, many of the projects, even in the best-case scenario, are likely to show low profitability. [43] One reason for this low profitability is because some projects actually serve strategic, rather than financial, goals. One example would be CPEC, the main purpose of which is linking China with the Pakistani port of Gwadar, so oil can be transported to China. This will help PRC tankers avoid the Strait of Malacca, which is patrolled by foreign navies. [44] Gwadar Port is so important strategically that Beijing would never risk its successful completion simply to earn a profit. This is fine for SOEs guided by the central government, but will not attract investment from the private sector.

Chapter 2: Southeast Asia

The Association of Southeast Asian Nations (ASEAN) is a regional economic cooperation grouping of ten countries: Indonesia, Malaysia, the Philippines, Singapore, Thailand, Brunei, Cambodia, Laos, Burma (Myanmar), and Vietnam.

US withdrawal from the TPP

Many economists believe that US President Donald J. Trump's decision to remove the US from the Trans-Pacific Partnership (TPP) created opportunities for China in Southeast Asia. However, this opinion ignores several key points. The TPP never actually existed, so the US pulling out could not have changed anything. The US is heavily engaged with Southeast Asia, and US trade within the region has not decreased as a result of the decision to disengage from TPP. The US already runs trade deficits with most ASEAN countries, and the TPP would not have dramatically increased US imports from ASEAN as ASEAN products are already cheap for Americans and the current duties are low. Similarly, decreasing duties on US exports to ASEAN would most likely not have had much impact on US exports as US products are generally higher-end products which, even duty-free, would be expensive for the great many ASEAN residents who may earn as little as 2% of what the average American earns. For example, the average per capita GDP of Cambodia is below US$1,400 per year compared with US$56,000 per year in the US. The US abandoning the TPP does not represent a reduction in US engagement with ASEAN. It is simply that the US prefers to maintain bilateral trade relations rather than engage in multinational trade agreements.

Another point disproving this idea is that China is already heavily involved economically with ASEAN, meaning US withdrawal does not create any new opportunities for China. China is the largest trading partner of ASEAN. By 2015, total trade between China and ASEAN had reached US$471 billion. [1] In the first half of 2017, China invested US$4.8 billion in ASEAN. [2]

Although China is not a member of ASEAN, it is a member of ASEAN Plus Three, which also includes Japan and South Korea. The economies of ASEAN and China are also linked through a large number of China-led agreements and institutions such as the Regional Comprehensive Economic Partnership (RCEP), the ASEAN-China Free Trade Area (ACFTA), Asian Infrastructure Investment Bank (AIIB), China-ASEAN Investment Cooperation Fund (CAF), New Development Bank (NDB), Free Trade Area of the Asia-Pacific (FTAAP), Asia-Pacific Economic Cooperation (APEC), ASEAN-PRC Comprehensive Economic Cooperation Agreement, and the Asia-Pacific Trade Agreement. China also has bilateral free trade agreements with Thailand and Singapore. Clearly, China is already deeply involved in Southeast Asian economies, and these various trade groupings and financial institutions will be investing in BRI projects.

Sovereignty over the South China Sea is most politically sensitive issue associated with the ASEAN component of BRI. In the past, China has taken a more aggressive stance in asserting its claim over the region. However, more recently, Beijing has been using the BRI as a bargaining chip. When Singapore said it would uphold the International Court of Justice's ruling against China's South China Sea sovereignty claims, China decided that it might be better to reroute part of the BRI transportation links to a port in the Malaysian peninsula rather than continuing on to the port of Singapore. [1] In Malaysia, China is investing US$1.9 billion in the Melaka Gateway port, on the Strait of Malacca and the Kuantan port on the South China Sea. [2] China also considers Indonesia an integral component of BRI and has consequently invested heavily in the country. Indonesia's President Joko Widodo has publicly stated that the South China Sea claims are so complicated that he does not want to get involved. [3] Similarly, even the Philippines and Malaysia have quieted their disputes with China regarding sea sovereignty. As ASEAN countries become more dependent on BRI funds, they lose their ability to resist China. [4]

China is the largest trading partner of ASEAN, a nd over the last decade, trade between China and ASEAN has more than tripled. Chinese foreign direct investment (FDI) in ASEAN hit US$8.2 billion in 2015. [5] China is also among the top five trading partners of each ASEAN member taken individually. [6]

Some notable Chinese automotive investment projects in ASEAN include the joint venture between Shanghai Automotive Industry Corporation (China), General Motors (USA), and Wuling Automotive Company (China) that began constructing a US$700 million automobile plant in Indonesia in 2005. [7] In addition, Beijing Auto International Cooperation set up a plant in Malaysia and Zhongce Rubber opened a tire plant in Pattaya, Thailand. Energy infrastructure projects in the region are being carried out by PRC companies such as Power Construction Company, Hubei Electric Engineering, China National Heavy Machinery Corporation, China International Water and Electric, China National Electric Engineering, China Investment Corporation, and Energy China. In telecommunications, Huawei and ZTE from China are among the region's top players. [8]

The economic relationship between China and ASEAN is expected to continue to grow. At the China-ASEAN Summit held in Burma, PRC Premier Li Keqiang dubbed the next ten years a "diamond decade" for China-ASEAN relations. [9]

ASEAN economies facing Chinese investment
When analyzing international trade, ASEAN is often compared to the EU, but the similarities are quite superficial. While both represent a collection of member countries, ASEAN is an international organization. The EU, however, is a supranational organization, effectively moving towards having the member states under a single government. There is an EU commissioner of trade, an EU Court of Justice, and a common currency. In contrast, ASEAN represents ten separate economies, with ten separate currencies, and almost no unified ruling bodies. " ASEAN remains a very weak economic entity." [10]

The economies of ASEAN and China are also linked through the Chinese-led RCEP, and the ASEAN Plus Six, which includes Australia, New Zealand, and India. China has created, or participates in, a number of other transnational institutions that aim to facilitate trade and investment in ASEAN, such as ACFTA, which removed 90% of tariffs when trading with China when it was signed in 2010. This represented the first trade agreement between ASEAN and an outside party. Covering a population of 1.9 billion people, ACFTA is the largest free trade area in the world. [11]

ASEAN has a combined population of more than 639 million and a combined GDP of US$2.76 trillion. As a block, it is a significant economy. When the countries are examined individually, disparities become apparent. Indonesia is the largest country by both population (an estimated 269 million) and GDP (just over US$1 trillion). Thailand, has the fourth largest population, 68.9 million, but the second largest GDP, US$406 billion. [12] Some ASEAN members have small but wealthy populations. In 2017, the per capita GDP of Singapore's roughly 5.6 million inhabitants was US$57,700 USD, whilst Brunei's 428,000 residents were earning about half that. For other ASEAN countries, GDP per capita figures varied from US$9,800 in Malaysia to US$3,800 (Indonesia) and just US$1,390 in Cambodia. [13]

PRC trade and investment is important throughout the grouping, but Cambodia, Laos, Burma (Myanmar), and Vietnam – the least developed economies in ASEAN – are highly dependent on trade with China. The six more developed economies, however, enjoy a much more diversified trade base. [14]

China-ASEAN economic interaction
Economic interaction between China and ASEAN is facilitated by geographical and cultural proximity. Another commonality is rapid GDP growth. From 2005 to 2014, ASEAN's GDP grew by an average of 5%, while China's grew at an average of 8%. To put this growth in perspective, during the same period, Japan, a major trading partner of both, grew at an average rate of only 0.4%. [15]

ASEAN's dynamic growth comes largely from the concept of Regional Value Chains (RVCs) whereby the various member states have different comparative advantages and through division of labor are able to achieve a total productivity which is more than the sum of its parts. [16]

ASEAN enjoys an advantage in terms of labor costs, as salaries tend to be much lower in ASEAN, particularly in Cambodia, Laos, Myanmar (Burma), and Vietnam (the so-called "CLMV" countries) than in China.

Consequently, Chinese companies can shift labor intensive production work from China to ASEAN. [17] In addition, advanced manufacturing can be done in the wealthier ASEAN countries. Therefore, electronics, car parts, and components all feature in RVCs between China and the more developed ASEAN countries of Singapore, Malaysia, and Thailand. Lower-end manufacturing can be done in the less developed countries. Thus, Chinese companies manufacture clothing and textiles in CLMV. [18]

As both a manufacturing hub and an important source of capital, China has the potential to buoy the ASEAN economies, but also to create structural imbalances that damage the region in the long run. Chinese investment and the jobs it creates are welcome in the region, but the jobs come with a price. Local economies can become too dependent on China. Since ACFTA took effect in 2010, ASEAN has run a trade deficit with China. Apart from Thailand and Malaysia, all ASEAN countries consistently run a trade deficit with China. [19]

China represents one of the largest FDI sources for some ASEAN countries, yet the total volume of Chinese FDI into ASEAN is small, accounting for only 2.3% of the total. FDI compared to trade is also extremely small at only 10.7%. [20] Additionally, China – unlike the US – runs a trade surplus with most of ASEAN. Some suggest that increasing their trade surplus is one of Beijing's motives for establishing so many free trade agreements with ASEAN.

China-ASEAN trade agreements

China has created a myriad of trade agreements and institutions to facilitate trade, investment, and lending to the ASEAN countries. Some of the major agreements and institutions include:

China's office of Official Development Assistance (ODA) extends loans and export credits to ASEAN partners, particularly CLMV through the China-ASEAN Investment Cooperation Fund (CAF). [22]

- Regional Comprehensive Economic Partnership (RCEP) – which focuses on trade;
- New Development Bank (NDB) – which funds basic services and grants emergency assistance in conflict-affected states. NDB also invests in infrastructure such as electricity, transport, telecommunications, and water and sewage;
- Asian Infrastructure Investment Bank (AIIB) – which funds infrastructure and communication;
- China-ASEAN Investment Cooperation Fund (CAF) – funds infrastructure projects;

- Free Trade Area of the Asia-Pacific (FTAAP) – had been endorsed by all Asia-Pacific Economic Cooperation (APEC) members;[23]
- ASEAN-People's Republic of China Comprehensive Economic Cooperation Agreement, and the Asia-Pacific Trade Agreement;
- China also has individual free trade agreements with Thailand and Singapore.[24]

China-led Regional Comprehensive Economic Partnership (RCEP)

Singapore has traditionally been a US ally with lukewarm relations with Beijing. However, most likely due to increased Chinese investment, Singaporean Prime Minister Lee Hsien Loong has expressed his support of Chinese President Xi Jinping and global free trade.[25] Every ASEAN leaders has said they were concerned about increased protectionism in the West and that they supported the ASEAN-Hong Kong-China Free Trade and Investment Agreements signed in Manila in 2017.[26] Many ASEAN governments have turned down the volume on their complaints about South China Sea sovereignty, with possible exception of Vietnam. Philippines President Rodrigo Duterte has gone so far as to propose a resource-sharing arrangement with China covering disputed areas. For the most part, it seems that with Singapore as acting chair of ASEAN, the organization exists to facilitate free trade, while steering clear of sensitive issues, behavior which favors China.[27]

The following pages will take a look at some individual ASEAN economies and their economic interaction with China. Before doing so, however, a basic profile of both China and the US is given both for comparison and in order to set context. Readers may think that some ASEAN countries are poor or in need of infrastructure investment, but just how poor are they? There may be a perception that some countries have authoritarian regimes, low degrees of business freedom, or high levels of corruption that may drive countries closer to China or entice unscrupulous leaders to make poor long-term decisions about their country's future debt and sovereignty in order to gain short-term benefits. Therefore, it would seem helpful to begin each country section with an economic and governmental snapshot of each country.

Data from the Heritage Foundation will be used to measure the degree of economic and business freedom in each of these countries. The Heritage Foundation assigns various indicators of score between 0 and 100 with 100 being the greatest degree of freedom and 0 being the lowest. The author has selected a number of indicators including: population; per capita GDP; property rights; government integrity; business freedom; labor freedom; trade freedom; investment freedom; financial freedom; GDP growth rate; and trade as a percentage of GDP. Transparency International's Corruption Perception Index, which runs from 0 (most corrupt) to 100 (least corrupt), will also be used. Finally, the Democracy Index published by the Economist Intelligence Unit will be used to evaluate the quality of democracy in select countries receiving BRI investment. The index awards scores between 1 and 10, with 1 being an authoritarian regime and 10 being a full democracy.

CHINA

The PRC has a population of 1.4 billion with a per capita GDP in 2016 of just over US$8,100. [28] The Heritage Foundation assigns China a property rights score of 46.7, government integrity of 47.3, business freedom 54.9, labor freedom 61.4, trade freedom 73.2, investment freedom 25, and financial freedom 20. China's economy is moderately dependent on trade, with total trade, imports and exports combined, equal to 37% of GDP. China's GDP growth in 2017 was 6.9%. [29] China has a Corruption Perception Index of 39%. [30] The Economist Intelligence Unit awards China a Democracy Index score of 3.1. [31]

THE UNITED STATES

The US has a population of 325 million, with a per capita GDP of over US$59,000 per year. [32] The Heritage Foundation awards the US a property-rights score 79.3, government integrity of 71.9, business freedom 82.7, labor freedom 91.4, trade freedom 86.7, investment freedom 85, and financial freedom 80. The US is moderately dependent on trade, which comprises 28% of GDP. In 2017, GDP growth was 2.4%. [33] The US has a Corruption Perception Index of 75%, [34] and a Democracy Index score of 7.98. [35]

SINGAPORE

Singapore is a small high-income country. [36] The Heritage Foundation awards Singapore a property rights score of 97.1, government integrity of 87.9, business freedom 95.1, labor freedom 90, trade freedom 90, investment freedom 85, and financial freedom 80. Singapore's economy is heavily dependent on trade, with total trade, imports and exports combined, equal to 326% of GDP. The Heritage Foundation reports that Singapore enjoys a stable government enacting prudent macroeconomic policies and reasonable GDP growth of 2%. [37] Singapore boasts a Transparency International Corruption Perception Index of 84%. [38] The

17

Economist Intelligence Unit's Democracy Index score for Singapore is 6.3. [39]

Apart from good governance and a relatively open economy, another tremendous advantage is the Port of Singapore, one of the busiest ports in the world by way of tonnage handled.

In 2010, Singapore's economy grew by 15.2%. However, more recently, in spite of having so many advantages, economic growth has been lackluster. In 2016, the economy only grew by 1.8%, and for 2017, the government predicted a mere 1.3% growth. [40] Roughly 19,000 Singaporeans lost their jobs in 2016, the highest in seven years. *South China Morning Post* reports that, in the past, Singapore's economy was based on foreign investment and inexpensive labor. As the rest of Southeast Asia now offers opportunities for investment and cheap labor, Singapore needs to find another way to compete. The government's new strategy is to refocus the economy on other, more profitable areas. One such area is manufacturing. In contrast to the overall economic slowdown, Singapore's manufacturing sector expanded 21% last year. [41] Another area where Singapore could expand is banking and finance. It has long been a regional financial center and now aims to become an international financial center. To this end, Singapore is already tightening its money laundering and terrorism financing regulations. [42]

Two specters now threaten Singapore's economic future. One is that Washington's new, protectionist stance may negatively impact Singaporean exports. [43] Another threat to economic growth involves Singapore's two largest trading partners, China and Malaysia. [44] China has more or less decided to exclude Singapore from the One Belt One Road (OBOR) project because of Singapore's continued relationship with Taiwan, which Beijing sees as a violation of its "One China" policy. [45] Instead of investing in Singapore, China had been planning to invest in Malaysia's ports and railways; however, the new Malaysian government headed by Prime Minister Mahathir Mohamad has canceled or reviewed major PRC-backed projects. [46] Currently, Singapore's maritime activity contributes an estimated 7% to GDP. [47] If the Malaysian projects are revived, a great deal of shipping business will literally pass Singapore by, resulting in billions in lost revenue.

Singapore's economy will feel additional pressure as surrounding countries tighten monetary policy and restrict capital outflows. This will

most likely cause a reduction in liquidity in Singapore's banking sector. [48]
The irony of course is that tighter monetary policy and the possibility of reduced trade with the US comes at a time when Singapore is courting at-risk China trade and investment. For most of the last decade, China has played a major role in Singapore's economic development. The future, however, seems somewhat uncertain.

Singapore is China's largest source of foreign investment, while Singapore is also the largest recipient of Chinese investment in Asia. Singaporean investment in China has mostly been in the service sector, including dental services, education, and banking. Singapore is also a major player in China's real-estate market. In 2014, China was Singapore's largest trading partner and Singapore was China's no. 3 trading partner. [49]
Consequently, the two countries' economies are closely aligned. In fact, China's sovereign wealth fund, the China Investment Corp. (CIC), was modeled on Singapore's sovereign wealth fund, Temasek Holdings. [50] In 2010, the Monetary Authority of Singapore established a bilateral currency-swap agreement with People's Bank of China which was a major step toward the internationalization of the Chinese currency. [51] The countries have enjoyed cooperation in a number of large scale projects, including development of Datansha Island in the provincial capital of Guangzhou, the Sino-Singapore Guangzhou Knowledge City, and a sustainable city initiative called Sino-Singapore Tianjin Eco-City. [52] Similar joint ventures include Guangzhou Science City and Guangzhou International Biological Island which, like Sino-Guangzhou Knowledge City, receive significant financing from Temasek Holdings. [53]

In 2018, Singapore's Ministry of Trade and Industry and China's National Development and Reform Commission agreed to strengthen economic ties between the two countries. Both China and Singapore recognized the BRI as the base for this cooperation, specifically citing the Chongqing Connectivity Initiative/Southern Transport Corridor which connects the overland Silk Road Economic Belt to the 21st Century Maritime Silk Road. The Singaporean trade minister for said that Singapore's role as a regional infrastructure, financial, and legal hub, will add value to Chinese companies along the BRI. This cooperation will be managed under the Joint Council for Bilateral Cooperation. [54]

THAILAND

Thailand is the fourth most populous country in ASEAN and has the second largest GDP. The country enjoys a relatively high standard of living with a per capita GDP of US$6,595 in 2017. [55] Historically, Thailand has been considered an economic success story, moving from a lower-income to an upper-middle-income country in a single generation. From 1986 to 1996, its GDP grew at an average rate of 7.5%. From 1997 to 2005, GDP grew an average 5% per year. However, in recent years, average GDP growth has slowed, to an average of 3.5% for the period 2005 to 2010. Since 2014, the average has been around 2%. [56] Thailand has a Transparency International Corruption Perception Index of 37. [57] The Economist Intelligence Unit assigns Thailand a Democracy Index score of 4.63. [58]

The Heritage Foundation reports that the Thai business climate is mixed, with both positive and negative indicators. Property rights were scored at 51.3, government integrity 40, business freedom 69.9, labor freedom 62.8, trade freedom 82.8, investment freedom 50, and financial freedom 60. The foundation identified corruption and political instability as the biggest hindrance to Thailand's economic development. Since becoming a democracy in 1932, Thailand has experienced 19 military coups. The country is trade dependent with total trade equal to 132% of GDP. [59] The king's death in 2016 has caused speculation about the country's economic and political future. [60] Many wonder if the upcoming elections will be fair, if they will be contested, if there will be violence, and if the business climate will be dramatically altered.

China-Thailand trade and investment

China is Thailand's no. 2 trading partner, behind the US. [61] The China-Thailand Free Trade Agreement was signed in 2003. [62] In addition, China is the second largest investor in Thailand, after Japan. PRC companies are being offered bridge loans from Siam Commercial Bank to encourage their investment in 161 projects which Bangkok is promoting, such as the Eastern Economic Corridor development project. So far, the largest recipients of Chinese investment have been the sectors of automotive and auto parts, petrochemicals, smart electronics, agriculture and biotechnology, tourism, medical, digital, robotics, aviation, and textiles. [63]

Since seizing power in 2014, Thailand's military government has bolstered economic relations with China, whilst pivoting away from the US. [64] In January 2016, the military government approved Thailand's entry into the China-led AIIB in order to finance its many plans for infrastructure expansion. [65]

Bangkok is hoping to use US$40 billion in Chinese investment to jump start the economy, but so far the cash has failed to materialize. Plans to build a Thai-Chinese rail line, for example, have not moved beyond the discussion phase. [66] The railway is expected to cost US$13 billion, for which Beijing is offering financing at 2% In addition to political uncertainty, the railroad faces opposition from inside Thailand as some doubt that Thailand needs or wants the railroad. [67]

Despite large investments failing to materialize, the local economy has attracted increasing investment from Chinese private and state-owned enterprises. The Thai-Chinese Rayong Industrial Zone, established in 2012, hosts numerous Chinese-owned solar, rubber and industrial manufacturing businesses. [68] As labor becomes cheaper in other ASEAN countries, such as Cambodia and Burma, Thailand, like China and Vietnam, is trying to move up the value-added chain, leaving low-skilled manufacturing jobs and increasing its competitiveness in the manufacture of computers and digital equipment. To achieve this, the Thai government is courting additional Chinese investment in the high-tech sector. [69]

Increasing Chinese investment and tourism has led to Thailand becoming home to one of the largest overseas populations of PRC nationals. Chinese visits in 2018 exceeded 10 million. [70] In some parts of the country, particularly in places like Pattaya, Mandarin is heard at least as often as English. [71]

Around one third of Thailand's population has Chinese ancestry but acceptance of this group has only recently materialized, as China's economic importance has increased. [72] Thai-Chinese are influential in the business sector, and China has been able to utilize these local ethnic connections to facilitate investment.

China, unlike the US, has not pressured Bangkok to improve human rights or strengthen democracy. Washington has recently toned down its criticism of Thailand's current military government. [73] To counterbalance Beijing's growing economic power in the region, the US has been strengthening military ties with Thailand. [74] This relationship goes back to the Korean War, and was strengthened during the Vietnam War.

BURMA (MYANMAR)

Burma has a per capita GDP of just under US$1,300 and a population mainly engaged in agriculture. [75] The Heritage Foundation indicators on Burma stand as follows: property rights 32.5, government integrity 28.2, business freedom, labor freedom, trade freedom, investment freedom, financial freedom 54.2, GDP growth rate 7%, and trade as a percentage of GDP 43%. [76] Burma has a Corruption Perception score of 30. [77] The Economist Intelligence Unit assigns Burma a Democracy Index number of 3.83. [78]

Burma runs an overall trade deficit, as well as a trade deficit with its no. 1 trade partner, China. [79] In 2017, China was the largest investor in Burma, investing US$18 billion in 183 projects. China accounts for 26% of all foreign investment in Burma. [80]

Under the dictatorship that ruled Burma between 1992 and 2011, the country became isolated from the West, suffering under sanctions and a lack of development aid. During that period, China was one of the few countries willing to build economic links with Burma. Additionally, China forged alliances with many of the ethnic rebel armies, in order to facilitate the transport of minerals and energy from Burma to China. Beijing even gave heavy weapons to the most powerful ethnic force, the United Wa State Army. [81]

In spite of Burma's reliance on China, the relationship began to cool in 2011, when Yangon called a halt to a PRC-backed hydropower project. The reason given was that the dam was against the will of the people. The project would have redirected the flow of the Irrawaddy river, submerged 766 km^2 of forest, and 90% of the power generated would have gone to China. [82]

In 2012, Aung San Suu Kyi's National League of Democracy won a majority of seats in the parliament, and the promise of improved democracy and human rights instantly moved Burma back into the Western sphere of influence. Reflecting official concern, Chinese state media began running stories analyzing worsening ties with Burma, and exploring ways to improve them. This lead to a PR campaign to improve China's image in the country. Beijing began forging ties with local political parties, utilizing a "government-to-government," "party-to-party" and "people-to-people" approach Beijing has employed elsewhere in the region. [83] Local intellectuals, journalists, and politicians were invited to China. Beijing was careful to avoid criticizing Yangon for mistreatment of the Rohingya ethnic minority. [84] China's PR campaign, plus its largesse, seems to have shifted Burma again, toward China and away from the West.

Burma plays a crucial role in the BRI because of the deep sea port at Kyaukpyu in southern Rakhine state, which would grant China access to the Indian Ocean. Gaining access to Kyaukpyu would be another way for China to avoid the Strait of Malacca choke point. Beijing has been pressuring Yangon to construct a high-speed railway to Kyaukpyu, and a joint memorandum for the railroad was signed in 2011. However, it lapsed in 2014, because the Burmese side lost interest. [85]

CAMBODIA

The following section on Cambodia is much longer than the sections on other ASEAN nations, because Cambodia is a model for China's BRI objectives.

The Kingdom of Cambodia is a relatively small country and ranks as the second poorest in ASEAN in terms of per capita GDP. Cambodia's business climate indicators, according to the Heritage Foundation, are generally poor. The kingdom has extremely low rule of law with property rights of 42.4, government integrity 12.8, business freedom 29.6, labor freedom 62, trade freedom 80, investment freedom 60 and financial freedom 50. [86] Cambodia's economy is heavily dependent on trade with a total trade volume (imports plus exports) equaling 142% of GDP. The largest obstacles in Cambodia's economic development, according to the Heritage Foundation are corruption and lack of rule of law. Cambodia has a Corruption Perception Index of 21. [87] The Economist Intelligence Unit assigns Cambodia a Democracy Index score of 3.63. [88]

Cambodia is sandwiched between two huge neighbors: Thailand, which has about four times' Cambodia's population; and Vietnam, which has about six times' as many people. Throughout its history, Cambodia has suffered incursions and domination by one or the other of these behemoths. As a result, Cambodia's relationship with China, Asia's no. 1 power, helps to balance the region. Chinese influence and Chinese money has made Cambodia less dependent on other countries, and gives Phnom Penh the ability to negotiate from a position of parity with its two neighbors. In 2015, China's investment in Cambodia exceeded all other sources of FDI [89] and accounted for 35% of Cambodia's total FDI. [90]

China-Cambodia trade and investment

China is Cambodia's third largest trade partner and second largest import partner. [91] Cambodia runs a trade deficit with China. China receives 4.4% of Cambodia's exports while 24% of Cambodia's imports come from

China. [92] Cambodian exports to the PRC are largely agricultural products and raw materials, such as wood, plastic and rubber. [93]

China has invested in Cambodia's infrastructure steel industry. Guangxi Nonferrous Metal Group is constructing a steel mill Preah Vihear province, Cambodia Iron & Steel Mining Industry Group and China Railway Group, Ltd. have agreed to build a railway. Cambodia's Power Partner Profit Group has signed an MOU with Chinese companies in the fields of agriculture, electronics, and minerals. The Civil Aviation Administration of China signed an MOU with Cambodia's State Secretariat of Civil Aviation. [94] Other PRC investment projects in Cambodia include telecoms and the Russei Chrum Krom hydroelectric plant built by China Huadian Corp. [95] Additionally, at a meeting in 2015 with Prime Minister Hun Sen, President Xi Jinping promised US$500 to US$700 million of additional aid. [96]

The first Cambodia-China Business Forum and Financial Development Forum was held in Phnom Penh in December 2016 with the theme: Cambodia: The Kingdom of Opportunity Along the 'One Belt, One Road' – and the aim of boosting China-Cambodia trade. In 2015, trade between the two countries increased by US$3.75 billion compared to the previous year, reaching US$5 billion. China is also Cambodia's no. 1 investor, focusing on agriculture, agro-industry, manufacturing, tourism, energy, construction, real estate, and the financial industry. [97]

Cambodia also has direct economic relations with individual Chinese provinces. In March 2017, an MOU was signed between Cambodia and China's Shaanxi province, to strengthen ties and increase trade. Shaanxi alone accounts for about a quarter of China's total investment in Cambodia, focusing on irrigation systems, telecommunications, hydropower, and infrastructure. Cambodia has established a trade center in Xi'an (the biggest city in Shaanxi) to facilitate investment in the kingdom. [98]

The US and other Western countries require improvements in democracy in exchange for aid. Cambodia, which never ranked well in terms of democracy, has slid further and further into a single-party autocracy led by Prime Minister Hun Sen and the Cambodian People's Party. The lack of aid from the West has pushed Cambodia toward China, a willing donor. A tremendous blow came to US-Cambodia relations came in 2017, when US President Donald J. Trump announced he was cutting aid to Cambodia because recent elections "failed to represent the genuine will of the Cambodian people" [99] Germany placed visa restrictions on members of the Cambodian government, including the prime minister. [100]

Backed by Chinese money, Hun Sen has dissolved the main opposition party, jailed dozens of critics, and closed dissenting news media outlets. *New York Times* claimed, " Laos and Cambodia seem on the path toward becoming client states of Beijing." [101] Around 70% of Cambodia's roads and bridges were built by China, financed through about US$2 billion of loans. Senior Cambodian officials have said that only Beijing has responded generously to requests for aid. [102]

Work has commenced on a rail link from Sisophon and Battambang which is meant to continue to Poipet on the Thai-Cambodian border, eventually linking with a Chinese-built railroad in Thailand. So far, however, the Thai side has been stalling construction, raising the question: How badly do ASEAN nations want to be connected with each other or with China? [103] Is it possible that Beijing is the one actually wanting these links? And if so, why should Southeast Asian nations go more deeply into debt with China in order to support projects which will ultimately benefit China the most?

The BRI, as outlined by Xi, is much more than roads, railways, and seaports. It was to be a comprehensive makeover, impacting all facets of host societies, bringing development and advancement to all. Consequently, the initiative is meant to offer educational human-resource development through spreading Chinese language and culture, and increasing the education and competency of the countries it touches. The Chinese language is being promoted in participating countries through the network of PRC-funded Confucius Institutes. In addition, Beijing has been offering university scholarships to students from BRI countries to study in China for language or degree programs. Courses on offer range from engineering to medicine, which help increase the human capital of these developing nations. A further benefit has been that increased Chinese investment has led to an increase in recognition of Chinese identity by ethnic Chinese minorities living along BRI. Nowhere is this educational and cultural influence more profound than in Cambodia, where Chinese investment has led to a dramatic upsurge of Chinese-language study as well as a resurgence of Chinese identity among Sino-Khmers.

A history of Chinese education in Cambodia

Just after the fall of the Song Dynasty in the thirteenth century, Chinese communities largely composed of Hokkien people established themselves in Cambodia. Later, Cantonese, Hainanese, Teochiu, and Hakka also migrated to Cambodia, creating a sizable community of ethnic Chinese by the 20th century. [104] Under French colonial rule from 1865 until 1953, this community was essentially autonomous; they were permitted to establish their own schools to see to the education of their youth.

Under French rule, the majority of the Phnom Penh's population was ethnic Chinese, and divided along dialect lines. The Cantonese worked the rivers, the Teochiu were business people, and the Hokkien were administrators. [105] The French relied on the Chinese as middlemen. [106] In 1875, Tuan Hoa Chinese School was founded , marking the beginning of formal Chinese education in Cambodia. [107]

By 1970, Cambodia was home to 231 Chinese schools, 50 being in the capital. Chinese schools were considered to be among the best in the country, but this was not enough to save them. [108] When General Lon Nol seized control of the government that year, he ordered the closure of all Chinese schools in the country. During the Khmer Rouge years, 1975 to 1979, all schools were closed nationally. [109] Roughly 20% of the country's population and about 50% of the country's Chinese population were killed during that period. [110] The Sino-Khmer population was further diminished when many of those who survived the genocide fled overseas.

After 1979, when schools began to reopen, the Vietnamese rulers of the country blocked the reopening of Chinese schools. A Vietnamese edict called all Chinese Khmers "suspects." As a result, many Sino-Khmer families stopped speaking Chinese to avoid unwanted attention. [111] By 1984, it was estimated that the Sino-Khmer population had dwindled to just 60,000. [112] The ban on Chinese education was lifted in 1992. [113] Tuan Hoa, the largest and oldest Chinese school, reopened; by 1999, it boasted 2,800 students. [114]

Rebirth of Chinese identity in Cambodia

From pre-colonial times through to the 1970s, Sino-Khmers dominated the country's economic and business sector. However during Lon Nol's regime, Cambodia was rife with anti-Chinese feelings. [115] As a result of Khmer Rouge murder and Vietnamese suspicion, many Cambodians of Chinese descent stopped speaking their language, adopted Khmer names, and simply became Khmer. [116] Amid the general suppression of "Chinese-ness" in Cambodia, Chinese families began disassociating from their Chinese identity until sometime after 2000, when China began its economic engagement with Cambodia, and the situation changed for Sino-

Khmers. Michiel Verver argues that "Chinese family businesses, trust-based networks, patronage arrangements, and cultural representations have indeed been greatly revitalized over the last few decades." [117]

This revitalization has come in part because of heavy investment by China into Cambodia, which has also led to the reemergence of the Chinese language. Sino-Khmers, who just a few short years ago did not want to identify as Chinese, now find that employment and economic success are dependent on their Chinese-language skills, and that being Chinese has become an integral part of their identity. [118] Beijing's funding of Mandarin-language training for both Sino-Khmers and other Cambodians has been instrumental in helping Sino-Khmers recognize their own Chinese identity.

Historically, a number of Chinese dialects were spoken in Cambodia, and people tended to live, work, and marry within their dialect group, so there was less of a unified feeling of "Chinese-ness". However, from 1999 onward, partly due to Beijing's financial support of Chinese schools, Mandarin has become the lingua franca among Sino-Khmers. Having a unified language is one of the first steps to establishing an ethnic identity. Additionally, Chinese Khmers now find it easier to work with and for Chinese from the PRC as they share the same dialect.

The rebirth of Chinese identity and Chinese education comes not only because of Sino-Khmers, but also from Sino-Vietnamese who cross the border to attend Chinese schools in small Khmer towns such as Kampong Trach. [119] Another boost to Chinese education in Cambodia has been the increasing number of parents from the Chinese mainland who work in Cambodia and send their children to Chinese schools in Cambodia. At Zhongchua International School, for example, about half of the children in the Khmer-Chinese medium program are children of mainland parents working in Cambodia. [120]

Michiel Verver reports that a Khmer tuk-tuk driver told him: " It is good to have a Khmer-Chen (Sino-Khmer) in your family; these families are not poor like mine." [121] This very telling quote reveals two aspects of the new "Chinese-ness" in Phnom Penh: The Chinese, including Sino-Khmers, are seen as being good at business and rich; and it demonstrates that intermarriage is viewed as desirable.

From 1991, the ban on celebrating Chinese festivals, particularly Chinese New Year was lifted. [122] In 2014, *Phnom Penh Post* reported that nearly one million Sino-Khmers celebrated Chinese New Year. [123] Just two years later, Xinhua estimated that nearly 60% of Cambodians had celebrated Chinese New Year. [124] The reverse assimilation effect of local Khmers adopting this Chinese holiday clearly demonstrates not only a rebirth of Chinese-ness among Sino-Khmers, but also acceptance by the population at large.

The current state of Chinese education in Cambodia

By 2011, Chinese was already the second most popular foreign language, after English, being studied in Cambodia. [125] Chinese schools, such as Tuan Hoa, have seen an increase in enrollment; by early 2016, Tuan Hoa was reported to have over 10,000 students. [126]

The situation of the Chinese minority in Cambodia has improved dramatically over the past three decades, partly due to the growing economic relationship between China and Cambodia. Numerous Chinese-language newspapers are printed in Cambodia, and during elections, political parties print campaign literature in both Khmer and Chinese. [127] In 2010, a Confucius Institute opened in Phnom Penh, offering Chinese-language classes for Khmer learners and teacher-training for local teachers of Chinese. The Cambodian government's support for the institute was evident: The first group of 50 students was all employees at various ministries. [128]

More Cambodian students are pursuing degrees in Chinese language because investment and tourism from China has grown. In 2007, The Royal University of Phnom Penh began offering a Chinese language program designed to help local students pass the HSK 6, the highest level of the international Chinese proficiency exam. [129] Asia Euro University (AEU) currently offers a degree in Chinese literature. AEU provides degree-level courses in Chinese, with support from the Confucius Institute of the Royal Academy of Cambodia and the Chinese Embassy in Phnom Penh. Additional Chinese support to Cambodian education comes through the establishment of exchange programs with Chinese universities. The director of AEU's Department of International Cooperation stated that, apart from the growing economic ties between China and Cambodia, many students are motivated to study Chinese because they are Sino-Khmers who have observed Chinese culture and festivals their whole lives. [130]

One private Chinese language school, founded in 1915, has reported a surge in ethnic Khmers enrolling. Of the school's 16,000 students, 5% are now ethnic Khmers. The school is partially funded by donations from alumni and the PRC embassy. According to the school's headmaster, students learn Chinese not only because it affords them more employment opportunities, but also grants them access to higher order positions in engineering or banking. [131]

    Hybrid schools are also becoming popular, such as the bilingual American Chinese International School of Phnom Penh, and Abundant Life International School, the first trilingual (English, Chinese, and Khmer) school in Cambodia. [132] Countless small tutoring centers have also opened around the capital.

Economic factors driving the study of Chinese language

China is Cambodia's largest donor. In 2016, Prime Minister Hun Sen announced that China would be granting an additional US$600 million in aid loans to Cambodia. [133] During a consequent visit to Phnom Penh by President Xi Jinping, the PRC leader announced Beijing that a US$90 million debt owed by Cambodia to China would be forgiven. [134] Just as Cuba was once a place where the benefits of being a Soviet client state were shown to the world, one of China's motives for investing in Cambodia's education system is to demonstrate to other poor countries the benefits of participating in the BRI. [135]

    China is Cambodia's largest single source of investment, and when it comes to capital spending, China accounts for 20% of Cambodia's total. [136] The PRC has invested so heavily in construction and infrastructure, *The Diplomat* reported, "Chinese money is literally changing the shape of Cambodia's landscape" [137] To tap into this investment, Khmers and Sino-Khmers alike are signing up for Chinese language classes. Other major sources of investment include Hong Kong, Taiwan, Singapore, and Malaysia, all of whom use Chinese to communicate." [138]

    China already dominates Cambodia's construction sector, and is a major player in the garment sector. Now, China is becoming the major force in tourism. [139] In 2016, the total number of Chinese tourists was expected to be close to one million. Cambodia's tourist industry is promoting the "China-Ready" program in the hopes of attracting even more Chinese tourists. To this end, they are encouraging workers in the tourism sector to learn the Chinese language. [140]

    Many Cambodian parents, even those who are not Sino-Khmer, send their children to Chinese schools because they see Chinese as an important language for business. [141] Hanban News reported that Cambodians who speak Chinese earn an average of 50% more than those who do not. At a time when the monthly minimum wage was US$140, those able to speak English were earning US$260 per month, while Chinese speakers made around US$300 monthly. [142]

China's educational aid to Cambodia

Chinese aid differs from that of other countries because the PRC government observes several self-imposed rules:

1. Prioritize national development. Beijing has repeatedly said that education is a cornerstone of development, and thus invested heavily in the educational development of its aid-recipient countries. This also provides China with a growing number of sympathetic Chinese speakers in each country. Those Chinese speakers often find work in Chinese companies, or local companies or government departments who deal with China. Either way, it gives China more allies in any negotiation.

2. Allow each country's leadership to decide what sort of help that country needs. [143] This differs from aid from Western governments, which often follow up to see how money was spent.

3. Chinese aid is always request-driven. This dovetails with the PRC policy of preserving the sovereignty of aid recipients. Finally, in regards to educational aid, culture and education are closely linked in the Chinese way of thinking. Consequently, at Chinese embassies a single office is generally responsible for culture and education, whereas the oversight of professional and vocational training falls to the Ministry of Commerce. [144] It is often difficult to separate the spread of culture from the spread of propaganda.

PRC educational aid in Cambodia is diverse. Aid given helps fund language teaching, university and vocational training, school construction (financed by China and led by PRC construction companies), support local and joint educational initiatives such as conferences and fairs, as well as university scholarship programs and opportunities for Cambodian students to study in China. Additionally, China also offers teacher-training programs to improve Cambodian educators. When students become qualified Chinese teachers, they will work as teachers or translators by the government or in industry, or they may open their own language schools. Training teachers has a multiplier effect in terms of building a Chinese-speaking human resource within a host country.

The Diplomat has referred to Cambodia as China's mouthpiece in Southeast Asia. The kingdom earned this title in 2012, when Cambodia was hosting the ASEAN conference, and managed to have the South China Sea sovereignty issue dropped from the agenda. [145] In late 2017, Hun Sen defiantly told the world he was rejecting all US aid after Washington had criticized him for canceling elections. He felt that, after dissolving the opposition party, there was no need to hold an election. [146] Washington estimated that in 2014 its aid to Cambodia, including health, education, governance, and economic programs, as well as clearing unexploded ordnance, totaled more than US$77.6 million. [147] China spends much more; in fact, Cambodia is the no. 1 recipient of PRC aid in the world. [148] Cambodia is a clear example of the strategic and political benefits that Beijing derives from the BRI.

LAOS
The population of the Lao People's Democratic Republic is almost 6.8 million, with a per capita GDP of US$1,818 according to the World Bank. The business climate, according to data from the Heritage Foundation is not encouraging, the score for property rights being 35.3, government integrity 32.6, business freedom 66.3, labor freedom 54.4, trade freedom 74.6, investment freedom 35, and financial freedom 20. [149] However, average GDP growth has been 7% per annum in recent years, despite corruption and burdensome bureaucracy. In addition, an underdeveloped financial system, which suffers from too much government regulation, high credit costs and lack of access to financing, have slowed the country's development. Total trade volume is equal to 79% of GDP. The Laos Corruption Perception Index score is 29. [150] The Economist Intelligence Unit gives Laos a Democracy Index score of 2.37. [151]

China-Laos trade and investment
The PRC is the no. 2 trade partner of Laos, in both exports and imports, behind Thailand and ahead of Vietnam. [152] Trade between China and Laos has increased steadily, nearly tripling from US$1.3 billion in 2011 to US$3.6 billion in 2014. However, the economic slowdown in China caused trade to contract to US$2.78 billion in 2015. [153]

In particular, Laos trades with China's Yunnan province, accounting for 40% Yunnan's total trade. China is also the top investor in Laos, with over 760 projects underway. Yunnanese companies lead many of these investment projects, including roads, electricity transmission lines, water supply, and economic zones. [154]

PRC investment is also helping to modernize Lao's underdeveloped financial markets. The state-owned Lao Development Bank signed an MOU with China's Fudian Bank to facilitate trade and investment, country-to-country services, capital management, credit cooperation, and currency exchange. [155]

31

The Lao economy has been growing at an average rate of 7% per year, and VOA credits China with being a major driver in the country's development. Chinese investment is significant in a number of sectors, such as mining, energy, agriculture, banking, and commercial real estate. Credit extended by the Bank of China accounts for 40% of the country's total foreign debt, with most of these funds being used in infrastructure and power projects. In Vientiane, PRC investors are building office, residential and commercial complexes. Another project underway is the high-speed railway from Vientiane to the Chinese border. [156]

However, international agencies, among them the Asian Development Bank, believes that Laos is too dependent on China, as demonstrated by the Chinese slowdown of 2015 resulting in a slowdown in Laos. The World Bank has also recommended that Laos diversifies its economy. [157] The railway project is still scheduled to be completed on time in 2025, but many Laotians have complained that the labor working on the railroad is predominantly Chinese, reducing knock-on benefits to the local economy. Development banks worry that the US$6-billion rail project will exacerbate Laos' already precarious debt levels, which reached 68% of GDP in 2016, increasing the debt distress level from "moderate" to "high" in the most recent World Bank/IMF Debt Sustainability Analysis.

Laos' budget deficit in 2017 was 4.8% of GDP, compared with 4.6% in 2016. China and Laos have set up a 70/30 joint venture to finance the railway project. Each side needs to contribute 40% of their investment commitment in cash, which means that Laos, with 30% of the joint venture, needs to contribute US$715 million over the five-year construction period. Of this, US$250 million will come from the national budget. The remaining US$465 million will be borrowed from the Exim Bank of China at 2.3% interest with a five-year grace period and a 35-year maturity. Some are asking who will bear the cost if the railway does not make money, and think that may be more of a concern for Laos than for China. One commentator said the railway is likely "not a commercially viable project in the timeframe of a Western bank," but that given "China's objectives.... it makes sense for China." [158]

VIETNAM

Vietnam's 97 million inhabitants have a per capita GDP of US$1,835. [159] Vietnam has averaged about 6% GDP growth for the past five years, making it one of the fastest growing economies in Asia. [160] Vietnam has made impressive progress, nearly doubling per capita GDP since 1984. As impressive as Vietnam's development has been, the country could be developing even more quickly if its business climate was better. The

Heritage Foundation reports that Vietnam had a Property rights score of 49.7, government integrity 24.6, business freedom 61.2, labor freedom 62.2, trade freedom 83.1, investment freedom 25 and a financial freedom score of 40. Like China, Vietnam is transitioning from communism to "market socialism" whereby SOEs are being privatized and the general economic climate is being liberalized. Economic development are also held back by an opaque bureaucracy and a weak judicial system. SOEs still account for about 40% of GDP; all land is still owned by the state. The Communist Party of Vietnam controls much of the judiciary and membership of the party is seen as a way to achieve economic success; nepotism and corruption are rife.

Vietnam's total trade equals 179% of GDP [161] and the state still controls certain sectors, such as financial services and banking. As a result, non-performing loans (NPL) remain high. In 2016, across Vietnam's entire banking system, the percentage of NPLs reached 5.84%. [162] Having more than 3% NPLs is considered a warning sign, but because Vietnam's GDP growth has been robust, debtors are likely to be able to repay some of their debts, and thereby reducing the NPL rate over time. [163]

China-Vietnam trade and investment
While the US is Vietnam's no. 1 export partner, China is Vietnam's largest total trade partner, in terms of both exports and imports. Vietnam's imports from China are roughly three times the value of its exports to the PRC. [164]

China Daily reported that in 2015 there were 1,300 PRC investment projects in Vietnam, and the country is expected to be a conduit for China to trade with ASEAN through China's Guangxi province. [165] Because PRC investment in Vietnam increased in 2017, China went from Vietnam's no. 8 source of FDI in 2016 to the Indochinese country's no. 3 source. [166] However, this figure includes Hong Kong, Macao, and Taiwan, which are usually considered separate entities for investment purposes. [167]

Chinese FDI usually takes the form of Build-Operate-Transfer (BOT), Build-Transfer (BT) or Build-Transfer-Operate (BTO) agreements. [168] Chinese investments in Vietnam focus on labor-intensive industries such as garments and textiles, hydropower, as well as sectors which produce a lot of pollution, such as steel production, chemicals, and cement. [169] Some major PRC investments in Vietnam include: the Vinh Tan 1 Thermal Power Project in Binh Thuan; the Hung Nghiep Formosa Dong

Nai Textile Limited Company project in Nhon Trach Industrial Park; Texhong Group's textile factories in the north; the Viet Luan tire project in Tay Ninh; plus rubber-processing plant and metallurgy projects. Chinese companies are also heavily involved in building the Cat Linh-Ha Dong urban railway (part of the planned Hanoi Metro) and the troubled Da River water pipeline. [170]

Prospects for China-Vietnam trade and investment were damaged when the US withdrew from the TPP. PRC firms had been planning to establish manufacturing and assembly plants in Vietnam so they could export duty-free to the US. [171] Now that the US has removed itself from the TPP, there is less incentive to invest in Vietnam.

INDONESIA

One of the most prominent BRI projects in Indonesia is a high-speed railroad that will drastically quicken travel between Jakarta, the capital, and Bandung, the country's third-largest metropolitan area. Indonesia awarded the contract to a Chinese consortium in 2015, and the railway was expected to begin operating in 2019.

The 142-km-long rail link was supposed to illustrate China's expanding economic power and influence. However, the completion date has been pushed back to 2021, "amid obstacles that include budget overruns, land acquisition delays and political uncertainty." [172] Paperwork and permit problems halted the project in its first several months, after which land acquisition proved to be a major headache. Rising land prices during delays is partially responsible for the project's growing price tag, from US$5.5 billion when first announced to US$6.1 billion by late 2018. [173]

New infrastructure and an expanded maritime presence has allowed China to establish more secure sea lines of communication through the vital waterways of the South China Sea and Straits of Malacca. These efforts include ambitious port projects in Southeast Asia, including a US$6 billion investment by China in Indonesia's Tanjung Sauh Port on the island of Batam. [174]

PHILIPPINES

Philippines President Rodrigo Duterte has forged closer ties with China, while simultaneously embarking on the Build, Build, Build infrastructure program. In keeping with the BRI, Beijing has pledged millions of dollars in aid to the Philippines, but according to the president of the Philippine Chamber of Commerce and Industry, the money has yet to materialize, and neither is the Philippines feeling the benefits of the BRI. However, others in the Philippines see some advantages to the country joining the BRI, such as the chief of the Employers Confederation of the Philippines, who felt that Chinese markets would now be more open to Philippine exports. Also, Asia-Pacific Pathway to Progress program convenor Aaron Jed Rabena cited Manila's membership of AIIB as another benefit of BRI participation. He blamed the slow progress of Chinese infrastructure projects on the careful approach taken by the Philippine government and not on failings by the Chinese side. A local analyst cited the local real-estate boom and growing numbers of PRC tourists as additional benefits. 175

Beyond the economic impact, Renato C. De Castro, a professor of international studies at De La Salle University, expressed worries that becoming too dependent on China and Chinese money may result in the PRC taking a leadership role in shaping Manila's foreign policy. He also warned that, like BRI projects elsewhere, construction projects in the Philippines will be carried out by Chinese companies, with Chinese workers and Chinese materials. He also spoke of the need to avoid a debt trap. On top of these fears, some say many of the projects may become underutilized "white elephants," or be started but never completed. 176

Chapter 3: The Pacific

Micronesia and the Pacific Islands is an area of the world often overlooked by journalists, but which has tremendous strategic importance. It is an area where China, through the Belt and Road Initiative, is playing out a modern Great Game with the US, but not enough people are watching.

The Federated States of Micronesia (FSM) is located in the Caroline Islands, an archipelago in the Western Pacific. The Federation is composed of four states. The independent countries of Kiribati, Nauru and the Marshall Islands lie to the east. Palau, which is also independent, is nearer China and the Philippines, as are Guam and the Northern Mariana Islands. Like Wake Island, Guam and the Northern Marianas are US territories. The FSM has a population of just over 104,000 and an average per capita GDP of just over US$3,000 per year. 1   The official language is English, although local languages are also spoken. F ishing and US economic assistance to Micronesia account for 40% of its GDP. 2   Guam is unique in that its main source of income is US defense, followed by tourism. 3   Both the US Navy and US Air Force maintain major bases on Guam and other islands, making Micronesia America's most important outpost in the Pacific. 4

In 2013, through the Compact of Free Association (which also covers Palau and the Marshall Islands), US assistance accounted for roughly 58% of the FSM's GDP. When this arrangement ends in 2023, the FSM will not be cut off completely, as Washington has established a Trust Fund to provide an income beyond the year 2024. [5]

Micronesia is facing a number of systemic problems. "Present concerns include large-scale unemployment, overfishing, overdependence on US foreign aid, and state perception of inequitable allocation of US aid." [6]

In recent years, Chinese investment in the region has increased dramatically. The economies of the countries of Micronesia are so small that in many cases Chinese investment can comprise a significant percentage of GDP. As arrangements with the US run out, Beijing seems eager to supersede Washington as the major power in the region.

The PRC's engagement with the Pacific Island countries (PIC) began in the 1970s, when many of these nations were gaining independence from various Western powers. At that time, Beijing and Taipei were in fierce competition for international recognition. [7] Over the past 40 years, these two rivals have abandoned their recognition race and the PRC is now focused on economic expansion. The 2006 visit of PRC Premier Wen Jiabao to Fiji established the China-Pacific Island Countries Economic Development and Cooperation Forum (CPICEDCF). [8] Since then, economic activity between China and the Pacific islands has steadily increased with Beijing distributing US$1.4 billion worth of aid to the region. By 2012, China was the no. 3 source of foreign aid. [9]

In 2014, PRC President Xi Jinping attended a summit in Fiji, which included leaders of the eight Pacific Island countries that have diplomatic ties with China. The purpose of the meeting was to discuss Xi's desire to increase the level of engagement between China and the region to one of so-called "strategic partnership." "Xi's visit symbolizes China's growing presence in the Pacific Islands region, and its far-reaching consequences for the evolving regional order." [10]

Apart from economic engagement, China has been increasing its cultural influence on the region. In addition to offering thousands of scholarships to young people who wish to study in China, in 2006, a Confucius Institute was established at the University of South Pacific in Fiji. [11] In 2015, the China Cultural Center in Fuji was inaugurated. [12] Chinese communities in the region have been growing through immigration, and have become dominant in particular business sectors, such as retail and restaurants. [13]

China's economic interest likely stems from the fact that many PICs are resource-rich, and China would like to obtain commodities such as timber and fish. Strategically, the islands lie along important shipping lanes, which also interest China. " Some one-third of global trade and almost 50% of energy commerce passes through waters controlled by these island states ." [14]

Since the end of World War II, the US has been the dominant power in the region, particularly in the FSM, providing military protection, currency, language, and financial support. The growth of both Chinese economic involvement and cultural influence may challenge the US role in the region. The US dollar is the official currency and the largest sources of income are American aid and farming.

Micronesia: Caught between the US and China

Following Japan's defeat in 1945, the UN awarded former Japanese territories, including Micronesia, to the Allied nations. It was at this time that the US became responsible for the Trust Territory of the Pacific Islands and the Compact of Free Association began. Under the compact, the Trust Territories were free to become independent states . Originally, the arrangement was set to expire in 2023. In the mid-1960s, however, Micronesia began taking early steps towards independence. This led to the establishment of the Commonwealth of Northern Marianas, Republic of Marshall Islands, Republic of Palau, and the FSM. [15] Under the terms of association, these nations are independent, but the US provides aid money as well as defense. [16]

Citizens of Guam, Northern Mariana Islands, and Swains Island are US citizens from birth. Those born in American Samoa are US nationals, but not citizens. Citizens of the FSM are not US citizens, but they have many special rights normally reserved for US citizens. For example, FSM citizens are permitted to join the US military. They are also permitted to move to the US to live and work without a green card, and they are fast-tracked to US citizenship. Micronesians generally choose to immigrate to Hawaii, Guam, American Samoa, and the Commonwealth of the Northern Marianas Islands. [17]

Currently, the relationship between the FSM and the US is managed by the Joint Economic Management Committee (JEMCO). In 2015, the FSM congress drew up a resolution to end its relationship with the US in 2018. Ending the compact early means that annual US funding will stop and FSM citizens living in the US will lose their legal advantages. 18

Since 2001, Beijing has been courting Micronesia in anticipation of an end to the US compact. China has hosted a number of leaders from the region, including the king, queen and crown prince of Tonga, the president of Micronesia, the prime ministers of Samoa, Fiji and Vanuatu, the vice president and finance minister of Kiribati, and the foreign minister of Papua New Guinea.

In addition, there has been considerable unofficial contact between the PRC and various regional leaders. The foreign minister of the Solomon Islands (which recognizes Taiwan, not China) made a quiet trip in 2000, and a group of West Papuan separatists visited the following year. [19]

China's growing relationship with the PICs

The recognition race between the PRC and Taiwan ended with six states recognizing Taiwan (Republic of China): Kiribati, Marshall Islands, Nauru, Palau, Solomon Islands, and Tuvalu; and the PRC being recognized by eight countries: the Cook Islands, the FSM, Fiji, Niue, Papua New Guinea, Samoa, Tonga, and Vanuatu. All eight have received large amounts of PRC aid. In fact, Beijing is now the no. 2 aid donor for Samoa and Tonga. Between 2014 and 2015, trade between China and the PICs increased by 60% reaching US$8.1 billion. Chinese trade with Fiji alone reached US $333 million by 2013. [20]

"The [Chinese] are buying, or investing in, plantations, garment factories, fishing and timber-cutting licenses." [21] Since the military coup in 2006, ethnic Indians – once the main drivers of Fiji's economy – have been leaving the country in droves, due to political and economic uncertainty. As a proportion of Fiji's population, Indians accounted for 35% in 2013, down from 50% in 1987. As the Indians exit, their plantations and other businesses are being bought by the Chinese. [22]

In 2000, the total value of PRC trade with its eight diplomatic allies in the Pacific stood at US$248 million. By 2012, that number had increased to US$1.767 billion. China was received 45% of the exports of the Solomon Islands. China is also the largest purchaser of timber from Papua New Guinea. Chinese companies, between 2003 and 2012, invested more than US$700 million in PICs. Papua New Guinea, with a total US$313 million, has been the no. 1 Chinese investment destination in the region. The largest single investment in the region is China's stake in the PNG Ramu Nickel Project. The second and third largest recipients of Chinese investment are Samoa (US$265 million) and Fiji (US$111 million). [23] China has also bid for large-scale infrastructure projects funded by agencies such as the World Bank and Asian Development Bank. By 2012, Chinese companies had been awarded US$5 billion in construction projects. Beijing "reportedly deploys more diplomats in the region" than any other government." [24]

Chinese aid to PICs

"The weakness of these countries creates real opportunities for rising powers like China to exercise more influence over their governments," says Ben Reilly, a political scientist at Australian National University's Center for Development Studies. [25] The allegiance of the PICs could shift from the US to China. [26]

Beijing sponsored the first CPICEDCF in 2006. Through this and other multinational economic organizations, China has handed out a great deal of aid to the region. " Since 2006, China has provided US$1.4 billion in foreign aid to eight Pacific Island countries – the Cook Islands, Federated States of Micronesia, Fiji, Niue, Papua New Guinea, Samoa, Tonga, and Vanuatu ." [27]

Concessional loans, many of which have been used to build infrastructure, comprise 80% of China's total aid to the region. Since 2006, the largest recipients of PRC aid have been the region's two biggest economies, Fiji and Papua New Guinea. As a result of these loans, many of the Pacific islands are facing a debt crisis. Tonga, for example, now has external debt equal to 44% of its GDP. Concessional loan debts to China account for 65% of this total. [28]

Fiji is the largest recipient of PRC aid. From 2005 to 2009, Fiji received US$865 million in Chinese aid. Since 1995, Fiji has been receiving military aid from China. After the 2006 military coup, Western donors halted aid but China increased its assistance. China also provides training for Fijian officers at its National Defense Academy in Beijing. [29]

Papua New Guinea is another major recipient of PRC aid. From 2005 to 2009, the resource-rich country received US$236 million. In 2012, Chinese aid to PNG included government office buildings, education, sports and cultural venues, medical facilities, roads and bridges, hydropower, bulwarks, and model villages, emergency aid, climate change assistance, and development of human resources. In 2013, Beijing announced it would grant a US$1 billion concessional loan to PICs. [30]

Chinese tourism and investment in Palau

The Republic of Palau, an archipelago with a population of 21,000, gained independence from the US in 1994. [31] Palau shares maritime boundaries with Indonesia, the Philippines, and the FSM. Palau's GDP growth rate in 2015 was 9.4%. According to World Bank data, the annual per capita GDP of Palau is US$15,100, which is much higher than that of other Pacific islands. Both Tuvalu and the Marshall Islands, for instance, have annual per capita incomes of less than US$4,000. [32]

After Palau established formal diplomatic relations with Taiwan in 1999, Taiwanese businesses began to establish themselves on the island. Business people also invested in land and hotels. At that time, Taiwanese accounted for 45% of foreign tourists entering Palau. Taiwanese companies dominated tourism, and when media reports of Taiwanese dominance of local business appeared, local politicians began to express resentment. [33]

In 2014, 100 million Chinese tourists travelled abroad, [34] and Palau has become a favorite destination. Unlike other PICs, its growing tourism industry was built largely for ethnic Chinese visitors. [35] Tourism now accounts for 42.3% of Palau's GDP. [36]

Before PRC citizens began travelling to the island, the majority of visitors were Japanese, Korean, or Taiwanese. Chinese tourism to the island increased by a staggering 500% in 2013, reaching 10,955. In 2014, Palau tourism reached 141,000, up 34% from February the previous year. Many Chinese go abroad in February, the month in which they have their long lunar new year vacation. [37] In January 2015, Chinese represented 62% of tourists to Palau, up from 16% the previous year. For a period, hotels were focusing heavily on PRC tourists. For instance, when the AFP visited At Sea Passion Hotel, 74 of the 75 rooms were occupied by Chinese visitors. [38] In 2015, the Chinese diaspora established the Palau-China United Association to help PRC citizens who wish to do business on the island. [39]

Despite some positive economic impacts, this increased investment and focus on mainland tourists has also come at a cost for the local communities. Palau natives have accused Chinese tourists of breaking coral, littering, being loud, and showing disrespect to the environment. Palau was having so many problems dealing with the inundation of Chinese tourists that the island reduced the number of incoming flights by half. [40]

In 2018, it was reported that Palau's refusal to end its diplomatic relationship with Taipei had led to Beijing ordering tour operators to stop selling package tours to the country. [41] Even so, PRC investors have been investing in tourism infrastructure. Chinese have bought apartment buildings and converted them into bed-and-breakfasts. While this investment has been good for the national economy, it has hurt small, local tour operators. [42] A Chinese company, Palau Pacific Star Corporation is building a 300-room hotel on Airai Island, which will be the country's biggest hotel. [43]

In 2013, FDI in Palau was US$18 million. The following year, FDI peaked at US$40 million, then dropped in 2015 to just US$9 million. Foreign investment in Palau is mostly in tourism and real estate. While investment from China is increasing, by far the major investing partners are still the United States, Singapore, and Japan. Palau maintains a number of barriers which could discourage FDI, especially for newer investors such as the Chinese. For example, the fee for a work permit is US$500. In addition, a number of local industries are not open to FDI. In the 2016 World Bank Doing Business Report, Palau ranked 136th out of 189 countries.

Chinese investment in Micronesia
Historically, the FSM have relied on an annual assistance grant from the US, which in 2013 was US$92 million. This grant was equal to 40% of GDP. [44] This type of grant, as well as diplomatic services and military protection, extends to Palau and the Marshall Islands, two countries which have similar arrangements with Washington. However, the US has been reducing the amount of aid every year. Between 1987 and 1991, the annual US grant to the FSM and the Marshall Islands was US$430.5 million. Between 1992 and 1995, however, it fell to US$365.5 million. From 1996 to 2001, it dropped further to US$295.5 million. Part of this grant is paid into the trust fund established by the US to support Micronesia after the compact ends in 2023. [45]

China first began investing in Micronesia in the early years of the 21st century. In 2003, Chinese aid was roughly US$23 million. "Chinese investment is more noticeable now than ever. Overseas development assistance from China has increased steadily since 2003." [46] The continual decline of US aid to Micronesia has created opportunities for Beijing. US aid to Micronesia decreased by nearly a third in 2008, because of the Global Financial Crisis, at which point China began pouring money into the region. [47] PRC aid to the region is now thought to be quadruple that of 2003. [48]

Much of China's overseas investment is related to food security. Chinese companies have established fishing interests in the FSM; they now enjoy a monopoly over the local fishing industry, which they obtained by

41

loaning money to Micronesia and accepting fishing resources as collateral.
49

In 2011, Yap State, one of the four federated states of Micronesia, was negotiating a deal with a Chinese company, Exhibit and Travel Group, to build tourism infrastructure, including a casino. [50] Another of the states, Chuuk State, is also negotiating a massive casino deal with a PRC developer. [51]

Chinese investment in the PICs

Until recently, Palau gained most of its tourism revenue from Chinese visitors. Guam, on the other hand, only receives 1% of its tourists from China. PRC investments already dominate Palau and Saipan, and Guam is hoping to benefit from similar Chinese investment. So far, however, Guam has not been able to arrange visa-free entry for PRC citizens. Chinese investors in Saipan are building casinos and hotels. When these projects are completed, Saipan will have more hotel rooms than Guam, despite Guam being dramatically larger in terms of population. [52] Guam's close relationship with the US complicates Guam's involvement with China.

Guam's most important source of revenue is US defense spending. Local economists hope that disputes over the South China Sea could boost US defense spending in the region. [53] Heightened tensions in the South China Sea would most likely be good for Guam in terms of increased US military spending, but would probably make it even more difficult for Guam to benefit from Chinese tourism or investment. Meanwhile, China is still playing a long-term waiting game with Guam. " Beijing is making huge investments via banks in Guam, and this is increasing every year." [54] Basically, what Beijing seems to be doing is establishing a large bank account in Guam and adding to it, as a carrot, with the implication that Guam could keep the money if Guam should decide to leave its association with the United States in 2023. At the same time, the US has announced plans to move thousands of US Marines from Japan to Guam. This move will cost about US$8.5 billion, which the US has also deposited in a bank on Guam. [55]

In addition to competing with the US, China is also investing in Pacific islands which are aligned with European powers. China invests more in French Tahiti than does France, which may lead to Tahiti declaring its independence. "Since 2014, China has been planning to install its first military base in the central Pacific Ocean in Tonga, which can't pay its debts to China." Chinese investment already accounts for 40% of Tonga's

GDP. Similar situations exist in Samoa and Papua New Guinea, who also owe money to China. [56]

Between 2000 and 2012, Chinese trade with the Pacific nations with which it has diplomatic ties grew from US$248 million to US$1.766 billion. Bilateral trade has increased by an average of 27% year-on-year since 2006. China mainly exports electronics; processed food; machinery; textiles; equipment for fishing, farming, and mining; clothing and footwear; furniture; and construction materials. China imports timber, seaweed, seafood, and minerals. China runs a trade deficit with the PICs because it imports large amounts of raw materials. [57]

The Pacific islands that recognize Taiwan and consequently do not have official diplomatic ties with China include the Solomon Islands, Nauru, and French-ruled New Caledonia. PRC trade with this trio is actually higher than PRC trade with countries which recognize Beijing. The 2012 total for all bilateral trade between China and the PICs was US$4.5 billion, of which only US$1.7 billion was with nations with embassies in Beijing. [58]

In addition to Chinese FDI (much of which has come from large and mid-sized state-owned enterprises investing in resource development, fisheries, real estate, and service industries), Chinese companies have won infrastructure contracts in the region totaling US$12 billion. [59]

Problems with the BRI in the Pacific Islands

Debts caused by the BRI are a problem for many countries, but are especially acute in smaller countries. One in three countries receiving BRI loans face "debt distress." [60] Among countries listed by the Center for Global Development as "highly vulnerable" to BRI debt problems are some of the very small economies in the Pacific. [61]

The growing influence of PRC business interests in the PICs has caused friction with local populations. Many locals resent the growing economic success of local Chinese communities, and have even targeted them for attack. Honiara, capital of the Solomon Islands, was the site of anti-Chinese riots in 2006, when Beijing had to evacuate 300 of its citizens. [62] There have been ongoing PR problems for a Chengdu-based company, Exhibition and Travel Group, which wants to bring tourism to the FSM island of Yap in a relatively big way. Locals oppose the plan, fearing it will destroy their traditional way of life. [63]

In 2006, after a military coup in Fiji, Australia and New Zealand imposed sanctions on the country. Fijian Prime Minister Frank

Bainimarama then turned to Beijing for financial help. [64] China now accounts for 40% of Fiji's foreign debt. [65] Across the Pacific, countries are feeling the strain of debt to China. In order to make its loan payments, Vanuatu was forced to increase its consumption tax from 12.5% to 15%. Tonga had to call upon the IMF to negotiate a five-year loan amnesty. [66]

During her stint as Australia's minister for international development, Concetta Fierravanti-Wells criticized Beijing for building unnecessary roads and projects in the region. One such project was a a 600-seat stadium built by China in Vanuatu as a gift. Theoretically, the stadium could never be filled because, even if Vanuatu managed to stage an event large enough to draw 600 spectators, there aren't enough hotel rooms on the island. Additionally, the government has been struggling to cover the electricity bill. To deal with crippling debt, Vanuatu has had to establish a debt management unit. One option being considered is to begin charging income tax, but that would nullify Vanuatu's advantage as a tax haven. Tonga is also suffering under foreign debt equal to 44% of GDP, 60% of which is owed to China. [67] Frustration with China is mounting in the region; many business owners told *The Australian* that they felt helpless and that their own governments had sold them out. Residents even went so far as to say they felt as if China were holding them for ransom. Tongans felt the Chinese were putting them out of jobs and dominating the retail sector, opening Chinese shops which sold goods manufactured in China. [68]

Not settling for economic domination alone, the PRC is also increasingly militarizing the region. Beijing has said its medium-range "Guam Killer" missiles are now in service. [69] Now, if China feels the need to attack US soil, it could decimate Guam. China is also considering establishing a full military base on the island of Vanuatu. No official statement has been made, according to Reuters, but the plan calls for an initial access agreement, whereby PRC ships could be serviced and resupplied in Vanuatu, eventually leading to a permanent base. [70]

Even though some of Beijing's actual and potential partners have expressed concerns about "transparency, debt sustainability and usefulness, as well as questioning China's underlying strategic aims," [71] in late 2018, Vanuatu and the PRC signed a fresh batch of BRI-related agreements. [72]

Chapter 4: Russia and Central Asia

Russia is a vast country with a population of over 142 million and a nominal per capita GDP of US$11,441. [1] The Heritage Foundation assigns Russia a property-rights score of 48.7, a government-integrity ranking of 38.1, business freedom 77, labor freedom 52, trade freedom 79.4, investment freedom 30, and financial freedom 30. Russia's economy is moderately dependent on trade, with total trade, imports and exports combined, equal to 46% of GDP. [2] Russia's GDP growth was 1.3% in 2017. [3] Russia's Transparency International Corruption Perception Index score is 29%. [4] The country's Democracy Index score, according to the Economist Intelligence Unit, is 3.17. [5]

Russia is a major energy supplier and commands a strategic geographic location, connecting Central Asia, China Europe, and the northern Arctic. [6] Three of the six corridors of the BRI directly affect Russia; the China-Mongolia-Russia Economic Corridor; the New Eurasian Land Bridge; and the Central and West Asia Economic Corridor. [7] Russia is thus a very desirable partner for the BRI.

Prior to the BRI, Moscow and Beijing have had a long history of interactions, not all of them good. In 1858, the Treaty of Aigun between the Russian Empire and the Qing Dynasty set the border at the Amur River, with Russia receiving a large chunk of land, known as Primorye, on the left bank of the river. In a separate treaty signed two years later, Russia also acquired land on the right bank of Amur, which gave them control of the entire Primorye region all the way to Vladivostok. [8]

Beijing resents both treaties, which were signed while China was weak. As a result, military clashes between the two countries broke out in 1969. Bilateral relations were finally normalized in 1989, while sovereignty over two small islands remained unresolved. [9] Sino-Russian partnership agreements were signed in 1994 and 1996, followed by a treaty of friendship and cooperation in 2000. In 2004, roughly half of the disputed territory was transferred to China. In Russia, this agreement was seen as yielding too much. In 2008, all border issues were considered settled, but many in China still felt they had been cheated. [10] In spite of these ambiguities, in 2011, the Russian Direct Investment Fund (Russia's sovereign wealth fund) and China Development Bank (CDB) signed an agreement, creating the China-Russia RMB Investment Cooperation Fund. [11] In 2012, a Russian-Chinese strategic partnership deal was signed. Additionally, both Russia and China are members of the Shanghai

Cooperation Organization (SCO), BRICS, the G20, and the UN Security Council. [12]

In 2013, when PRC President Xi Jinping first announced the BRI, Russia was skeptical about participating. In 2015, Russia launched its own initiative, the Eurasian Economic Union (EEU or EAEU), linking at first Russia, Kazakhstan, Belarus and Armenia, then joined by Kyrgyzstan seven months later. [13] Russia was concerned the BRI would compete with the EAEU. [14] The fact the initial BRI announcement was made in Kazakhstan was particularly worrisome for Moscow, as Kazakhstan is a key economy in Central Asia and played an important role in the EAEU. Russia had overcome its skepticism by the end of 2014, however, due to the Ukraine crisis, which left Russia feeling more isolated from the West and suffering from a worsening economy, brought on by US-led sanctions. Losing the Ukraine as a potential participant in Russian markets was another factor, as Ukraine has the no. 2 economy in the region. Consequently, in March 2015, Russia decided to join the China-led Asian Infrastructure Investment Bank (AIIB). [15] Later that same year, Moscow and Beijing agreed to link the EAEU and the BRI. Due to concerns about a potential loss of sovereignty, Moscow promotes an image of "a larger Eurasian partnership" or "Greater Eurasia," a network of existing and emerging "integration formats," of which, the BRI would be just one more initiative alongside the EAEU. [16] Russia's plan is well suited to Central Asia, particularly in Kazakhstan and Kyrgyzstan, where Sinophobia runs deeper than resentment toward Russian imperialism. [17]

China-Russia trade and investment

Russia's top exports include crude petroleum, refined petroleum, petroleum gas, coal briquettes, and raw aluminum, making Russia an excellent target for Chinese trade. [18] China is Russia's no. 1 export partner, but Russia also incurred its largest trade deficit with China, amounting to US$9.1 billion in 2017. [19] China was among the top five sources of foreign direct investment in Russia. [20]

The single largest Chinese investment in Russia has been the Yamal liquid natural gas (LNG) project on the Siberian Arctic coast. [21] Between 2016 and 2018, the Russian Far East has received over US$7 billion in Chinese investment, accounting for 80% of its total. In 2017, the number of Chinese companies in the area increased by over 30%. Gazprom and China National Petroleum Corp. signed a 30-year deal in

2014 to provide gas to China. In 2017, Tianjin Port Group signed an MOU for cooperation with Commercial Port of Vladivostok Group. This cooperation is expected to save time and increase the transport of freight between the two countries. [22]

One of the most important infrastructure projects in the China-Russia-Mongolia Economic Corridor is the Tongjiang Rail Bridge, which connects the city of Tongjiang in Heilongjiang province to Nizhneleninskoye in Russia. [23]

Beijing and Moscow have set up a US$10 billion China-Russia RMB Investment Cooperation Fund, which provides access to RMB financing for Russian projects. Additional funding comes from CDB, China National Petroleum Corp., the Silk Road Fund, China Investment Corp., the RDIF, and the Russia-China Investment Fund. Moscow and Beijing have come to an agreement whereby settlement can be carried out in RMB through China's Industrial and Commercial Bank of China. [24]

The RDIF, together with China's sovereign wealth fund, the China Investment Corp. (CIC) jointly formed the Russia China investment Fund (RCIF) in 2012. [25] One of the first projects undertaken by the RCIF was the development of the former Tushino airfield in the northwest of Moscow. [26] China National Petroleum Corp., along with Russian companies Rosneft and Gazprom, signed agreements on oil and gas projects. [27] RCIF partnered with the China-Eurasian Economic Cooperation Fund (CEF), which is backed by China's Exim Bank, to invest in Eurasia Drilling Co and United Transport Concession Holding. Other investment projects range from light rail to highways, a railway bridge on the China-Russian border, Russian retail chain Lenta, and Chinese taxi-hailing service Didi Chuxing. [28] Additionally, the RDIF, in cooperation with CDB, has established an RMB investment cooperation fund. [29]

In Siberia's Trans-Baikal region, China and Russia have signed a 49-year lease agreement for 150,000 hectares of farmland. Some Russians oppose this deal, feeling that their homeland is being sold out. Other objections to PRC investment come from Russian monitoring authorities which have determined that the Chinese are using excessive amounts of chemicals, particularly nitrates, which in addition to destroying the soil, pose health problems for consumers. [30]

Many Russians resent an influx of Chinese, which they see as *de facto* occupation of Russian territory. A film titled "China – A Deadly

Friend," part of a series called "Russia Deceived," was released in 2015. The film, which claims Beijing is planning to invade Russia's Far East, was a major hit. [31] In spite of ill-feelings toward China, in the minds of Russians, the US remains their primary foe. One survey found found that 68% of Russians regard the US as an enemy, but only 2% see China as one.

The Sino-Russian alliance, as a counter to the US, is boosted by the close relationship between Putin and Xi, who have met dozens of times since 2013. [32] Additionally, some Russians feel the rise of China signals the decline of the US, and they are hoping that eventually China would be in a position to lift sanctions against Russia. There is also hope that China's building of transportation links from Russia to Europe could help Russia take advantage of wealthier Western European markets. [33]

Locals in Russia's Far East are afraid that the arrival of Chinese people, money, and technology is sinicizing their territory, and that Chinese will eventually seize political control. In 2018, an online petition, banning Chinese from purchasing land at Lake Baikal, was signed by over 50,000 Russians. Other petitions have been circulating, asking politicians to stop the Chinese from taking all of the local timber. [34]

Central Asia

It is unlikely that Central Asian nations will switch their allegiance from Russia to China. [35] Researchers have found that Central Asian countries are happy to participate in projects which help them in economic terms, but that they resist the spread of Chinese ideology, culture, or population. Throughout Southeast Asia, Chinese script can be seen on everything from hair cutters to construction companies and hotels. In Central Asia, by contrast, in major cities, such as Astana, while Cyrillic and English can be found everywhere, Chinese writing is almost non-existent. [36]

Kazakhstan offers the most direct overland route from China to Russia, making the country so significant to the BRI that its leaders refer to their nation as the "buckle" in the Belt and Road. [37] Kazakhstan believes so strongly in the benefits they stand to gain through the initiative that they have invested US$5 billion of their sovereign wealth fund in BRI infrastructure projects, such as Khorgos, a border city which has the world's largest "dry port" facilities. Kazakhstan has also received around US$30 billion in Chinese investment; the PRC is now the no. 1 investor in all five former Soviet republics in Central Asia. [38] Apart from investment, however, the Central Asian republics have seen very little increase in actual business.

Even Kazakhstan, the country where the BRI was first announced, has not experienced a major upsurge in business with China. [39] The two countries have signed deals for more than 51 projects, worth US$27 billion, but so far little has materialized. On a state visit, Xi claimed that China had carried out US$42.8 billion of projects in Kazakhstan, but what he was referring to was unrelated to the BRI. In 2009, China loaned money to Kazakhstan for oil projects which were finally completed in 2015. [40] This further illustrates one of the criticisms of the BRI: Because the initiative lacks a clear definition or scope, and as there is no published list of projects or timeframe for completion, China can pick and choose which projects to tout as having been part of the BRI. Consequently, only successful projects, regardless of when they began, are likely to be counted as part of the initiative.

The backlash in Central Asia has been similar to that in Russia's Far East, namely the loss of sovereignty and land. In 2016, Kazakhs protested because they believed new laws would result in China buying up too much land in Kazakhstan. [41]

China is utilizing soft power to further its aims in the region, building 11 Confucius Institutes across Central Asia and offering education to 23,000 Central Asian students at Chinese universities. [42] Further soft power initiatives involve Sino-Russian cooperation, such as a Russia-led initiative involving China and Pakistan seeks to broker a settlement in Afghanistan's civil war. If successful, this could eliminate much of the US influence in the region. [43] Both Russia and China stand to gain from such involvement in Central Asia. Moscow wishes to re-establish its former dominance in the region, while Beijing sees an opportunity for investment and economic gain. Russia and China's gambit depends on the US withdrawing its troops from Afghanistan, something previous US administrations were considering. But US President Donald J. Trump reaffirmed his pledge to maintain American forces in Afghanistan for fear of creating a power vacuum. [44]

China is Afghanistan's biggest investment partner, having taken a 30-year lease on the Aynak copper mine, as well as constructing a railway link, connecting China's far east with the Afghan rail port of Hairatan. Additionally, by further developing transportation routes through Afghanistan, China could decrease the time and cost of trading with Iran. [45]

China is definitely playing a softer game in Central Asia than in the South China Sea, where many believe there is a real threat of a military clash. In Central Asia, however, "the logic of BRI in Central Asia is one of connectivity, cooperation, and large-scale investment. All China needs to make BRI work in Central Asia is open borders and receptivity to Chinese capital." [46] China is racing against time, however, as India, a country whose aid is more welcome in Afghanistan, is prepared to invest in hospitals and dams. [47]

Central Asian companies suffer from poor corporate governance which precludes many of them from working with AIIB. This leaves an opening for China to provide much needed financing. [48] Of all of the Central Asian nations, Tajikistan has the highest China-debt to GDP ratio of 49%. [49] Roughly 40% of Kyrgyzstan's public debt, and 50% of Tajikistan's, is owed to Chinese institutions, primarily Exim Bank. [50] Exim Bank holds 36% of Kyrgyzstan's government debt. [51]

The reason for the high level of debt and for the lack of an increase in local business is the fact that PRC aid to Central Asia is classified as "tied aid," meaning it comes with certain conditions, such as concessional loans, a requirement that at least 50% of raw materials, equipment, technology, and services should come from China, as well as a minimum percentage of participation by Chinese companies. [52] There are concerns that the competitive advantages of Chinese firms may destroy local industries in countries that receive BRI financing. These advantages range from sheer size and lack of competition from other Chinese firms, to government subsidies, preferential access to raw materials, and advantageous financing arrangements through state banks. When these advantages are combined with loan conditions requiring that 50% of materials and equipment be purchased from Chinese firms, it seems unlikely that local firms could survive, much less compete with the Chinese. In those countries where China is buying local commodities, there is a trend toward becoming too dependent on China. Since 2016, China has been the only buyer of Turkmenistan's gas exports. [53]

Chinese aid is frequently tied to trade agreements and investment deals, and may include such political concessions as the host country agreeing to reject recognition of Taiwan. [54] Additional geopolitical demands include "refusal to support the Uyghur cause, collaborating in the 'hunt for dissidents' within the framework of RATS (Regional Anti-Terrorist Structure of the Shanghai Cooperation Organization), limited relations with Taiwan, silence on the Tibetan issue, and (in some cases) alignment with China at the UN Security Council." [55]

Aid can also be granted in exchange for natural resources. In 2006, China offered Kyrgyzstan a US$1.2 billion railway package in exchange for access to mineral resources. [56] A pipeline was built in Turkmenistan with Chinese investment but because the payments are being made in gas, Turkmenistan has experienced no increase in income. [57] Similarly, in 2009, China granted Turkmenistan US $4 billion in exchange for the right to exploit natural gas fields. [58] Many see China as more or less assuming the role Russia once played in the republics, namely that China now provides the republics with finished goods and technology, and the republics provide China with energy and natural resources. [59] For example, up to 80% of all goods sold in the bazaar in Kyrgyzstan are Chinese products. [60] And China controls 30% of the oil extracted from Kazakhstan. [61]

Another concern is that many of the projects within the context of the BRI have motivations other than profit. In fact, some experts go so far as to say that Chinese banks may not even have the ability to evaluate the profitability of investment projects as they have little experience. [62] On the other hand, it is the Chinese side which conducts the profitability research which is presented to potential host countries. Therefore, Central Asian countries may be going into debt in order to further a Chinese strategic or political objective, which has little or no chance of turning a profit or even covering loan payments. Chinese banks may be given the option to write some of these loans off, but Central Asia will not.

Not all Chinese investment in the region has been bad. China has invested in the New Silk Road Agriculture and Textile Industrial Park in Tajikistan, where Chinese textile firms are already operating. Similarly, Chinese textile firms have invested in the Uzbekistan's Jizzakh Special Economic Zone. These investments have introduced new technology to local industry which could have long-term positive effects, but other investments just make Central Asia more dependent on the PRC. One example would be a US$26 billion China–Kazakhstan agreement, signed in September 2016 and spanning a range of industries, including mining, smelting, engineering, chemicals and petrochemicals. Part of the deal was that 100% of the output would be sold to China. While this may positively impact GDP, it does not help Kazakhstan develop new markets or connect with the rest of the world. [63] Meanwhile, locals often do not benefit from jobs created by Chinese investment. In Kyrgyzstan, Chinese migrants openly compete with locals for work. [64] Reportedly, some Chinese projects reserve as many as 70% of the jobs for Chinese workers.

Consistent with Beijing's requirements that Central Asia support its campaign against terrorism, both Kyrgyzstan and Kazakhstan have deported alleged Uyghur terrorists to China. In June 2004, at the Shanghai Cooperation Organization (SCO) summit, Uzbek President Islam Karimov publicly stated that Uzbekistan was in full support of China in its fight against the three evils, "international terrorism, extremism, and separatism." [65] While most people in the West would agree with the first two issues, the third was clearly a reference to Uyghur separatist movements in Xinjiang and possibly a further reminder of Beijing's policy regarding Taiwan.

One of the many reasons that Central Asia is so important to the BRI is because it serves as a land-bridge between China and South Asia. The China-Pakistan Economic Corridor (CPEC), which became operational in 2016, represents a modern "Great Game" played between China, Pakistan, India, Russia, the US, and UK, with the Central Asian countries acting as pawns. The China-Pakistan-India dynamic is particularly volatile as both China and Pakistan have fought wars against India. CPEC strengthens the relationship between China and Pakistan, causing India to move closer to the US and to also form relationships with Afghanistan and Iran. [66] Xi's visits to Pakistan have further alienated India by offering concessions to India's Central Asian neighbors and allies.

Russia has always been a bit of a wild card in the region, periodically swinging towards or away from China. Russian Ambassador to Pakistan Alexey Y. Dedov has said that Moscow is in discussions with Islamabad to merge CPEC with Russia's Eurasian Economic Union. [67]

Russia's joining of CPEC creates an opportunity for China, Russia, and Pakistan to improve their relationship. [68] As a result of Russia's acceptance of CPEC, Russia is now being permitted to export through Gwadar Port in Pakistan. CPEC will be looked at in much greater detail, later in this book.

Chapter 5: The BRI and Soft Power

In a 2014 address, PRC President Xi Jinping said that part of China's commitment to the world is to increase China's soft power, linking China's likability to its economic rise. Soft power can be an important tool in transforming a country into a world leader, "a country's perceived legitimacy, attractiveness of ideology and culture, and societal norms play an important role in shaping international politics." [1]

A primary element of Chinese soft power is doublespeak. For example, the Belt and Road Initiative is not called the Chinese Global Expansion Program or the Chinese Global Domination Program. China's economic rise would appear to be in direct violation of socialist ideals. But China refers to its economy as socialism with Chinese characteristics, a term invented to mask the apparent capitalist motivation behind global economic expansion. The removal of term limits for Xi has not been described as making him "president for life," simply a removal of limits. Each time PRC government spokespeople are asked if Xi will be president for life, vague answers are given, effectively saying that it is obvious at some time one could become too old or mentally no longer nimble enough to rule, but there is never a direct mention of a lifetime term for Xi. The Chinese Dream and Xi Jinping Thought are all forms of propaganda or soft power which soften the reality that China is an autocratic state which hands down political edicts to lower levels of government and to private citizens, driving them toward the completion of state objectives, such as securing supplies of energy and natural resources, as well as controlling world financial and trade markets, through the BRI. [2]

Apart from doublespeak, a country's image can be improved by throwing cash around. The total amount of money China spends each year to improve its image and likeability is difficult to determine, but experts estimate the figure to be somewhere around US$10 billion. [3] This includes money spent to sponsor BRI-related events such as the May 2017 BRI forum in Beijing which was attended by 30 world leaders and representatives from 110 countries and international organizations. [4]

The initiative itself can be seen as a tool to establish China's soft power, as it brings investment and development to countries where China hopes it will be perceived China as a friend. In BRI-participating countries, PRC leaders have also promoted "Chinese language, educational exchanges, media expansion, and pop culture." [5] Confucius Institutes are government funded and function like the British Council, Alliance Française, Germany's Goethe Institute, or Spain's Cervantes Institute. As of 2018, there were over 500 Confucius Institutes around the world, teaching courses and holding events related to Chinese language and culture. [6]

Student exchanges are another important aspect of soft power. In 2016, nearly half a million foreign students traveled to China. The following year, China was ranked as the no. 3 most popular destination for foreign students. While the majority of foreign students studying in China are self-funded, China also provides a number of scholarships. [7] In the 2006–2007 school year, only 1,200 Kazakh students studied in China, but by the 2014–2015 academic year, the number had increased to 11,200. [8] By 2018, Xi had announced that the Chinese government would award 30,000 government scholarships to Shanghai Cooperation Organization (SCO) member states, as well as extending invitations to 10,000 teachers and students from Confucius Institutes in these countries. [9]

Media is another element of soft power, and Beijing is funding a number of international news outlets. The government's primary news service, Xinhua, now boasts 170 foreign bureaus and continues to grow. Other government-backed media, *China Daily* and *Global Times* , publish English-language editions available worldwide. In 2016, the state TV network, CCTV, renamed itself China Global Television Network and now has reporting teams based in more than 70 countries feeding its six channels, which broadcast in English and as well as in Arabic, French, Russian, and Spanish. [10]

"China Radio International (CRI) broadcasts 392 hours of programming a day in thirty-eight languages from twenty-seven overseas bureaus." [11] CRI, working through front companies, operates more than 30 radio stations in 14 countries. These overseas media are targeted at the estimated 50 million Chinese diaspora, living mostly in Southeast Asia, as well as non-Chinese around the world. [12] In March, 2018, Beijing approved funding for what has been called the largest propaganda machine in history. A new broadcaster will be formed, called "Voice of China," perhaps as a parody of the US-funded Voice of America (VOA). [13]

In the entertainment industry, Chinese soft power is projected through film director Zhang Yimou, actor Jackie Chan, pianist Lang Lang, former NBA stars Yao Ming and Li Na, ballet dancer Tan Yuanyuan, and pop singer Jane Zhang. [14]

Chinese companies are working with Hollywood production companies to expand China's influence into the world of entertainment. Chinese firms, such as Dalian Wanda, participated in recent films including *Godzilla* , *Jurassic World* , and *Interstellar* . US production companies agree to these joint ventures because they need investment capital from China as well as a way in to the Chinese market which dramatically boosts their total ticket sales. [15]

The Marvel film *Iron Man III* represented a co-production with a Chinese company. In China, a different cut of the film was released, expanding the subplot about the Chinese doctors who performed surgery on Ironman. [16] *Kung Fu Panda III* was another hit movie produced by a US joint venture company called Oriental DreamWorks. [17] In China, *Kung Fu Panda III* was the highest-grossing animated film ever. Abroad, the film positively portrayed Chinese culture, mythology, and kung fu, winning over new fans for China. [18] Real pandas are at the focus of Beijing's so called "panda diplomacy," enacted through China's zoo exchanges. [19] The ancient Chinese martial art of kung fu is also the subject of the PRC's "Shaolin Diplomacy," sending Shaolin Temple kung fu performers around the world, even to Harvard University and the UN. [20]

International sport can also serve as a vehicle for soft power. Hosting the 2008 Olympics was a milestone in the development of Chinese sport as well as a major step in promoting a positive image of China. At the 2016 Olympic Games in Rio, China took home 71 medals, almost double the number of medals they had earned in Los Angeles in 1984. [21]

Tourism as soft power
Tourists bring much needed revenue to host countries, as well as spreading Chinese language and culture. Chinese outbound tourism has increased steadily over the past decade, reaching 120 million outbound trips in 2016. [22] This dramatic increase has been a result of the country's rapid economic growth whereby the average citizen has seen the average yearly salary increase from under US$2,000 per year in 2002 to about US$7,000 today. [23] More recently, the BRI has also become a significant driver of Chinese outbound tourism. According to the Silk Road Tourism Cooperation Forum and the Eleventh Outbound Tourism Forum held in Beijing on June 29, 2015, China increasing tourism is in keeping with the government's strategic goals behind the initiative. [24] To further promote the growth of Chinese tourism in line with the BRI, the Beijing-based World Tourism Cities Federation (WTCF) has proposed the "Belt and Road Tourism Corridor" including the 55 WTCF member cities which lie along the Belt and Road from Asia to Africa, accounting for 70% of global tourism. [25]

WTCF reported on the One Belt One Road Tourism Forum held in Beijing in July 2015, one of numerous government-sponsored tourism expos held around China, including the China Western Tourism Exposition, the South China Sea Tourism Development Strategy High-end Forum, and the Beijing International Tourism Expo. [26] This demonstrates Beijing's commitment to increasing tourism which is both a part of trade and a component of the Belt and Road Initiative.

The BRI includes the development of transportation infrastructure which will facilitate tourism, such as the railway network linking Association of Southeast Asian Nations (ASEAN) countries to China. [27] PRC tourists already account for 12% of arrivals across ASEAN; with support from Beijing, the number is expected to grow. [28] Xi has promised increased tourism from China as a form of aid to countries connected by the BRI. [29] Recognizing the importance of Chinese tourism in ASEAN, Secretary-General of Malaysia Inbound Tourism Association Mint Leong has urged tour operators to upgrade their services and focus on higher-end travel to service the new Chinese customers.

English-language social media and soft power

When Xi announced his Thirteenth Five-Year Plan, which included the BRI, the Chinese government commissioned an English-language cartoon video called "The Shisanwu!" (pinyin transliteration for the Thirteenth Five-Year Plan). The video is done in a hip, humorous style with native English speakers singing a catchy song "If you wanna know what China's gonna do, best pay attention to the shisanwu! The shisanwu, The shisan what? The shisanwu!" [30] The content is short on explanation about the actual contents of the Thirteenth Five-Year Plan, but the Westerners in the video seem to be very excited about it and suggest viewers should be too.

Another PRC government propaganda video, "The Communist Party of China is with you along the way," attempts to explain the Chinese Dream to the world, giving it the most positive spin possible. The video portrays China as an "ancient and youthful country." What's not to like about that? "Our people's dreams are our goals," and the entire Communist Party is working towards the achievement of those goals. Just as with the Thirteenth Five-Year Plan video, there is no significant explanation as to the contents of the China Dream or why it would benefit people outside of China. Nonetheless, the video is upbeat and reminds people that the 80 million members of the Communist Party of China stand together. [31]

Another video, "How Leaders Are Made," explains how Xi became the leader of China, and compares it to becoming the president of the US, which the video claims costs lots of money and takes a lot of campaigning. The implication is that the levels of exams and selections one passes while climbing the political ladder in China mean one is smarter and more qualified than the US president. [32] The video was produced in English and is available on YouTube, so was clearly intended for a foreign audience. Perhaps the message being sent to other countries is that – if they side with China, rather than the US – they would be siding with a leader who is smart and capable, rather than rich and full of showmanship. The video goes on to say that one of the secrets of the Chinese economic miracle is that the government has been able to maintain a fairly unified policy and vision which includes policies on the environment and GDP. The video also claims that Chinese netizens can criticize their leaders online, but this is not exactly true.

"When China met Carolina," is another English-language video which portrays Americans in North and South Carolina explaining how great it is to work for Chinese companies. The central message is "China is not here to steal your jobs, it is here to save them." [33] The video goes on to claims that Chinese investment has created over 80,000 jobs in the US. By extrapolation, North and South Carolina benefit from Chinese investment, as could the entire United States and the world. In the video, a Chinese factory owner, who goes by the English name of Jeff, explains that by buying this factory and producing in the US, his products now bear a Made-in-USA logo. While this is true, there is no doubt that this means the Chinese are circumventing US import duties. [34]

Yet another piece of propaganda, "Britain meets China," explains what close friends China and the UK are. According to the storyline, the friendship is apparently based on the fact that Xi likes soccer. The first half of the video focuses on student exchanges, language and soccer, while the second half shows employees at a Chinese-invested automotive factory in Britain and how happy they were to still have jobs. [35]

One of the most egregious propaganda videos is The Belt and Road music video produced by Fuxing Road Studios, which also produced the shisanwu video. This video features multiethnic children, singing in English: "The belt moves on the land, the road moves on the sea. The promise that they hold is joint prosperity." [36] The video goes on to extol the virtues of the BRI and how they will benefit all of the world's people. "The trade routes open up. That's when the sharing starts. Resources changing hands... we're sharing a world of prosperity. [37]

At the 2017 World Economic Forum in Davos, Xi began a narrative of China being the new champion of global free trade. [38] A similar message seems to have been attached to the BRI, projecting China as a benevolent force bringing as much peace and prosperity to as many countries as possible. The BRI video echoes this sentiment: " We're paving new roads, building more ports, finding new options with friends of all sorts; it's a culture exchange, we trade in our wealth, we connect with our hearts, it strengthens our health." [39]

Chinese-produced English-language media exalting the virtues of the BRI do not end with that music video. The PRC government even made a series of videos for YouTube (which is blocked in China), depicting an allegedly-American father telling a bedtime story to his five-year-old daughter, Lilly, explaining why he has to go to the BRI conference in Beijing. Lilly asks her father, "It's a Chinese initiative, right?" and the father answers, "It's a Chinese idea, but it belongs to the world." [40] Later, Lilly asks, "Globalization? What's that?" and the father explains, "That's where people from different parts of the world cooperate more. They buy and sell things to each other. And they visit and even live in each other's countries.... It's good for people. We lead happier lives when we cooperate." [41] The father goes on to explain that the BRI is necessary because some countries do not want globalization right now. Lilly smiles and enthusiastically reveals that she approves of the initiative and suggests that we should too.

In the fourth video, Lilly asks where the countries will get the money to build all of these projects. The father says, "That's a big question and I will tell you that one tomorrow." [42] In part five, the father explains the financing of the BRI. [43] Rather than use the terms "concessional loans" or "crippling debt," he tells his daughter that the initiative is like her piggy bank. Only Lilly puts money into Lilly's piggy bank, and only Lilly can take money out. The father explains that the BRI is like a piggy bank. A lot of countries put money in, and they are the only ones who can take it out; however, the countries can take out more than they put in because "they build new things that help all the countries make more money to share." [44]

Although the Chinese people appear share Lilly's enthusiasm for the BRI, and the singing multiethnic children also seem to approve, not everyone is convinced. Chinese soft-power initiatives have paid off more in some countries than in others. In Africa, China has the highest approval ratings. In surveys, citizens of countries such as Burkina Faso, Ethiopia, Ghana, Liberia, Mali, and Niger all rate China positively. China is generally well-perceived in Latin America. Pakistan and Russia also have a positive view of China, while in Japan and the West, China's popularity has steadily declined. [45] The US, Australia and many EU leaders have also pushed back against or outright rejected the BRI. [46]

In the bedtime-story video, Lilly tells her father that she wished everyone understood the BRI as well as she did, because then they would definitely go along with it. Apparently, neither Donald Trump, nor a lot of people in India, Pakistan, or Thailand understand the BRI as well as that five-year-old.

Africa is one of the places where China enjoys a relatively good reputation, and the positive view survives despite China's soft-power blunders. In the 2018 Chinese New Year state TV special, in an attempt to celebrate the allegedly close relations between China and Africa, a Chinese actress appeared on stage in black face, with her bust and bottom padded. Her dance partner was a black man in a monkey costume. [47] An issue with China's soft power along the BRI seems to be that China is trying to promote the concept of brotherhood with countries where the Chinese have no commonality, no shared history, and no cultural understanding. Not only does the average Chinese person have very little in common with the average African, but the average Chinese person has never seen, much less met, an African. Still, it seems shocking that this would prevent Chinese propagandists from knowing that Africans probably do not like people wearing black face or dressing black people up like monkeys.

One of China's classic soft-power fails was the government funded English-language hip hop video "This is China Rap," which has such compelling lines as "The Red Dragon ain't no evil. The song also goes on to explain that "we all know that China is a developing country. It has large population and it is really hard to manage, especially after WWII almost perished." [48] It has been suggested that one reason why China fails so miserably in its propaganda attempts is because the current generation of leaders grew up in an era essentially without media. The young people featured in the "This is China Rap" video grew up in an era where American movies dominated China's cinemas. They have watched foreign music videos and may have some concept of how to be "cool," but the people commissioning the videos and ultimately approving the texts do not.

The Confucius Institutes have also proven to have been a failed vehicle of soft power. At numerous top universities, including members of the Ivy League and the University of Chicago, professors have banded together to sign petitions driving the institutes off campus. One reason they give is that the institutes repress freedom of speech, prohibiting students from discussing sensitive topics such as Tiananmen Square, Taiwan, or

Tibet. [49] In Australia, intelligence analysts have warned against having a PRC-funded body imbedded in an Australian government institution, such as a public university. [50] Doris Liu, a Chinese-Canadian journalist and filmmaker, in her film, *In the Name of Confucius* , goes so far as to accuse the Confucius Institutes of both spying and being used to recruit intelligence assets. [51]

Beijing's soft-power initiatives are facing to major hurdles. The first is that China has no history of people-to-people diplomacy. The authoritarian nature of the PRC and the fact that China restricts the flow of information and even the emigration of its people makes it difficult for China to open up to the world. Next, while soft power, kung fu exchanges, and free education may help China's image abroad, they will not make people in Sri Lanka forget that they lost control of both an airport and a seaport to China because they could not repay their loans. Moving forward, when Pakistan feels the crunch of its massive BRI-related debts and sees no increase in its revenue because of the one-sided nature of the contracts, will the so-called Iron Brotherhood survive?

Chapter 6: South Asia

Pakistan and the BRI

In 2017, Pakistan had a population of 197 million and a per capita GDP of US$1,547. Recent GDP growth has been 4.7%. Unemployment stands at 6%, while public debt as a percentage of GDP is 65%. [1]

The China-Pakistan Economic Corridor (CPEC), which runs from China's northwestern Xinjiang Province to Gwadar Port on Pakistan's Arabian Sea coast, is considered to be the flagship of the BRI. [2] In agreeing to participate in CPEC, Pakistan has signed agreements to have the PRC finance and build a massive amount of infrastructure in the country, including highways, roads, seaports, fiber-optic cables, telecommunications grids, banking networks, and power generation facilities. CPEC was the first project to receive funding from China's Silk Road Fund, a dedicated investment fund established to finance projects associated with the BRI. As of mid-2018, US$19 billion in projects had been completed or in progress. [3]

The project was meant to boost Pakistan's GDP, and thus provide the government with the tax revenues needed to repay the Chinese loans. Unfortunately, so far, the plan seems to be somewhat backfiring for Pakistan, putting a strain on the country's public finances and currency. In part, this is due to a sharp increase in imports from China and sweetheart deals given to Chinese companies and Chinese investors linked to CPEC. In addition to an underperforming Pakistan rupee, the country's foreign currency reserves are being depleted.

China is the no. 1 source of foreign direct investment (FDI) in Pakistan, accounting for almost half of Pakistan's total received FDI in 2016 to 2017. [4] CPEC investments helped Pakistan's GDP grow by 5.3% in 2017, better than the 2016 figure of 4.9%. However, Pakistan fell well behind its larger neighbor, India, where growth was 7.4%. [5] Consumer spending in Pakistan has been good as a result of CPEC investment. This, however, is only a short-term economic gain; the medium-term outlook is more bearish, as Pakistan's imports are outpacing exports. [6]

One benefit of large-scale foreign investment is that it normally attracts additional investment from other countries. Since the beginning of CPEC, domestic investment has increased, but so far investment from countries other than China has not increased appreciably. One specialist has said he did not believe Chinese investment will attract investment from other countries, saying: "Chinese investment is largely strategic." [7]

China's engagement with Pakistan through CPEC has been called "debt trap diplomacy." The projects are mostly being built by companies from China, the lender country. The projects often hemorrhage money or fail to meet deadlines, putting the borrower, Pakistan, in the unenviable position of having to throw good money after bad. The borrower then has to borrow more money from the lender and is soon saddled with so much debt that it cannot keep up with payments. This leads to an effective loss of sovereignty, as the borrower must yield to the lender's political influence. [8] By joining CPEC and accepting these loans, Pakistan must agree to create markets for Chinese exports, grant access to natural resources, and support China's geostrategic interests. [9] Additionally, the loan agreements often lack transparency, making it unclear just what Pakistan owes or how the loans will be repaid.

Sri Lanka serves as a cautionary tale for countries associated with the BRI. Due to its inability to repay loans, Sri Lanka has been forced to turn over control of its largest seaport to a PRC state-owned company on a 99-year lease.

The BRI in Sri Lanka and the Maldives

Construction of Sri Lanka's Hambantota Port began in 2008 and was 85% financed by China. By 2017, Sri Lanka's debt equaled 81.6% of GDP with the country's annual external-debt financing roughly equal to its entire tax revenue. [10] Sri Lanka's debt to China is said to be US$8 billion and carries an interest rate of 6%. As a result, Sri Lanka transferred control of its largest port and airport to China to cover the debt. The Maldives is similarly in debt to the PRC and may have to cede territory as payment. This region is important to China as two thirds of Chinese energy supplies pass through its sea lanes. [11] The Maldives may have to give up land as soon as 2019. Meanwhile, China has already warned that the UN and other countries should respect the sovereignty of the Maldives by not intervening. [12]

Former Maldives President Mohamed Nasheed claims that Beijing has already taken control of 16 islands. Additionally, he charges that apart from useful infrastructure, Chinese-built roads lead nowhere and there are airports that sit idle, all of which have further increased Maldives' debt. In addition to debt and loss of sovereignty, the former president expressed concerns that civilian ports could become military assets. [13] This allegation is strengthened by the fact that a PRC military submarine docked in Colombo, the Sri Lankan capital, in 2014. [14] In 2018, a PRC combat force entered the Indian Ocean for the first time in four years. Beijing claimed the forces were there as a result of civil unrest which might prompt the Maldives government to call on China to protect Chinese investments on the islands. [15] In mid-2018, the Sri Lankan government announced that it would base its navy out of the Chinese-controlled Hambantota Port. [16] In August that year, a PRC navy force made a goodwill visit to Colombo. [17]

To avoid a similar debt-trap and a loss of sovereignty, Nepal backed out of a US$2.5 billion dam-construction deal with China. The reason given was that the Nepali government found the financing agreement unacceptable and because it required transfer of ownership. [18] Similarly, in November 2017, Islamabad canceled a US$14 billion joint venture with China to develop the Diamer-Bhasha dam. This came after authorities determined that under the terms of the agreement, Chinese companies and labor would be used. Continuing with the project would also have increased Chinese imports to Pakistan, further worsening the country's trade deficit with China. Additionally, China wanted a transfer of partial ownership, which Pakistani officials said was out of the question. [19]

As a direct result of CPEC, Pakistan's trade deficit hit a record US$37 billion in fiscal 2018. The IMF has determined that the country's capital outflows, including loan repayments, profit repatriation and imports of inputs, will peak at US$3.5 billion to 4.5 billion by 2025. The IMF warned that running such unhealthy current accounts risks the country's macroeconomic stability. There is also speculation that power generated by CPEC projects will be too expensive for Pakistani consumers. [20]

Islamabad is now facing a financial shortfall, unable to meet its 2018–2019 service payments for foreign loans. If Pakistan were to go to the IMF for the bailout, the IMF would review Pakistan's finances and challenge Pakistan's participation in CPEC. Consequently, Pakistan has gone to China for a bailout, and Beijing is expected to grant the additional loans, so as not to threaten CPEC. This result is that Pakistan's debt to China will increase, as Islamabad borrows money from Beijing to repay its previous loans to China and other foreign countries. [21]

Backlash against CPEC

Pakistani industry representatives have complained that the terms of CPEC forces them to award contracts to Chinese companies, sometimes even if a local company's bid is lower. [22] PRC contractors are also awarded "tax breaks and exemptions for CPEC-related imports (from China), putting local companies at a disadvantage." [23]

Islamabad apparently recognizes the problem of its growing trade imbalance with China, and is now requesting that Beijing " give it concessions in the revised free trade accord." [24] Much of this imbalance comes as the result of the China-Pakistan Free Trade Agreement (CPFTA), which grants incentives to Chinese imports. Local manufacturers are complaining that they were not consulted during negotiations between Islamabad and Beijing, and that the concessions given to Chinese imports render domestic products uncompetitive. Tariff concessions by Islamabad have probably cost Pakistan considerable lost revenue. The Federal Board of Revenue has opposed the CPFTA because the country already has a large trade deficit with China. Industry representatives have warned that the CPFTA could cripple local industry. The president of the Federation of Pakistan Chamber of Commerce & Industry (FPCCI) warned that moving ahead with the CPFTA will subject Pakistan to "an industrial slump, massive unemployment and a further erosion in the balance of payment position." [25]

The chief of the Sarhad Chamber of Commerce & Industry told *Asia Times* that China already enjoys a zero tariff on 35% of tariff-lines, and that could now increase to 70%. He said that all local industries have complained to the FPCCI and warned that if the government does nothing to even out the playing field, local industry will have no option but to start a protest movement. [26]

The IMF determined that Pakistan's fiscal deficit was about to reach 5.5% of GDP, and that the country was quickly depleting its foreign reserves. The IMF warned that if Pakistan did nothing to reverse this trend, the country might be unable to repay US$17 billion worth of debt-servicing. Pakistan has received a total of US$87 billion in foreign loans, including CPEC-related borrowing from China. [27]

Security risks in CPEC

Security is a major concern for Beijing. CPEC runs through disputed territories as well as separatist regions where acts of terrorism have been committed against CPEC projects and workers. The US, the UK, and France are used to seeing reports of their nationals being killed abroad, but this is a new experience for China, as the country has only about 20 years of experience operating beyond its own borders. Deaths of Chinese workers overseas appears to be a consequence for which the Chinese have little tolerance. This was demonstrated in 2011, when China's navy evacuated thousands of PRC nationals from Libya, and again in 2014, when terrorist attacks forced Chinese workers to abandon northern Iraq, retreating to the relative safety of Baghdad. In 2015, China's military evacuated 600 Chinese from Yemen. [28]

Beijing has pushed Pakistan to increase security along CPEC. Pakistan has complied, recognizing the importance of CPEC-related investments and not wanting to see the financial taps turned off because of terrorism. As the military presence is increased around the country, this further complicates the separation of military and civil rule. Now that the US has now cut off military aid to Pakistan, the only place Islamabad can seek increased military spending is Beijing. In the end, this means that Pakistan is accepting money from China, to build up the Pakistan military, to fight against Pakistani people, to protect China's economic interests in the country. [29]

Geopolitical implications

China is already Pakistan's largest import partner, accounting for 28% of Pakistan's imports. China is also Pakistan's no. 3 export partner, behind the US and the UK. [30] The US canceling hundreds of millions of US dollars in military aid to Pakistan has driven Islamabad deeper into its relationship with China. [31] The day after Trump tweeted that the US had "foolishly given Pakistan more than US$33 billion in aid over the last 15 years, and they have given us nothing but lies and deceit," Pakistan's central bank announced that it would now allow business with China to be carried out using the Chinese yuan. [32] Imports and exports, as well as financing transactions for bilateral trade and investment activities can now be conducted using the yuan. [33] The move could be a tremendous hit to the US dollar, or the first of many moves by Beijing to erode the dollar's dominance in global commerce.

Working with Pakistan, China is now planning to extend CPEC to Afghanistan. The three countries met in Beijing in December 2017 for the first China-Afghanistan-Pakistan Foreign Ministers' Dialogue. Another agreement, the Quadrilateral Traffic in Transit Agreement (QTTA) links China, Pakistan, Kyrgyzstan, and Kazakhstan. Via Kyrgyzstan, QTTA links Pakistan with Russia. [34] Russia is another country which has agreed to use Chinese yuan in its business dealings with China. [35]

India, an ally of the United States, opposes CPEC on grounds that it runs through territory disputed by India and Pakistan. [36] While India, which has fought wars against both Pakistan and China, should be happy that Pakistan is receiving less military aid from Washington, India is also concerned that a decrease in US support may drive Pakistan closer to Beijing. India sees the increased Chinese presence in Pakistan as a security threat. [37] Eventually, India fears that China will build a military base in Pakistan. [38]

US sanctions on Iran have also had a direct impact on CPEC. China is the no. 1 purchaser of Iranian oil, and Iran is also one of the countries which has agreed, at least in theory, to conduct business using the Chinese yuan. [39] Additionally, Pakistan's Gwadar Port will be used to transport Iranian oil to China.

As much as Pakistan is sliding into the Chinese sphere of influence, Pakistan is a large, multiparty democracy, built on the Western model. Despite problems of corruption, on paper at least, Pakistan has a civil government like those in the UK and the US. Consequently, the country has more in common with the US than with China. [40]

Western aid, from the US and institutions such as the World Bank and the IMF, have come with some sort of accountability, encouraging the development of civil society, human rights, and accountability in Pakistan. PRC aid, on the other hand, is available in spite of a country scoring low on measures of good governance. [41] In theory, according to domestic laws and norms, Pakistan should have a transparent society with checks and balances. The details of CPEC, however, the financing, debt repayment, and sovereignty transfer are all being kept from the public, with a handful of top government officials making all the decisions, while keeping the populace in the dark. [42]

Pakistan is a democracy which is supposed to have freedom of the press and freedom of speech, yet government ministers have lashed out at journalists who challenge the government's line or push too hard for solid information. Additionally, CPEC has caused an even greater blurring between military and civil government in Pakistan. Beijing has repeatedly shown that it prefers to work with military governments and that it sees public or press criticism of government projects as a failing of the democratic system. [43] Beijing is not used to being criticized, as all China's media are state-owned.

When Trump cut military aid to Pakistan, he was thinking like a businessman. He felt that Islamabad was being paid for a job, helping the US to combat terrorism, but had failed to do this. Consequently, he did what any manager would do to an employee who fails to carry through on a task he has been paid for. He fired Pakistan. While a businessman's acumen can be beneficial to international trade negotiations, the scope is often too narrow for geopolitical matters. By cutting aid to Pakistan, Trump has saved US taxpayers some money, but potentially cost it its alliance with Islamabad. Further, as Pakistan still needed money, it turned to the only friend willing to write checks, China. As Pakistan slides deeper into Beijing's debt, it will move further away from Western alliances and closer to a new association comprised of China, Iran, and possibly Central Asia and Russia.

CPEC has been called the flagship project of the Belt and Road Initiative, but may actually be the dividing line that separates the new from the old global economic order. CPEC could be the turning point which shifts global alliances with Pakistan, Russia, and China on one side, and the US and India on the other.

India and the BRI

In April 2018, after a meeting of the Shanghai Cooperation Organization (SCO), India sent a communique, once again refusing to support the BRI. One of New Delhi's many objections is that part of CPEC runs through the disputed territory of Kashmir. [44]

Although India has refused to join the BRI, the country is the no. 1 recipient of loans from the Asian Infrastructure Investment Bank. India was also a founding member and, after China, owns the largest share of the bank. [45] India is also a member of the SCO along with Russia, Kazakhstan, Uzbekistan, Tajikistan, Kyrgyzstan, and Pakistan. [46] The SCO which now represents 40% of the world's population, consists of a long-term treaty of friendship, drafts of five-year plans, such as the SCO Action Plan for 2018–2022, and the Treaty for Long-Term Neighborliness. [47]

In lieu of BRI participation, India is involved in a number of multinational infrastructure projects designed to link Iran with Russia via India. To this end, India has acquired a portion of Iran's Chabahar Port and is working with Iran and Russia to complete the 7,200-km-long International North-South Transport Corridor, a sea, road, and rail network among India, Iran, Afghanistan, Armenia, Azerbaijan, Russia, Central Asia, and Europe. By moving goods by sea to and from Iran and then overland through Russia and Europe, India can bypass Pakistan altogether. Other India-led projects include the reopening of a 1,360-km-long road linking north-eastern India with Thailand. There is even talk of expanding the route to Myanmar, Cambodia, Laos, and Vietnam. [48]

Chapter 7: Financing the BRI

One of the biggest questions about the success of the BRI has been whether or not China can finance it. Financing is key to the success of any overseas economic expansion. To this end, Beijing created the China Investment Corp., China's sovereign wealth fund.

Sovereign-wealth funds are financial vehicles owned by governments which invest a government's cash reserves, national retirement pension funds, or revenue from commodity sales, such as oil. In addition to increasing the returns on a country's reserves and diversifying its investments, sovereign wealth funds often invest in foreign countries as a means of gaining political influence. [1]

The first sovereign wealth fund was the 1953 Kuwait Investment Authority, established to invest oil income. Following suit, Abu Dhabi created an Investment Authority in 1976. The Government of Singapore Investment Corporation was launched in 1981, and Norway's Government Pension Fund in 1990. [2] Today, countries including Japan and South Korea have sovereign wealth funds. Combined, the world's sovereign wealth funds now have US$7.2 trillion in assets under management, double the assets they held in 2007. [3]

China is unique in that it has four sovereign wealth funds, two of which are among the ten largest sovereign wealth funds in the world. China's National Social Security Fund, with US$236 billion of assets under management, is the world's no. 10 sovereign wealth fund by size. [4]

China Investment Corp. (CIC, 中国投资有限责任公司; zhōngguó tóuzī yǒuxiàn zérèn gōngsi) with over US$941 billion under management, is the world's no. 2 such fund. Established in 2007 to diversify the investment of China's currency reserves, [5] CIC is registered as a wholly state-owned enterprise (SOE) and maintains very close ties to the Chinese government. [6]

CIC's overseas investments
Beijing's Tenth Five-Year Plan (2001-05) announced the "going out" strategy whereby Chinese corporations, both SOEs and privately-owned enterprises (POEs), were encouraged to make direct investments overseas in order to gain access to foreign markets, secure natural resources, and acquire advanced technology. [7]

Chinese investment in the US comes from three sources: People's Bank of China (PBOC) buying US Treasury notes, CIC and other sovereign wealth funds investing in US equities and businesses, and finally outward foreign direct investment (FDI) by both Chinese private companies and Chinese SOE's. While private firms account for the largest number of investments in the US, the Chinese government accounts for a greater percentage of dollars invested. [8]

Research has determined that China's POEs have been more market driven in their behavior compared to Chinese SOEs such as CIC. [9] However, the larger investments were made by SOEs at least in part because they have had more access to capital as a result of their close ties to state-owned banks. In order to obtain government capital, POEs must link their business objectives with government strategic objectives, such as acquiring foreign firms in the hopes of obtaining advanced technology. Often, if financing is granted to an SOE, the government stands as a guarantor which can result in the SOE transforming into a joint ownership company with the government as an owner. [10]

After the Global Financial Crisis, the Chinese government seized the opportunity to purchase undervalued assets in developed countries. [11] Six tenths of all Chinese FDI comes from Chinese SOEs. [12]

About 25% of CIC's assets are invested outside the PRC. [13] To increase China's food security, the corporation has invested in agriculture, buying up farms in Asia, Africa and Latin America. [14] In Europe, it has the purchased a 10% stake in London's Heathrow Airport. [15] China has joined the European Bank for Reconstruction and Development, facilitating Chinese FDI, in large part through CIC, in central and eastern European states. [16]

In the US, CIC has made a number of real-estate investments, such as purchasing a stake in a skyscraper on Madison Avenue in New York City. [17] In 2009, CIC announced plans to invest heavily in distressed US real estate, in coordination with the US Treasury Department's Public-Private Investment Program. [18] Beyond real estate, the corporation has taken a seat on the board of US energy giant AES and other foreign firms. [19] CIC has purchased small stakes in American International Group Inc., Apple Inc., and News Corp., which owns *Wall Street Journal* . CIC has taken much larger stakes in investment banks Morgan Stanley and BlackRock Inc. In addition to these direct investments, CIC owns shares in an array of US companies which were purchased through external money managers who handle a portion of CIC's investments. [20] As of mid-2013, nearly half of CIC's equity investments were in the US. [21]

CIC has been building relationships with buyout firms and " CIC said it plans to raise between US$50 billion and 100 billion for the creation of a new unit to specialize in making overseas direct investments ." [22]

CIC investment performance

After racking up tremendous losses in overseas investments, China's National Audit Office accused CIC of, "mismanagement, dereliction of duty, a lack of post-investment management, and poor due diligence." Between 2008 and 2013, 12 of CIC's overseas investments showed losses. [23] In fact, roughly 70% of China's overseas investments have been unsuccessful. [24]

CIC was particularly unsuccessful in Canada, investing a total US$1.9 billion in four Canadian projects which all went badly. CIC invested in Athabasca Oil Corp., considered the most overpriced IPO in Canadian history, as well as Penn West Petroleum Ltd., which was later the subject of an accounting scandal. Other investments included Sunshine Oil Sands Ltd., which had to halt production because it ran out of money, and MEG Energy Corp., whose shares have plunged 45% since the 2010 IPO. On average, CIC's Canadian investments are now worth 20 cents on the dollar. [25]

Over the last several years, Beijing has suffered additional losses in the Arab world due to political instability in that region. In the face of so many failures, Chinese netizens have used social media to complain that citizens should not be required to finance these failures. Adding fuel to the fire, two thirds of the overseas investments made by China's sovereign wealth funds, including CIC, are thought to have suffered losses. [26]

Political implications of CIC's overseas investments

CIC's first overseas office was in Toronto, but after racking up severe losses in Canada, the corporation moved that office to New York City. [27] According to a CIC spokesperson, the move was made in order to maintain CIC's existing relationships with New York investment banks and to look into new investment opportunities in the US. [28] Some US politicians oppose CIC's increasing investment in the US on grounds of national security. [29]

Wall Street Journal reported that here have been concerns that sovereign wealth funds investing abroad "might be directed by political agendas in addition to financial goals." [30] US politicians have for years expressed concerns about foreign entities buying US real estate. [31] Similar concerns have been expressed about Chinese entities, particularly CIC, buying US properties. In 2005, US political opposition prevented SOE China National Offshore Oil Corporation (CNOOC) from buying Unocal Corp. [32]

Although China has four sovereign wealth funds, the PRC Ministry of Finance, which oversees CIC's management, has designated the corporation as China's primary outbound investor leading a government strategy to decrease the cost and ensure control over raw materials and natural resources. [33]

CIC's lack of transparency

CIC is a signatory to the "Generally Accepted Principles and Practices" (GAAP) for sovereign wealth funds. Also called the Santiago Principles, GAAP is a set of voluntary guidelines for transparency and governance of sovereign wealth funds established in 2008. [34] Because Beijing regards the holdings of CIC as sensitive, the company has had limited transparency, failing to disclose its holdings, domestic investments, shareholder relations, and auditing practices. [35]

In addition to investing overseas, CIC has purchased shares of Chinese SOEs on the Hong Kong stock exchange. [36] This creates a number of additional issues of transparency and potential conflicts of interest as some of the SOEs invested in are banks. CIC itself is an SOE, so it is required under PRC law to maintain a Communist Party committee.

Additionally nearly all of the board members are former government officials. [37] Therefore CIC's close ties to the Chinese government are undeniable. Furthermore, tracing those ties requires working through a chain of ownership which may be murky, as much of CIC's activity is clouded behind the veil of conduit companies. For example, CIC purchased a large stake in US real-estate developer General Growth Properties Inc. through whom local properties can be acquired. [38]

In some instances, CIC holds stakes in the very banks that loan money to CIC and other, potentially competing, Chinese SOEs and POEs. CIC sometimes obtains financing from state-owned banks which compete against banks CIC owns. CIC's Madison Avenue property was refinanced through Wells Fargo and a Chinese state-owned bank. [39] US politicians have pressured CIC to disclose its domestic assets at the same time that CIC's banking subsidiaries were applying to open US branches. [40]

Furthermore, many of the companies CIC invests in are "strategic industries" where Beijing is reluctant to allow external auditing on the grounds of national security. China's seven strategic industries are: energy, IT, biotechnology, high-end equipment, new energy, new materials, and new energy cars. [41] CIC has invested in many if not all of these industries.

In 2015, China backed the Asian Infrastructure Investment Bank (AIIB) as a multilateral development bank, focusing on infrastructure development in the Asia-Pacific region. According to its president, AIIB will soon be expanding into South America, Africa, and further into the Middle East. He told *South China Morning Post* that this expansion will bring South America and Asia closer, as well as reduce transaction costs and time. The newspaper speculated that this expansion was meant to cause Latin American countries to abandon their support of Taiwan, while driving them further away from the American sphere. Currently, AIIB has 84 members, with the US and Japan being the only G-7 nations not to have joined. [42]

Funding is also provided by other Chinese institutions such as China Development Bank, Exim Bank of China, the Silk Road Fund, and the New Development Bank. PBOC Governor Yi Gang said those lenders "basically have a low profit margin," and relied largely on government subsidies. "[Now] they are trying to build sustainability in long-term finance." [43] He said that, as a consequence, China would be diversifying its funding sources by working together with financial centers such as

Hong Kong and London. [44] Additionally, the China-IMF Capacity Development Center, launched in May 2017, "could go some way to help Beijing unlock more funds, by clearing bottlenecks in debt, private participation, environmental compliance, and social and governance sustainability." [45] The center will focus on training and capacity development in foreign countries, including those associated with the BRI. [46]

Experts already see a decrease in BRI investment. In 2017, for example, energy investment along the BRI dropped 28% year-on-year. [47] The question therefore remains: Can China finance the BRI? Meanwhile, it must also be considered that some of China's lending clearly serves a strategic purpose, for example, by building bridges to the global Islamic community.

The growth of Islamic banking

Beijing's agreement to fund the China-Pakistan Economic Corridor (CPEC) utilizing a combination of Chinese and sharia-compliant Islamic financing will be a boon to Islamic financing in the region and around the world.

For financing to be sharia-compliant, it must meet several basic criteria: The investment must represent legitimate trade and be asset-based investment; the use of money to make money (interest or *riba*) is forbidden; and investments must be ethical. What is more, risk should be shared; harmful activities are prohibited; and investments should contribute to the public good. As Islam strictly prohibits gambling, certain types of extremely complex or risky financial investments are also off limits. This includes speculating on the stock market, exotic and derivative stock options, shorts and margin selling. [48] Islamic financing may be in the form of "murabaha" (a form of trade credit), "ijara" (a lend-lease agreement often used in Muslim mortgages), and "sukuk" (Islamic bonds). Emirates Airlines regularly use ijara for its expansions. [49] Sukuk are often used by governments to finance major projects and are being used in CPEC. [50]

Between 2000 and 2016, Islamic banks' capital grew from US$200 billion to around US$3 trillion. In spite of this massive growth, Islamic banking still only accounts for around 5% of the global total. However, it is one of the fastest growing sectors. [51]

Asia accounts for about 20% of the global total of Islamic banking, [52] and projects across the continent are increasingly turning to Islamic financing. Factors that are helping boost the popularity of Islamic banking include more companies trying to enter markets in Muslim countries, plus the increased sophistication of Islamic financial instruments, which makes them more viable for use in a modern financial system. [53] Islamic financing tends to be concentrated in oil-producing countries, and when these states experiencing general economic slowdowns due to dropping in oil prices, the growth of Islamic financing slows. [54] The US turning inward under President Donald J. Trump may hinder the future growth of Islamic finance; however, China turning outward and demonstrating a willingness to experiment with Islamic finance may help the development of Islamic banking. Additionally, the lifting of sanctions placed on Iran will help the sector grow, although Iran will need to review its policy of not allowing sukuk to be traded in foreign currencies. [55]

Islamic banking in China

The first Islamic financial institution founded in China was Hezhou Islamic Financing Company in 1987; it provided both deposit and lending services. In 2006, Deutsche Bank launched its first sharia-compliant family of mutual funds, DWS Noor Islamic Funds PLC, which included DWS Noor China Equity Fund. Bank of Bahrain launched the first ever sharia-compliant real-estate investment fund, Shamil China Realty Mudarabah. This fund invested in the Xuan Huang China Realty Investment Fund Limited, a joint venture between Shamil Bank and China International Trust Investment Corporation (CITIC Group), a state-owned investment company. [56]

In 2009, Malaysian banking group CIMB established the CIMB Islamic Greater China Equity Fund, which mostly invests in sharia-compliant investments. The same year, Saudi Arabia's Al-Rajhi Investments (ARI) brought sharia-compliant investments to China through the Shariah Asia Investment Fund in cooperation with the state-owned China Resources Corporation (CRC), a dominant player in PRC real estate. Together, CRC and ARI plan to invest US$200 million in the Islamic fund. [57] Later that year, China became an associate member of the standard-setting body of the Islamic Financial Services Board with the aim of expanding Islamic finance in China. [58]

Hong Kong is a fast-growing center of Islamic financing, in line with a goal declared by the Hong Kong authorities. In 2014, Hong Kong passed a law allowing the Hong Kong Monetary Authority to issue sukuk. Later that year, Hong Kong became the first AAA-rated government to issue a sukuk. [59] The 2014 sukuk used an ijara (lease back) structure to issue US$1 billion worth of bonds denominated in US dollars, which were sharia-compliant while being both S&P: AAA and Moody's: Aa1. [60] This first sukuk was so successful that in 2015, Hong Kong issued a second one worth US$1 billion using a wakalah structure. Under this structure, one third of the assets were collateralized by units in an office building and two thirds by sharia-compliant commodities. These bonds also had a credit rating of S&P: AAA and Moody's: Aa1. [61]

Another connection between China and Islamic financing is that Muslim-majority countries have issued sukuk related to the PRC economy, such as the exchangeable sukuk issued in China's water utility sector by Malaysia's sovereign wealth fund. [62]

Today, MSCI Golden Dragon Islamic Index measures the performance of large and mid-cap China securities and non-domestic China securities listed in Hong Kong and Taiwan which are relevant for Islamic investors. [63] Islamic financing is increasingly being used by Beijing as a form of diplomacy with the Muslim world. AIIB, which is also involved in financing CPEC, is increasingly offering Islamic financing as an option. [64]

China is uniquely poised to institute Islamic banking as China trades heavily with Organization of Islamic Cooperation (OIC) member countries. The OIC is the second-largest intergovernmental organization in the world after the UN, as it brings together 57 member states across four continents. China by 11% of OIC's exports. [65] In 2015, over 17% of OIC's total imports came from China, making China OIC's no. 1 trading partner. [66] Furthermore, 25 OIC nations have joined the BRI, and another 20 are founding members of AIIB. [67]

Chinese-Islamic financing in CPEC
The Islamic banking sector has grown faster in Pakistan than has the conventional banking sector. This is due in part to a five-year plan by the Central Bank of Pakistan. [68] Pakistan's Islamic finance industry has enjoyed double-digit growth for the last five years, and is targeting a 20% market share by 2020. [69] As a result, Pakistan ranks among the nine largest countries for Islamic Banking. Bahrain, Qatar, Indonesia, Saudi Arabia, Malaysia, United Arab Emirates, Turkey, Kuwait and Pakistan together account for over 90% of the global total. AIIB is prepared to integrate Islamic financing into CPEC.

An MOU was signed in 2016 between Pakistan's Meezan Bank Limited and China regarding the issuance of Islamic financing in connection with CPEC. [70] In order to integrate Islamic financing into the BRI as well as CPEC, a number of issues must first be resolved. Across the region, banks are struggling to demonstrate the viability of sharia-compliant financing vehicles in key sectors of the economy, including telecommunications and transportation. Another important area where Islamic financing is being considered is among SMEs along CPEC, as these will be instrumental in job creation. However, the banks are lacking in "talent development, advocacy, applied research, regulations, capital markets, product design, accounting and rating." [71]

Pakistan's Islamic banking sector is also suffering from a lack of liquidity, as well as cumbersome legal procedures, complex documentation requirements, a lack of Islamic finance talent, and a general distrust of sukuk among the populace. The result is a dearth of sukuk, driving issuers to rely on traditional corporate bonds. [72]

Proponents of Islamic financing see CPEC as a tremendous opportunity for public-private cooperation to promote the use of Islamic financing, particularly in hydropower, energy, and construction. It has been proposed that much of the US$45 billion CPEC investment could be parked in Islamic financial instruments. However, a lack of talent hinders the realizing of this proposal. To manage that quantity of money, an estimated 15,000 trained personnel will be needed. [73]

In conclusion

Islamic financing is one of the fastest growing areas of global finance. Many non-Muslim majority countries are expanding their Muslim banking business and even issuing sukuk to finance infrastructure development. China is perhaps the most important non-Muslim country currently promoting Islamic financing. CPEC projects seem to meet many of the requirements for Islamic financing; they represent legitimate trade, are ethical, and are asset-based with risk being shared. CPEC investments are not harmful and they contribute to the public good. The use of Islamic financing in CPEC will help build bridges between China and the Muslim world. CPEC will also add to the growth of Islamic financing in Pakistan, while showcasing Islamic financing to the world.

Chapter 8: The Middle East

Sino-Arab relations could be said to have begun centuries ago with the old Silk Road, which facilitated trade between China and the Middle East. More recently, economic and political ties between China and the Arab world have been growing, particularly during the last fifty years, as the

PRC supported Arab independence and opposed colonialism. Over the last two decades, during which China has risen to become a world economic power, ties and trade with the Arab world have increased dramatically. In 1993, China became a net energy importer. Since that time, energy security has been of particular importance to China, a need which is fulfilled through oil contracts with Arab countries that now provide more than half of China's petroleum. [1] China's top three trading partners in the Middle East are Saudi Arabia, the United Arab Emirates (UAE), and Iran. [2]

In 2004, PRC President Hu Jintao visited Egypt, where he met with Arab League Secretary-General Amr Moussa, and signed the Declaration of the China-Arab States Cooperation Forum. [3] Energy cooperation is at the heart of the relationship between China and the Arab world, and the Energy Cooperation Conference is a pivotal part of that relationship. [4] Much of Chinese commerce with the Middle East is based on China trading developmental loans, direct investment, infrastructure construction, and weapons in exchange for oil.

Seeking new opportunities, large numbers of Chinese companies, experts, workers, and individuals have been moving to the Middle East. In 2012 alone, Chinese enterprises signed US$19.94 billion in contracts in the Arab world and Chinese investment reached US$1.39 billion. [5] There are so many Chinese in the Middle East that when fighting broke out in Libya, more than 37,000 PRC nationals had to be evacuated. The UAE has approximately 200,000 Chinese residents. [6]

Put simply terms, the relationship between the PRC and the Middle East is based on the Gulf States trading oil to China, and China providing finance for infrastructure and capacity building. The reality, however, is much more complicated. The Middle East has historically been a region dominated by external forces such as the UK, France, Russia, and the US. In the last several decades, Washington has been the major player in the region; their relationships with Israel, Iran, and Saudi Arabia, and policies regarding Iraq, Syria, and Palestine, have had a direct impact on global oil prices and oil availability, as well as the flow of arms and money in and out of the region.

As China expands its interests further and further beyond its borders, its increased need for energy forces Beijing into the Middle East, where its policy places it right in the center of global affairs. China's relationship with Middle East nations is closely related to its relationship with the US and its engagement with the world community.

China's trade with the Middle East _

76

Between 1956 and 1990, China established diplomatic relations with all 22 Arab countries. [7] These relationships were often based on China's support for Arab independence movements. [8] The Chinese have often contextualized their relationship with Arab nations as being based on a common history of exploitation by Western colonial powers. "Chinese and Arab peoples have always supported each other in struggles against imperialism and colonialism and fight for national liberation and independence. They are close allies fighting in the same camp." [9]

China's continued economic development creates a demand for oil which drives China to involve itself in the Middle East. [10] The China-Arab Cooperation Forum is one result of this; forum members signed an action plan for 2014 to 2016, expanding trade and investment, particularly bilateral trade between China and the Gulf Cooperation Council. [11]

China's political engagement with the Arab World

Chinese Middle East scholar Wu Bingbing summed up China's Middle East policy as follows, "1. Refuse any single power's unilateral control of the region. 2. Prevent the emergence of any anti-Chinese regime in the region. 3. Oppose formal support of Taiwan independence forces or other separatist forces in China by Gulf countries. 4. Pursue potential support from the Gulf region for China's foreign policy." [12]

By engaging with the Middle East, China exposes itself to a host of geopolitical issues, as well as Washington's political agenda, as the US is the largest foreign player in the region. This sometimes works in China's favor, as some Middle Eastern countries see China as a counterbalance to US influence. [13] Arab League Secretary-General Nabil al-Araby has said that China was the only major power which supported Palestine and other Arab causes. He also said that China-Arab relations were ideal, as China plays an important role reducing Western influence in the region. [14]

Some Middle Eastern countries prefer developmental aid from China as it has fewer strings attached than US aid. "The China Model" for international development aid has been to offer investment and infrastructure in exchange for oil and natural resources, seemingly without taking sides in conflicts or becoming involved in the internal political affairs of China's trading partners. This strategy "has gained considerable attention in recent years as representing an alternative for developing countries to the 'conditionality' of Western-dominated aid agencies and the official development aid of the major economies." [15] Government in many developing countries now find PRC aid, particularly low-interest loans and investment packages, more attractive than Western aid (including aid from the World Bank or IMF), which is often accompanied by conditions regarding human rights, labor and political reforms, and environmental protection. [16]

Al-Araby went on to say that the Arab states will sign cooperation agreements with China in the fields of atomic energy and satellite navigation. [17] Atomic energy is a sensitive area where Western powers, particularly the US, have imposed restrictions on developing countries with nuclear ambitions. Policies and trade barriers related to nuclear energy most recently have impacted Iran, a country with whom Beijing is steadily increasing ties, and one commentator has written: "The endorsement of China is quite different from the ongoing suspicions the ayatollah has voiced concerning the nuclear agreement reached with the United States and its European partners." [18]

In 2016, Beijing's first ever Arab policy paper stressed a "win-win relationship" with the Middle East, citing both the original ties of the old Silk Road and renewed engagement symbolized by the BRI. The paper went on to say that China recognizes Arab countries' rights of sovereignty and to settle internal issues without outside intervention, which it then related to the Taiwan issue. In fact, the Taiwan issue was mentioned more than once in the paper. It seems that support of the "One China" policy is a requirement for taking advantage of the financial benefits of trading with China. As a result of their economic dependence on China, Arab states have historically refused to recognize the sovereignty of Taiwan. [19]

Apart from the One China policy, other predominant features of the paper included: the BRI, ene rgy cooperation, infrastructure, trade and investment, high technology, particularly in the field of nuclear energy, as well as a promise from China to finance these undertakings. "China is ready to continue to provide foreign-aid loan on favorable terms to Arab countries, as well as export credits and overseas investment insurance." [20]

Many Western observers have criticized China, claiming that while Beijing wants to benefit from economic engagement with the outside world, it is refusing to participate in world peacekeeping or military operations. China defends its lack of participation by citing its basic rules of international engagement which include support for sovereign states, noninterference in domestic affairs, and a "no enemies" policy. [21] One place where China has engaged in foreign military action is its navy participating in UN-mandated anti-piracy patrols near Somalia. As 12% of the world's oil supply flows through this region, China has a vested interest in seeing it protected. [22] These anti-piracy patrols represent China's first naval venture beyond the Pacific. [23] To support these patrols, China has constructed its first overseas military base in Djibouti, a country located in the Horn of Africa.

Apart from participating in the UN-led anti-piracy campaign, China has tried to engage with the Arab world without taking sides. In Syria, for example, China has tried to maintain good relations with the warring factions. In the Iran-Iraq war, China sold weapons to both sides. [24]

In trying to avoid direct military engagement, or taking sides, China " is the only one among the permanent members of the UN Security Council that has not taken military action against IS [Islamic State]." Military theorists believe that China lacks the capacity to fight a war and its military has no combat experience. [25] Meanwhile, Beijing fears that actively engaging against IS would make it a target for terrorism. The PRC has its own problems with Xinjiang's Muslim Uyghur minority who have committed domestic terrorist attacks and have been documented as joining IS by the thousands. Uyghurs have even been discovered to be fighting in Libya. [26] Beijing fears that sending Chinese troops to combat IS abroad would incite terrorism by Uyghur separatists at home.

China trades economic development for oil

Chinese economic ties to the Middle East region have been steadily increasing with China importing petroleum and exporting infrastructure investment. [27] China is the largest importer of oil from the Gulf region, importing fully half of the oil produced by Iran. [28] PRC national oil companies have been investing in the region, including heavy investment in Iraq's al-Ahdad, Halfaya, and Rumaila oil fields. [29]

According to a Chinese government paper on Sino-Middle East relations, the BRI has resulted in a three-part cooperation pattern with energy as the core, flanked by infrastructure construction and trade and investment. New cooperation focuses on three high-tech areas of nuclear energy, satellites, and new energy. [30] The paper also states that China will promote cooperation in scientific research, nuclear fuels, and reactors. [31]

In the Middle East and elsewhere, China has helped governments develop local technology and capacity in the oil sector, including the training of business managers, engineers, technicians, and workers. In places like the Sudan, Chinese investment and cooperation has created jobs. [32]

79

One component of China's bilateral cooperation agreements with 21 Arab countries has been the establishment of the Economic and Trade Committee, which oversees trade and technical exchange. Beijing has also signed investment protection agreements with 16 Arab countries, as well as dual-taxation avoidance agreements with 11 Arab countries. [33]

China's "oil and gas plus" cooperation model has created a petroleum triangle which includes China, Saudi Arabia, Iran, and Russia. Several banks and financial institutions have been formed to fund China's Middle East investments, among them the Asian Infrastructure Investment Bank. China is working with the UAE and Qatar to create US$25 billion of commercial loans, as well as a US$20 billion joint-investment fund to finance infrastructure development and high-end manufacturing. [34] China and Saudi Arabia set up a US$20 billion fund to invest= in infrastructure, energy, mining and materials. The two countries also signed US$65 billion in deals in 2017. [35] The Qatar Investment Authority, one of the world's largest sovereign wealth funds, signed a US$10 billion investment contract with China International Trust and Investment Corporation, a Chinese government-owned investment fund. [36]

As Pakistan teeters on the brink of an economic disaster, brought on by its inability to keep up with its balance of payments related to CPEC, Islamabad has begun looking for other sources of financing. In 2018, Pakistan invited Saudi Arabia to be the first third-party investor in CPEC. [37]

China profits from bilateral trade with Middle East
Since the declaration of the China-Arab States Cooperation Forum in 2004, China has been courting the Middle East, extending low-interest lines of credit, investing massively in local infrastructure, and in some cases even forgiving billions of dollars' worth of loans. In 2010, for instance, China forgave roughly 80% of Iraq's debt. [38] While China may appear to be losing money on some transactions, there is actually a payoff. As the largest importer of Gulf Oil, China has benefited most from falling oil prices. Since mid-2014, oil prices have been in steady decline, cutting China's import costs by almost 50%. As a result, China has been able to stockpile petroleum in order to secure its future energy security. [39]

Chinese trade with the Middle East is not limited to oil. Tourism represents another source of income for both China and Arab countries. Consequently, China has signed t ourism pacts with several Arab nations, making Egypt, Jordan, and Tunisia major destinations for Chinese tourists. Non-stop flights now link Beijing and Shanghai with Dubai, and Beijing with Kuwait and Doha. To further support tourism and economic cooperation, the Bank of China now has established an office in Bahrain. 40

Bilateral trade agreements have also opened new export markets for China. Chinese exports to the Middle East include light industrial equipment, textiles, food, clothing, grain, oil, food, metal and minerals, chemicals, and electronics. From the Middle East, China imports oil, fertilizer, chemicals, steel, copper, and aluminum. [41] Low-quality, low-cost PRC goods are now extremely common in Iraq and Iran. Chinese exports to Egypt now exceed those of the US. It is not just cheap products which China is selling overseas, however; they are also selling technical know-how. Algeria has become a market for Chinese engineering services, where Chinese firms have constructed a 1,216-km-long highway. Moreover, China maintains a trade surplus with some Arab nations. [42]

China becomes embroiled in Middle East politics

PRC President Xi Jinping visited Saudi Arabia and Iran, two countries which are stark rivals, to discuss the BRI, just weeks after sanctions were imposed against Iran because of Tehran's nuclear program. Iran has already been admitted to the Shanghai Cooperation Organization as an observer, and Xi has said he foresees Iran becoming a full member. Although Xi is courting both countries, and struggling to avoid showing favoritism to one over the other, the reality is that Saudi Arabia's strong relationship with the US may impede its relationship with China. Consequently, Beijing could develop a deeper relationship with Tehran than with Riyadh. [43] However, the road to friendship with Iran is made difficult by external geopolitics. In 2016, China diverted some of its oil trade from Iran to Saudi Arabia, both to comply with international sanctions against Iran and to increase ties with Saudi Arabia. [44] Although Iran is still China's largest oil supplier, China gets roughly 20% of its oil from Saudi Arabia. [45] Additionally, China accounts for more than a third of Iran's total foreign trade. [46] Iran's Supreme Leader Ayatollah Ali Khamenei openly stated that he preferred closer ties to China, as he has never trusted the West. [47]

Enmity and distrust toward the West, particularly toward Washington, creates a vacuum in the Middle East which Beijing hopes to fill. "Washington's preoccupation with the escalating violence and instability in Iraq and Afghanistan, as well as the Iranian nuclear crisis – combined with widespread popular opposition to the United States –

provide Beijing with a historic window of opportunity to enhance its position." [48] Middle Eastern countries with recent memories of colonization and interference from Western powers view China as a model of development. Beijing's state-led development program is seen as an act of defiance against the Washington Consensus, the prevailing US-led development model outlined by the IMF and World Bank; China often evokes these types of images in its communications with the Arab world. [49] As a result, China enjoys a relatively positive perception in the Middle East and is viewed as a counter to the unpopular influence of the US. As Russia failed to materialize as an influential global player who could support Arab interests in the face of the US, "China is widely perceived as the only credible alternative to US hegemony." [50]

China has found it increasingly difficult, however, to legitimize and codify its relationships with all of the Arab states. During the Cold War, Beijing was able to portray itself as protecting Arab states from the competing ambitions of Washington and Moscow. [51] Today, however, the political landscape has become increasingly complicated. Internal turmoil is more of a threat to Middle East stability than external powers. After the Arab Spring, China National Petroleum Corp. had to end its operations in Syria. When trouble broke out in Libya, thousands of PRC citizens had to be evacuated. [52] The Shiite-Sunni divide is another conflict which plays more of a role in regional political stability than does any ideological competition between the West and Russia. Saudi Arabia's recent execution of leading Shia cleric Sheikh Nimr al-Nimr was followed by the breaking off of diplomatic relations between several Sunni countries and Shiite Iran, further complicating China's relationships with the two factions. [53]

Another issue for China is that US dependence on Middle Eastern oil has decreased in recent years, whereas China's dependence on imported oil has steadily increased. "In 2011, China accounted for half of the growth in oil consumption worldwide." [54] Middle East relationships have thus become a higher priority for Beijing. Financial aid has been the primary tool through which China has tried to maintain stability in the region.

Through its state-owned banks and corporations, Beijing continues writing checks and investing in the Middle East. On his first trip outside the Middle East, Mohamed Morsi (briefly Egypt's president) flew to China where the China Development Bank granted the National Bank of Egypt a US$200 million line of credit. Sudan is another country receiving Chinese aid and investment. "Sudan is China's largest overseas oil project," and

"China is Sudan's largest supplier of arms." [55] Forty percent of the Greater Nile Petroleum Operating Co., which operates most of Sudan's oil fields, is owned by China National Petroleum Corp. [56] PRC companies employ Chinese laborers to pump petroleum in Leal, Sudan and send it through a Chinese-made pipeline to the Red Sea, where it is loaded onto ships for the its trip to China. Chinese workers are protected by Sudanese government soldiers armed with Chinese weapons. [57]

These expensive policies may not be well received back home in China. Around a third of China's population still live on less than two US dollars a day, and may oppose Chinese development aid to the Middle East region. [58]

China's geopolitical policy has been one of non-interference in the internal affairs of foreign nations, and to support the status-quo governments in other countries. This policy has won Beijing the support of long-term governments in the Middle East, particularly those which resent US interference. However, it has also created a number of difficulties in China's relations with governments in turmoil and countries in transition. China-Egypt relations, for example, cooled after the fall of President Mubarak. The opposition resented China's support for the president during the street protests that eventually lead to his government's collapse. China experienced similar problems in Libya after the fall of Muammar Gaddafi, who Beijing had openly supported. [59]

By becoming a significant player in the Middle East, China elevates its status to that of a global power. "With so many important issues interwoven, the chaotic Middle East is the intersection of the main contradictions of current international relations. It is also a focus of the US's global strategy and an important arena of international politics and power diplomacy." [60] As a result, China is now more susceptible to externalities, such as oil embargoes. [61]

Middle East stability directly impacts China's access to energy and thus could have long-lasting implications for its continued economic development. Other than the US and Iran, China has the greatest influence over whether or not there is another Gulf War. [62] While many political observers point to the importance of China in world affairs, Beijing itself claims not to be a superpower. "Many Chinese disavow responsibility for consequential decisions half a world away." It is undeniable; however, that Beijing's relationship with the Middle East, and Iran in particular, puts

China right in the center of Middle Eastern politics with global implications." [63]

In 1956, Egypt became the first Arab nation to recognize the PRC. Since then, Egypt has served as a gateway for Sino-African and Sino-Arab relations. In Cairo in 2004, the China-Arab States Cooperation Forum was established at the Arab League headquarters. Ten years later, China and Egypt established a comprehensive strategic partnership. [64] Egypt serves a crucial role in the maritime component of the BRI as the Suez Canal is a connection point between the Indian Ocean and the Mediterranean Sea. [65]

Egypt began working on its Suez Canal Corridor Project in 2014, with the intent of converting the region into an international business hub. The China-Egypt Suez Economic and Trade Cooperation Zone, will play a role in the project and has attracted the largest percentage of Chinese investment in Egypt. [66] China has promised an additional US$1 billion in financing for Egypt's central bank and US$700 million in loans to the National Bank of Egypt, "labelling itself the "new" choice as Middle Eastern relationships with the US sour ever further." [67]

China-Iran relations

China and Iran have been trading for at least 2,000 years. [68] In the days of Zheng He (1371–1433), the famous Chinese seafarer, China and Persia were major trading partners. After the 1979 Islamic Revolution, Tehran broke ties with Western countries and began forging relationships with Russia, North Korea, and China. In 1980, Iran began purchasing weapons from China. [69]

The Trump administration's opposition to the Joint Comprehensive Plan of Action (the Iran nuclear deal) as well as recent US sanctions on Iran have created opportunities for China in the Middle East. China has now become Iran's closest economic partner, with China's CITIC Trust extending US$10 billion in credit for projects in Iran. Other Chinese financial institutions are considering additional billions in financing. [70]

Since then, China has become Iran's most important trading partner and largest oil purchaser. China is also Iran's no. 1 investor. Meanwhile, Iran is important to the PRC because of its geostrategic location on the narrowest point of the Persian Gulf. Iran serves as a gateway for oil from other Middle Eastern nations, granting China access to the Arabian and Caspian Seas, as well as the Indian Ocean. The BRI will connect Iran with China's existing pipelines and trade routes, which will be good for both countries. On the whole, however, Iran needs China more than China needs Iran. Because of Western sanctions against Iran, Iran has been forced to adopt a "Look East" economic strategy, making China one of Iran's only powerful allies. [71]

The relationship between China and Iran is one of mutual benefit. In China, Iran obtains an ally who is a permanent member of the UN Security Council. China is also both a customer and an investor that steers clear of internal political affairs and questions of human rights. For China, Iran represents a trading partner, a market, where China will not have to compete economically with Western powers. In fact, Tehran's long-standing difficulties with the West may create a strategic advantage for China, as Iran provides a monopoly market for Chinese weapons. [72] For example, while Western nations refuse to sell arms to Iran, China saw an opportunity to make money by trading oil, weapons, and technology with Iran. "Supreme Leader Ayatollah Ali Khamenei said, 'The Islamic Republic will never forget China's cooperation during [the] sanctions era.'" [73] Today, Beijing and Tehran have deep military ties and Iran is a major purchaser of Chinese weapons. [74]

There are over 100 Chinese companies registered in Iran, which apart from oil have also invested in the extraction of aluminum, copper, and coal. Chinese companies, including state-owned Sinopec and China National Petroleum Corp., will be building a refinery in Hormuz, and upgrading one in Abadan. [75]

China's relationship with Iran is complicated by the fact that China is a member of the UN Security Council, and actually voted in favor of some of the sanctions against Iran. This may have been to maintain good relations with the West, or to support China's other Middle Eastern trading partners, such as Israel and Saudi Arabia, who wish to see Iran's military power reduced. [76] While China's trade with Iran is large, it is only one fortieth the size of China's trade with its three largest trading partners, the US, the EU, and Japan. [77] This puts Beijing in an awkward position. On the one hand, it wants to support Iran; on the other, it does not want to alienate its primary trading partners.

Meanwhile, India – a close US ally – has also invested in Iran, particularly in the development of Chabahar Port in an effort to link India with Iran's markets, as well as with energy resources in Afghanistan and Central Asia. By connecting India's Jawaharlal Nehru and Kandla ports with Iran, India can support its strategic interests in the Persian Gulf and Strait of Hormuz. [78]

Conclusion

China has been engaging with the Middle East ever since the old Silk Road. Following the formation of the People's Republic of China in 1949, Beijing has allied itself with the Middle East on the basis of a shared experience of colonial domination by Western powers and a subsequent struggle for independence. China's need for oil has increased dramatically over the past two decades, driving it to strengthen ties to the region. Middle Eastern countries see China as an alternative and a counterweight to US hegemony, and have largely received Chinese aid and investment with open arms. The basic relationship between China and the Arab world has been one of trading oil for money, weapons, technology, and nuclear energy. As Beijing becomes more deeply entrenched in the Middle East, it exposes itself to complex geopolitics which China has previously not had to contend with. Thus far, Sino-Middle East relations have been profitable for China. Whether those relationships will continue to be profitable, however, will largely depend on China's ability to juggle its relationships with polarized trading partners such as the US, Iran, Israel, and the rest of the Arab world.

Chapter 9: Africa

In July 2018, Senegal became the first country on Africa's Atlantic coast to sign up for the Belt and Road Initiative. Senegalese President Macky Sall described China as one of the greatest economic powers of our era, while the PRC ambassador to Senegal said that, in 2017, China had invested US$100 million in Senegal. However, foreign observers are warning that African nations, like many of the countries which have embraced the BRI, are in danger of falling into a debt trap. [1]

As US President Donald J. Trump pushes back against China, threatening trade, Beijing is struggling to win support from other countries. Having had little success in Europe and Asia, where several countries cite trade grievances similar to those complained about by Washington, China has found support among African nations grateful for Chinese investment. [2]

China-Africa economic interactions

Economic growth in Sub-Saharan Africa (SSA) has averaged roughly 5% per year over the past decade. Much of this growth can be attributed to foreign investment, including investment from China. During this time China's economic exchanges with Africa have grown dramatically, from 2.3% of SSA trade in 1985 to nearly a quarter of SSA trade in 2013.

Presently, China is SSA's largest export and development partner, with China acquiring approximately one-third of its energy from SSA. [3]

Chinese investment in Africa has skyrocketed in recent years, from US$7 billion in 2008 to US$26 billion in 2013. In 2015, PRC President Xi Jinping promised African states US$60 billion in loans, aid, and export credit. [4]

Between 2005 and 2018, China invested in at least 293 FDI projects in Africa to the tune of more than US$66.4 billion. One of the many economic benefits is that China gains access to Africa's growing middle class. Consequently, bilateral trade between Africa and China has grown to US$160 billion annually. As seems to be the norm in trade with China, Africa is running a tremendous trade deficit with the Middle Kingdom. [5]

Angola, South Africa, Sudan, and Nigeria have become China's largest bilateral trade partners on the continent. [6] From 1998 to 2012, around 2,000 Chinese firms invested in roughly 4,000 projects across 49 African countries. [7] China generally provides these countries with infrastructure such as roads, railways, stadia and government buildings, as well as healthcare programs. China exports heavy machinery and electrical equipment to Africa, and its largest import from Africa is minerals. [8]

PRC investment paid for a railroad connecting Kenya's capital, Nairobi, with the coastal city of Mombasa. This was the largest unfractured project in the country's history. [9] Another China-funded project is the 50-km-long highway linking Nairobi to Thika. The country's former president, Mwai Kibaki, launched a "Look East" policy in order to steer Kenya away from investment partnerships with Europe or the US. [10]

At the 2015 Forum on China-Africa Cooperation, China made a number of promises in the field of capacity building, including; 2,000 degree programs; 30,000 government fellowships; visits by 200 African scholars; and training for 500 African youths and 1,000 media personnel. In 2018, the number of government fellowships jumped to 50,000; youth exchanges increased to 2,000; and there were to be 50,000 training opportunities. Educating so many of Africa's youth and training its political leaders may shape the future of Sino-African relations in China's favor. [11]

Economists and politicians outside China have raised concerns about the effect of such massive Chinese government and SOE (state-owned enterprise) investment in Africa. Some see these investments as a form of economic colonialism, whereby China trades soft loans and infrastructure investment in exchange for natural resources and energy. It has even been said that China's investments in Africa, many carried out by large state-run companies, are not motivated by economic profits, but in pursuit of strategic benefits and geopolitical influence.

However, a closer look at China's Africa investments paints a different picture. The majority of Chinese investment projects in Africa are not being carried out by SOEs, but rather by private enterprises. Most of the more than 2,200 Chinese companies that have invested in SSA are privately owned. [12]

While there continues to be large investments which can be characterized as infrastructure or soft loans for natural resources, or other similar investments that appear to have geostrategic motivation, the main motivator for Chinese investment in Africa has been profit. "The reason the Chinese go there is because of cheap labor, since labor costs in China itself are rising." [13] At the same time, China invests in Africa in order to establish a solid base of critical raw materials, and extend its geopolitical influence in the undeveloped nations. [14]

Concerns have been raised that China is willing to trade with unstable governments which Western countries steer clear of. Once again, this is not exactly true. While China seems unconcerned with a country's rule-of-law measures, China generally confines its trading to countries with a healthy degree political stability. " Chinese ODI is indifferent to the rule-of-law measure, but on the other hand is positively correlated with political stability." [15]

This chapter will quantify Chinese investment in Africa, determine where the financing comes from, identify recipient countries and sectors, examine the motives behind the investment, look at the problems China faces when investing in Africa, and discuss some of the successes and failures.

Quantifying Chinese investment in Africa

Economists agree that PRC investment in Africa is increasing, but no one knows the total value. Loans and grants from Beijing are easy to quantify, but much of the investment is small, and carried out by individual Chinese starting or buying restaurants, hotels, or herbalist clinics. In 2012, the PRC's ambassador to South Africa estimated this type of direct investment as exceeding US$14.7 billion. [16]

Several of the largest investment projects are led by Chinese SOEs in the energy, mining, construction, and manufacturing sectors. China National Petroleum Corp. invested nearly US$6 billion in Sudan's oil sector. China Power Investment Corp. is planning to invest US$6 billion in bauxite and aluminum projects in Guinea. Other large investments come from private companies like Huawei and ZTE, which have become the principal telecommunications providers in a number of African countries. Other Chinese companies are investing in finance, aviation, agriculture and even tourism. Additionally, China is moving into Africa's financial sector. In 2007, for example, the Industrial and Commercial Bank of China (ICBC) purchased a 20% stake in South Africa's Standard Bank for US$5.6 billion.

China's African investment in perspective

A number of myths surround China's economic activity in Africa. Among them are: China is the no. 1 investor in Africa; Beijing is the largest aid donor in Africa; most Chinese projects in Africa are large-scale government-funded mineral or energy projects; China benefits economically from these projects, but local communities do not; Chinese investment is indifferent to the quality of local government; China only trades with countries which are rich in natural resources; China is willing to invest haphazardly in Africa, granting soft loans indiscriminately; China grants lump-sum loans and aid packages to dictators based on backroom negotiations. Each of these concerns will be addressed below.

The largest investor?

While China is Africa's largest trading partner, it is important to separate FDI from total investment, loans, aid, and other activities. Total Chinese FDI in Africa in 2013 to 2014 only accounted for 4.4% of Africa's GDP and only around 3 to 5% of total FDI. [17] Chinese direct investment in Africa has grown by approximately US$2 billion per year. [18] Between 2005 and 2014, Chinese direct investment in Africa increased eightfold, reaching US$3.2 billion. During the same period, the total value of all Chinese investment in Africa grew to US$32 billion. [19]

China also accounts for 13% of loans to Africa. One fundamental difference between loans from Western countries and loans from China is that the Chinese loans charge interest, whereas many of the loans from the West do not. [20] Although China forgives many of its loans to less developed nations, most African countries run a trade deficit with China. [21] EU countries, particularly France and the UK, are the largest investors by a tremendous margin, with the US not far behind. Even South Africa invests more in the rest of the continent than does China. Most of this investment, whether from Chinese or other sources, tends to be focused on countries which are rich in natural resources. [22]

The largest donor?

According to the OECD, PRC aid to Africa totals a little over US$2 billion each year, while US aid is around US$8 billion. In 2015, Xi pledged US$156 million in emergency food aid after having already pledged US$100 million in military aid to the African Union. These aid packages are much smaller than aid packages given by Western nations. Interestingly, they are also smaller than project financing offered by Chinese policy banks.

Large-scale energy deals

Large size deals by PRC SOEs often make the international news, and these deals tend to focus on natural resources. Investments in Africa by smaller private companies, however, are actually much more common, and most of these are in the service and manufacturing sectors, rather than in natural resources. [23]

Chinese SMEs, many of them privately owned, follow larger (often state-run) enterprises into Africa. The China-Africa Development (CAD) Fund has worked with PRC companies to make considerable investments in cement plants, solar and wind projects, and automobiles. [24]

It is a clear misconception that the PRC is only trading in African oil, but oil does play a major part in Chinese investment in Africa. For example, Nigeria is one of China's largest African trading partners; ties between the two countries date back to 1960 when Nigeria first gained independence. Although China's main interest in Nigeria seems to be oil, valued at US$2.83 billion in 2007, Ch inese financial interests in Nigeria also include telecommunications, railways, and small retail businesses. [25]

Benefit to local communities

Nigeria is central to China's economic strategy in Africa. The country is home to a wide array of Chinese projects; these range from producing building materials, light bulbs, and ceramics, to salvaging steel from decommissioned ships. Other projects include capacity building, such as a school established in the Nigerian capital by Huawei to train local engineers to build cell-phone networks. A Nigerian official has been quoted as saying: "The Chinese are trying to get involved in every sector of our economy ." [26] Today, in addition to providing training for locals, most contracts specify the number of African workers who must be employed on a project. [27] Reports that part of the US$60 billion in promised developmental funding will be used to fund the training of 400,000 African personnel in China, and that 100 villages will receive agriculture centers, on top of promises to provide emergency food aid and construct power grids should debunk the notion that Chinese economic activity in Africa benefits only China. Local economies benefit directly from these initiatives. [28]

China and African governments

Because the PRC has an official policy of not interfering in the internal affairs of other countries, they invest in countries regardless of their having good or poor governance. By contrast, Western countries tend to only invest in countries with good governance. As a result, the proportion of Chinese investment going to badly governed countries tends to be higher, but because Chinese ODI is designed to make profits, investment is still concentrated in countries which have political stability, if not necessarily good governance. [29]

Chinese trade with nations not rich in natural resources

Since 1994, Chinese investment and financing in Africa has steadily become more diverse. This is largely due to reforms in China's banking regulations and the establishment of policy and commercial banks. [30] Much of China's investment in Africa is presented at the triennial Forum on China-Africa Cooperation, which serves as the primary vehicle for China's economic engagement with SSA. [31]

Although much of China's economic engagement with Africa relates to natural resources, "Since 2004, China has undertaken investment projects worth around US$14 billion, which involve the exchange of commodities – ranging from oil in Angola to cocoa in Ghana – for infrastructure." Investment is also going into other sectors, and to countries which lack natural resources. [32] The Forum on China-Africa Cooperation, which includes delegations from 50 African countries as well as Beijing and the African Union, discusses trade related to and unrelated to resources. In some places, service-sector investments dominate, including restaurants, hotels and import/export furniture companies. [33]

Haphazard investment in Africa

A great deal of due diligence goes into Chinese investment in Africa. The process begins with a Chinese company's representative searching for projects. Next, they arrange meetings with African government representatives. After the Chinese company obtains government approval and signs an MOU, they conduct a feasibility study. If the project is deemed feasible, a contract is drawn up and taken to China's Exim Bank to obtain financing. Clearly, it is not true that China invests carelessly. What is true, however, is that China seems to be able to complete these steps and begin a project much faster than US companies. One example would be a dam project in Ghana. The US-led project was stalled for seven years, but the Chinese were able to start within a month of meeting the country's president. [34]

Lump-sum aid packages

The misconception that China will grant soft loans or lump-sum aid packages without due diligence or expectation of profit are so prevalent that even African leaders have been convinced they could receive free money. "Nigeria's Obasanjo, Gabon's Bongo, and, most recently, Guinea's Camara all believed that this was the definitive Chinese approach and pursued arrangements with Beijing on this basis. In most cases, however, their particular efforts to secure such a deal have been unsuccessful." [35]

Zimbabwe

Xinhua quoted Zimbabwe's president, Emmerson Mnangagwa, as hailing the BRI "as a progressive initiative that will enhance global trade," when confirming his country's participation. His first official foreign trip after taking office was to China, where he sought to strengthen ties with Beijing in order to repair his country's economy after years of international sanctions. Mnangagwa said that he had hoped to obtain money, technical expertise, and modern technology from China, his country's "all-weather friend." He also thanked China for standing by Zimbabwe through its time of need, and for helping Zimbabwe achieve independence in 1980. Additionally, he said that his ZANU-PF party hoped to continue to learn from the Communist Party of China. [36]

Zimbabwean opposition leader Nelson Chamisa said that, if he won the election, he would kick out Chinese investors, due to what he called "unacceptable deals." He accused PRC investors of asset-stripping the country and further pledged to "audit all business deals and those that fail the national interest will be reviewed." [37] In summer 2018, the ruling party won the elections, so it seems there will be no change in the status of Chinese investment in Zimbabwe.

Djibouti

In 2015, China announced plans to build its first overseas military base in the tiny African nation of Djibouti. China claimed that the base's purpose would be to mount anti-piracy patrols near Somalia. [38] Concerns have been raised that China will also build an overseas naval base in Pakistan, perhaps at Gwadar Port. [39]

Between 2016 and 2018, Beijing loaned over US$1.4 billion to Djibouti, an amount which exceeds 75% of the country's GDP. [40] This puts the country's debt-to-GDP ratio at 85%. [41] China has also loaned

US $20 billion to Guinea, one of the poorest nations on Earth, with a 2017 GDP per capita of only US$857 per year. [42] As is the case elsewhere, China's economic support is conditional on the recipient breaking off all official ties with Taiwan. To date, every African country, except Swaziland, has severed diplomatic relations with Taiwan. [43]

Zambia

By September 2018, it looked as if Zambia's debt to China was so high that the country would have to cede its national electrical supplier. In 2017, Zambia's debt servicing absorbed 77% of domestic revenue, leaving the country cash poor and needing additional Chinese loans. [44]

Financing Chinese investment in Africa

Infrastructure investment projects in Africa have been financed through the People's Bank of China, China Development Bank (CDB), and the Exim Bank of China. Much of China's financing activity on the continent has been focused on FDI, but this is only one piece of the puzzle. An FDI investment would involve a Chinese entity investing directly in an African entity and obtaining voting rights in it. As such, much of China's financial activity in Africa cannot be classified as FDI; many pledges are instead financed by China's policy banks. These financings represent a wide array of structures. China promised US$5 billion to the CAD Fund, a private equity and venture capital investment arm of CDB, as well as US$5 billion for the Special Loan for the Development of African SMEs, another branch of CDB, and US$10 billion for the China-Africa Fund for Production Capacity Cooperation.

Bilateral trade between C hina and Africa exceeded US$106 billion by 2008, with the terms, nature, and shape of these deals largely determined by the banks which provide financing. The diversity and scope of this trade and related investment and its financing represent a new approach in China's global economic strategy. [45]

PRC financing not only seeks advantageous geographical locations, but Chinese banks are also looking for "locations with relatively low efficiency in the banking system and with relatively light regulation ." [46] These conditions give Chinese banks opportunities to open local commercial branches serving the banking and finance needs of not only Chinese companies, but also the local market.

Some of China's funding activities in Africa are tied to oil. The government of Angola arranged several billion dollars' worth of credit with Exim Bank which was directly or indirectly linked to making oil concessions available to PRC companies. [47] Other funding activities are more diverse, and include pledges to the CAD Fund, which is expected to reach US$10 billion, CDB's African Fund, the Special Loan for the Development of African SMEs, and the China-Africa Industrial Cooperation Fund. [48]

The Ethiopian government tried for years to obtain financing for the Gibe III Dam project from the World Bank and the African Development Bank. Both refused because of armed conflicts in the region. Finally, ICBC granted a US$500 million loan for a turbine to be constructed by Dongfang Electric Corp. In September 2012, another Chinese bank signed an MOU with the Ethiopia Sugar Corporation for a loan of US$500 million for the construction of sugar factories. [49]

Large-scale conventional project financing is conducted through banks, such as t he CDB, which have close ties to Beijing. These banks are also involved in financing activities of the CAD Fund. [50] The CAD Fund is a key funding vehicle of China-Africa economic cooperation. " CAD Fund is the first fund in China focusing on investment in Africa and also to encourage and support further Chinese Enterprises to invest in Africa ." [51] Another fund, the China International Fund, is engaged in joint ventures in Guinea and Zimbabwe. [52]

Additional financing comes through policy banks, such as the Exim Bank of China, which has partnered with the World Bank and the African Development Bank. ICBC has become a principal financier in such projects as the Morupule power station expansion. In addition to pipeline and banking finance projects, ICBC and South Africa's Standard Bank (of which it now owns 20%) are now expanding into retail banking. The privately-held China Merchants Bank is also moving into Africa. Stanley Ho's Macao-based banks are moving into Portuguese-speaking countries, such as Mozambique and Angola. [53]

The expansion of Chinese banks into the retail sector is driven by the needs of local markets, which are going unserved by local banks. " To date the presence of Chinese banks in emerging markets like Africa has been limited, with these institutions unable to handle basic activities, such as remittances and advances, in African countries" [54] It appears t hat both local and foreign businesses have more confidence dealing with a Chinese bank, or a local bank partnered with a Chinese bank, than with a purely local financial institution. [55]

How Africans perceive Chinese investment

The African market is very price sensitive. Consequently, African nations have become dependent on competitively priced Chinese telecommunications infrastructure. Chinese construction companies can build roads and bridges faster and cheaper than other companies. China's commerce ministry estimates that 65% of Chinese FDI projects make a loss, compared with a 50% international norm. "From Africa's perspective, Chinese investment – especially in basic infrastructure – is more than welcomed." [56]

Africa's US$900 billion infrastructure deficit creates business opportunities for PRC companies. "Without potable water, all-weather roads, adequate power and reliable communication, African economies cannot thrive." [57] Chinese infrastructure construction is welcome, yet Chinese products are damaging local markets. Chinese textiles have destroyed South Africa's textile industry. Other countries, such as Ethiopia, have benefitted from PRC manufacturing. Chinese shoe manufacturer Huajian, has increased their staff from 600 to 3,500 employees over the last few years. While African workers welcome an opportunity to work, local business owners complain that poor labor and environmental practices give Chinese companies an unfair advantage, making it very difficult to compete with them. [58]

Beijing established diplomatic relations with Ghana in 1960. By 2011, 10,000 PRC nationals were living in Ghana, and bilateral trade had grown to US$3.5 billion, making China Ghana's no. 1 trade partner. There is a huge trade imbalance, however, with Ghana's exports to China totaling only US$400 million. Yet, Ghanaian students, academics, and government workers, "mostly welcome Chinese investment, believing it drives economic growth on the continent." [59]

Opponents of PRC investment in Ghana cite political motives behind the investment, poor working conditions, a lack of human rights, as well as concerns about the poor quality of Chinese products. Chinese shops are opening in Ghana, often run by Chinese, selling consumer products such as shoes and toothbrushes, as well as medicines. Locals complain that China only sends low quality products. While it is true that the small shops sell lower quality products, China also sells higher quality products in the supermarkets and department stores. [60]

China has become Cameroon's biggest development partner and investor, but there have been complaints that the Chinese use labor imported from China rather than employing local workers. China Harbor Engineering is building a US$567 million multipurpose seaport, employing 1,125 people. About half are Cameroonians, mostly employed as menial laborers. Some have complained they do not receive the wages they are promised, and are forced to work longer hours than contracted. [61]

Local suspicions regarding the behavior of PRC companies often prompt investigations by African media. In Uganda, for example, a media investigation led to a police investigation of a Tibet-based company accused of fraud in connection with their acquisition of a Uganda copper mine. [62]

In Zambia, Chinese mines pay lower wages than mines operated by local or other foreign companies. Chinese mines also have the lowest safety standards and worst working conditions. In addition to treating workers poorly, projects to extract natural resources often rob the local economy of opportunities for wealth creation. In Mozambique, some have complained that local authorities allow SOEs or Chinese businessmen to take logs and export them to China, gaining all the value there. [63] Mozambique, one of the world's poorest countries, is losing tens of millions of dollars in lost taxes from illegal logging trade with China. Illegal timber accounts for 48% of China's imports from Mozambique; the loss of tax revenue to the country has been estimated at US$29 million. [64]

At the 2018 Forum on China-Africa Cooperation, Xi countered push-back against PRC investment in Africa by stressing China's "five no's" policy: "No interference in the development paths of individual countries; no interference in their internal affairs; no imposition of China's will; no attaching of political strings regarding assistance; and no seeking of selfish political gains in investment and financing cooperation." [64]

Problems facing Chinese investment in Africa

A Chinese entity invested US$1 billion in a palm-oil plantation in the Democratic Republic of Congo, and later discovered that " there were no roads, the river was barely navigable and villagers were hostile ." [65] Even worse, as soon as planting began, the plants were stolen. In the same country, US$6 billion invested in infrastructure in exchange for profits from a copper mine has only yielded US$1 billion in returns, bureaucracy and power shortages having delayed copper production. [66]

Investment contracts often include an undertaking by the local African government to build transportation, water, or power infrastructure, but these improvements often fail to appear. "Public land turns out to be occupied by squatters, who may have farmed it for generations; private land may not be owned by the people selling it. Local politicians do not accept deals struck by national ones...." [67] *The Economist* explains that some problems of this kind can be circumvented by working with repressive governments, such as in Angola, but for the most part, it seems Chinese investment runs into the same roadblocks as Western investment. [68]

Chinese investment dropped by 40% in 2015, due in part to a slowing Chinese economy, but also because of a change in Chinese policy regarding investment in Africa. In past years, China focused on investing in natural resources. Now, China is more interested in technology and mature market investment. In its new five-year plan, Beijing has adopted a different developmental stance focusing more on the service sector, and reducing its reliance on heavy industries that consume huge amounts of resources, and cause massive carbon emissions. [69]

A problem faced by Chinese companies in Africa is competition from other Chinese companies. In Kenya, two Chinese companies, China Harbour Engineering Company and China Civil Engineering Construction Corporation, fought for a railroad contract. A similar situation occurred in Uganda. In 2012, China Civil Engineering signed a US$1.75 billion railway contract with Uganda's transportation ministry, but before construction began, China Harbour Engineering undercut them, causing the Uganda government to tear up the original contract and go with the lower bid of only US$1.25 billion. Two other SOEs, China Road and Bridge Corp. and China Railway Construction Corp., have waged a media war against one another while competing for Ugandan contracts. China Power Construction Corp. signed a contract with the Zambian government to rebuild the Kafue Gorge hydropower facility. When another Chinese firm tried to undercut them, the local government scrapped the contract and reopened the tender process. [70]

Another problem is that Beijing is inadvertently being pulled into complex geopolitics. In Kenya, Ethiopia, and South Sudan, China has become an unwilling spectator to armed conflict, a disputed dam project fueling border attacks. [71] Even though China has a policy of non-interference in local politics, by trading with the government rather than with the rebels, they are taking sides in conflicts which can adversely impact Chinese investment.

Chapter 10: Latin America and the Caribbean

Panama was the first country in the Latin America and Caribbean region (LAC) to join the Belt and Road Initiative. Shortly afterward, the May 2017 BRI summit in China was attended by Argentinian President Mauricio Macri and Chilean President Michelle Bachelet. Later that year, when Panama's President Juan Carlos Varela visited Beijing, PRC

President Xi Jinping stated for the first time that the BRI would officially be expanded to include LAC. [1] In a 2018 summit between China and the Community of Latin American and Caribbean States (CELAC), Chinese Foreign Minister Wang Yi invited more than 30 LAC countries to join the BRI. [2]

China-Latin America economic activity

Over the past two decades, China has steadily increased its investment throughout LAC, with bilateral trade growing 2,000% since 2000. [3] More recently, PRC investment in the region increased from US$7 billion in 2011 to US$29 billion in 2015. [4] To support their increased economic activity in the region, China became a permanent observer in the Organization of American States in 2004, and a member of the Inter-American Development Bank in 2009. Additionally, China participates in the UN Economic Commission for Latin America and the Caribbean. [5]

At a meeting of Latin American presidents, hosted in Beijing, PRC President Xi Jinping pledged US$250 billion over the next decade. [6] This money will come in various forms, such as the purchase of agricultural products, raw materials, and energy, as well as lending, infrastructure investment, and exporting finished products to Latin America.

China currently imports 40% of global soybean output, 75% of which it buys from Brazil and Argentina. China also imports a third of the world's iron ore and a fifth of its copper, much of which is purchased from Latin America. China buys oil from Venezuela, copper from Chile, and both copper and fishmeal from Peru. [7] "China is staying close to Latin America because they have many of the raw materials the Asian nation seeks, including iron, oil, and food." [8]

Other Chinese economic activity involves lending. In 2015, China loaned a total of US$30 billion to Latin American governments, double the previous year's total. This US$30 billion figure even exceeds monies loaned to Latin America by the World Bank and Inter-American Development Bank. Some of these loans are linked with infrastructure construction which will be carried out by Chinese firms, and China has offered an additional US$35 billion to be used for infrastructure investment. [9]

China's economic involvement in Latin America is not just about China making loans and extracting natural resources. China's exports to Latin America have grown year on year, reaching US$130 billion in 2014. According to data from the IMF, "China has become the top trade partner of Brazil, Chile and Peru," [10] and has free trade agreements with Chile, Costa Rica, and Peru, as well as institutional arrangements with several other LAC countries. [11]

However, not all PRC investment projects have been successful. In 2014, a Chinese-led business group was awarded a high-speed rail contract in Mexico, but the contract was rescinded because of public protests in Mexico against local government corruption. Similarly, in 2011, Chongqing Grain Group, began building a US$2 billion soy-processing plant, but the building site remained empty for several years. [12]

Why China invests in Latin America

China's goals in Latin America include obtaining energy, raw materials and export markets. Additionally, China utilizes its global trade to solve problems faced at home, such as ensuring the continued growth of its own economy. China uses its investment in overseas infrastructure projects to create opportunities for Chinese firms and contractors abroad. [13]

More than half of Chinese foreign direct investment (FDI) was invested in energy and oil companies, with mining, particularly copper and iron ore, accounting for another 25%. [14] Some of this investment is driven by China's insatiable need for raw materials. A second reason for heavy investment in raw materials is to build reserves and lock in current prices.

Other non-energy and non-mining investments have been focused on food. China is a net food importer whose government seems to be searching for various sources of raw food to ensure the country's food security. Therefore, China is investing in soybeans from Brazil and other foodstuffs from the Latin American region.

Early Chinese investment in Latin America focused on importing commodities China needed. The newest wave of PRC investment has focused on "a need to maintain economic growth by exporting its industries into other world regions." [15] By investing in large-scale projects, China is exporting both workers and pollution to LAC. Wages in the PRC have increased by a factor of between four and nine times over the past two decades, and this threatens to price Chinese manufacturing out of world markets. Seeking employment for its younger generation, China sends many of its workers to other countries, including LAC, where they can be employed, constructing highways, dams, railroads, and other Chinese projects. [16]

To further support the growth of the Chinese economy, the PRC uses its overseas investments as a way of creating markets for Chinese goods. This market-seeking behavior provides PRC companies with numerous advantages. Chinese firms can avoid Chinese import restrictions and flood LAC markets with cheaper goods from Southeast Asia and Africa. [17]

By exporting industrial projects, Chinese companies can avoid domestic regulations which may increase the cost of doing business. China also benefits by exporting pollution to LAC. Raw-material processing is an extremely polluting activity which China can avoid by processing its raw materials in LAC. [18]

Quantifying Chinese investment in Latin America

Today, LAC is the PRC's no. 4 trading partner, and as of 2014 China accounted for 12% of LAC's total global trade. [19] The two economies are so closely tied that a World Bank analysis estimates that, "for every 1% decline in China's economic growth, LAC's overall growth rate is reduced by 0.6%." [20]

In January 2015, the First Ministerial Meeting of the Forum of China and the Community of Latin American and Caribbean States (CELAC) was held in Beijing. [21] CELAC has 33 members including every country in Latin America, Mexico, and the Caribbean. [22] At this meeting, Xi announced the CELAC-China five-year cooperation plan which calls for bilateral trade to grow to over US$500 billion annually and for China's FDI to increase to more than US$250 billion over the next decade. The cooperation plan also established 12,000 scholarships and training programs for citizens of CELAC states. [23]

Xi also announced the 1+3+6 cooperation framework and the 3×3 cooperation model. [24] The "1" refers to China and CELAC, [25] and t he "3" to the three drivers of economic growth: trade, investment, and financial cooperation. The "6" is a reference to the six Chinese industries involved: energy and resources; infrastructure construction; agriculture; manufacturing; scientific and technological innovation; and information technologies. [26] The "3x3" means "Chinese and Latin American enterprises, societies, and governments" which will cooperate in "logistics, power generation, and information technology." [27]

Over the past five years, Chinese investment in LAC has averaged nearly US $10.7 billion annually. FDI has also increased steadily, with 87% coming from PRC state-owned enterprises (SOEs); 57% of this FDI was concentrated on raw-material acquisition. [28] Most of the Chinese FDI has been through mergers and acquisitions, over four-fifths of which was in raw-material extraction, with oil and gas accounting for 70% of this figure. [29]

Chinese FDI, while significant, is considerably less than that of some W estern countries: 20% less than the Netherlands, 17% less than the US, and 10% less than Spain. [30] "The figures that seem to reflect a flood of investment – the UN Economic Commission for Latin America and the Caribbean highlights that 13% of Chinese outward FDI is directed to LAC – are highly misleading. Much Chinese (and Korean) assets have been parked in the offshore tax havens of the Cayman Islands and the British Virgin Islands." [31] Even without discounting Chinese FDI for money parked in Caribbean banks, Chinese FDI in the region is still dwarfed by US FDI which is estimated at US$350 billion.

The US has long been the dominant power in the LAC and still overshadows China's influence in the region. China's role, however, is growing steadily. In 2000, China accounted for only 2% of Latin America's foreign trade, while the US had 53%. As of 2010, the Chinese share had grown to 11% of the total, while that of the United States had dropped to 39% ." [32] As much as Chinese influence in the region is growing, US economic dominance on the region still remains. In fact, US exports to the whole of Latin America are still three times those of China. [33]

China foreign aid to Latin America

Chinese aid to LAC began when the PRC opened an embassy in Cuba in 1960 and Cuba became the first recipient of PRC aid. Chinese aid to LAC during the Cold War focused on supporting the independence of LAC countries and creating an alliance of Third World countries, in keeping with Beijing's "three worlds theory." [34] More recently, Chinese aid to LAC has shifted largely to infrastructure construction in support of raw material and energy extraction.

Foreign aid and government-sponsored investment activities (FAGIA) is another of the many ways in which China engages economically with LAC. Beijing divides its FAGIA into three categories: grants, interest-free loans, and concessional loans – with the concession loans being financed by the Exim Bank. Other financing comes from the China Development Bank (CDB), while additional financing and technical support comes from SOEs such as National Overseas Oil Company, the China National Petroleum Corp., and the China Petrochemical Company. All China's FAGIA activities fall under the administration of the Ministry of Commerce. Most FAGIA cannot be categorized as foreign aid, however, because to qualify as aid, at least 25% of it must be a grant. Even so , China's total grant aid is many times larger than that of the US. [35]

Latin America has been the largest recipient of FAGIA from China. In 2010, Beijing's global FAGIA pledge was US$168.6 billion, followed by a pledge of US$189.3 billion in 2011, roughly equal to 3% of China's GDP. These figures are slightly misleading, however, because much of this money was in the form of loans which should be repaid. During 2011, US Agency for Development pledges totaled US$8 billion, and the US Export-Import Bank provided US$6.3 billion in loans. [36]

Financing Chinese investment in Latin America

Between 2005 and 2014, China committed to lending more than US$118 billion to LAC. [37] Loans in 2014 alone totaled US$22.1 billion, making the PRC Latin America's largest creditor. [38] Across the region, "From 2005 to 2014, 70% of China's Latin America loans went to infrastructure and energy projects and 25% to mining." [39] Venezuela is the no. 1 recipient of these loans, accounting for 50% of loans and 42% of infrastructure projects. [40]

China's lending to LAC comes through a variety of channels and institutions. "The CELAC-China Forum announced a China-LAC Special Loan for Infrastructure in its Cooperation Plan for 2015 to 2019. [41] China's policy banks, as well as the CDB and Exim Bank, have been major lenders to Argentina, Venezuela, and Ecuador – countries which have been unable to borrow from Western banks. In addition to direct lending to specific countries, China has created various Latin America funds such as a fund specifically for infrastructure investment, and another for Caribbean countries. [42] This lending is coupled with increased use of the Chinese yuan in the region. "Argentina, Brazil, and Chile already have bilateral swap arrangements totaling more than 280 billion RMB." [43]

Many of the investments China makes in Latin America are risky, because "Chinese loans to Latin American governments are often accompanied by fewer conditions and lack the traditional Western emphasis on fiscal rectitude." For example, ignoring Venezuela's low credit rating, Beijing lent US$50 billion to the country against future oil revenues. But the subsequent oil-price drop has made it nearly impossible for Venezuela to repay its loans. [44]

Problems with China's Latin America investments

China has faced many challenges and setbacks in its investments in the LAC region, such as protests and allegations of corruption surrounding proposed infrastructure projects. Other Chinese projects have been thwarted by local "social and political instability, environmental disputes, labor controversies, and disputes with local communities." [45]

In 2013, a private Chinese company, HKND, announced a plan to build a canal across Nicaragua, to challenge the Panama Canal, but so far, efforts have "often been largely exploitative and unsustainable ." [46] Other failures include, the government of Mexican President Enrique Peña Nieto cancelling construction of the U S $200 million Dragon Mart mega-mall near Cancun, because Mexico's environmental protection agency found that the project was doing tremendous harm to the environment. Not only was the project terminated, but it was also hit with US$1.5 million in fines. Local merchants and manufacturers praised the termination of the project as they felt it would have annually "flooded the domestic market with 300,000 tons of Chinese merchandise worth US$2 billion ." [47]

Some of China's planned projects in Latin America seem risky or even unnecessary, such as HKND's planned Nicaraguan Canal. Non-Chinese experts have said it is unclear if there is enough water in the region for the canal to operate. HKND believes that the project is viable because the new canal will cater to newer ships which the Panama Canal cannot accommodate. Shipping analysts have pointed out that very few modern ships need to pass through the canal. Meanwhile, the Panama Canal is being expanded to accommodate these modern ships. [48] Given these facts, it would appear that the project is doomed from the outset.

Other failures, and potential failures, come in the form of China ignoring obvious negative economic indicators. China has invested heavily in Brazil, which is in deep economic depression, and Venezuela which is faced with hyperinflation. China has loaned the most to Venezuela, US$65 billion, because Venezuela has the world's largest oil reserves. [49]

Many of China's investments in Latin America are failing for a variety of other reasons, "Corruption, cultural differences and bureaucracy in Latin America have halted momentum for many of them." [50] Business culture in the two regions is very different. China is used to moving very quickly from decision to implementation. Latin America, on the other hand, tends to move slower and with greater concern for the environment and indigenous people. A 3,750km railroad project, stretching from the Atlantic coast of Brazil to the Pacific coast of Peru was announced in 2011, but several years on, the project has yet to be realized. [51]

China's Exim Bank agreed to fund US$2.5 billion of Nassau's US$3.5-billion Baha Mar resort complex, to be built by China Construction America, Inc. (CCA, part of China State Construction Engineering Corporation Ltd.). In the end, the project went bankrupt after Baha owner Sarkis Izmirlian and CCA fell out. [52]

A final threat to Chinese investment in the LAC region comes from possible renewed competition from Western countries. China has long had the advantage of being almost the only lender willing to invest in countries such as Venezuela that were spurned by the developed world. Now that Argentina's credit worthiness has improved, China will face competition from Western lenders. [53]

Impact of Chinese investment in Latin America

After Argentina suffered a technical default on its international credit, China loaned them money to prop up their falling currency. Similar loans have been made to cover Ecuador's budgetary deficits. The PRC's continued lending to Latin American countries, in spite of their poor creditworthiness or default rates, is akin to the "good money after bad" strategies taken by Western countries who loaned money to Latin America in the 1980s, often loaning additional money to prop up failing economies to avoid losing money already invested. Beijing does not impose stipulations of fiscal austerity on loan recipients in the way Western countries do. Unrestricted lending may also be bad for the loan recipient, as this can encourage reckless spending by debtor governments. In 2016, Chinese policy banks extended US$2.2 billion in credit, compared with US$5 billion in 2015 and US$4 billion the year before that.

Much of China's financing activity in LAC supports infrastructure investment that is meant to benefit the local economy. However these benefits often fail to materialize. While large infrastructure projects do indeed create jobs, the total number of jobs is limited and most of the skilled and higher-paying jobs go to Chinese experts. The proposed Nicaragua Canal project could create 50,000 jobs, half of which – the lower half – will go to local people. Furthermore, over 100,000 locals would have to be relocated for the canal to be completed. [54]

A trade imbalance exists between LAC and China, partly because of the nature of the products being traded. Technological products only account for 5% of LAC exports to China, whereas technology and manufactured goods account for 60% of China's exports to LAC. [55] In 2013, bilateral trade between China and Latin America reached US$289 billion. This trade is imbalanced, however, because China imports raw materials from Latin America, but exports finished goods. This means that each dollar of raw materials purchased from Latin America is converted to several dollars' worth of finished goods exported back to Latin America. "In 2014, for every product Mexico exported to China, it imported 11 times that from the Asian giant." [56] Said another way, "In Mexico-China trade, for example, Chinese exports versus Mexican imports differ by more than 250%. [57] The LAC/China trade deficit has swelled from below US$20 billion until the mid-2000s to over US$75 billion since 2012. [58]

Most of China's imports from Latin America have been raw materials, the extraction of which harms the environment. Furthermore, this type of activity does not create as many jobs as manufacturing finished products. To make matters worse, Chinese LAC production employs laborers imported from the PRC, rather than hiring locals. Latin American governments are so desperate for Chinese loans that they often agree to terms which in the long term are a bad decision. For example, China already owns much of Venezuela's future oil output and controls 90% of Ecuador's oil sector. [59]

One benefit of Chinese investment in Latin America is that it shifts LAC countries' dependence away from the US. On the other hand, LAC countries risk deindustrialization, as it becomes easier to sell raw materials to China than develop domestic industries. Mexico also runs the unique risk of losing its favored NAFTA trade status if it becomes too heavily involved with China. Another problem unique to Mexico is that many of the products exported by Mexico are competing with similar Chinese products. It has been estimated that Mexico loses 11% of its total export markets because of Chinese competition. [60]

Chinese investment has modified the Latin American economy. In the 1980s, 52% of the region's exports were raw materials. During the 1990s, the region began to climb up the value-added ladder, lowering its dependence on raw-material exports to just 27%. In the 2000s, however, because of increased trade with China, the region began focusing on raw materials once again, which have returned to their pre-1990s level of importance. Much of this shift is the result of rent-seeking behavior by governments which find it easier to broker the sale of raw materials rather than try to develop a value-added economy. [61] Unfortunately, LAC trade with China is so heavily focused on raw materials that falling prices for raw materials in 2014 actually caused the total value of bilateral trade to drop for the first time since 2009. [62]

In contrast to Chinese FDI, which increases LAC dependence on raw-material exports, the majority of American FDI is focused on developing the manufacturing sector. [63] Chinese investment in Latin America frequently has long-term negative effects including a reduction in the local manufacturing sector and increased dependence on raw-material exports, increasing the region's exposure to fluctuations in global commodity prices. [64] Having the PRC as a major trading partner also ties local economies to China's economy; when the Chinese economy slows, China imports less energy and raw materials, sending local economies into recession. The economies of both Brazil and Chile grew dramatically as a result of China trade, but both also took a downturn when the PRC's economy slowed. [65]

The extreme case of Venezuela
The Hugo Chavez government of Venezuela forged close ties to Beijing which supported its socialist leanings. The friendship between China and Chavez coincided with the period where China's relationship with Latin America, based on commodity purchases and loans, peaked, which was between 2007 and 2016. These ties included developing an economy almost exclusively dependent on raw-material exports to China and money borrowed from the PRC. During the reign of Chavez, CDB extended over US$60 billion in loans-for-oil deals to the country. This means that most of the money given to Venezuela occurred before 2013.

PRC engagement with the country became even more critical as other developed countries refused to lend money or invest in the country because of its credit unworthiness. Of the US$120 billion China has loaned to Latin America since 2007, more than half went to Venezuela. In the absence of other outside help, the increased engagement with China may have seemed like a quick fix, but resulted in long-term negative side effects. In the case of Venezuela, "China's interaction with Latin America [has] been magnified by the willingness on the part of Chavez and Maduro to mortgage their nation's future massively for the sake of buttressing their own monopoly on power and for short term political gain." [66] Rather than invest the Chinese loans in developing economic infrastructure, Chavez used the money to finance social programs to keep himself in power. [67]

Foreign loans often create opportunities for corruption and rent-seeking behavior, while the inevitable payback hangs over the country like the Sword of Damocles. "Chinese monies have served to weaken the accountability of Venezuela's leaders to their own people." [68] Venezuela is now faced with the repayment of the Chinese loans, which means shipping so many barrels of oil to China that they have very little to sell on world markets to support other activities in their national economy. To make matters worse, under Hugo Chavez "PetroCaribe" policy, most Latin American countries received Venezuelan oil at a discount, further reducing the value of the oil remaining after payments are made to China.

Since then, the price of oil has dropped and Venezuela has descended into economic chaos. Venezuela's oil production has also decreased, making it difficult for the country to service its Chavez-era debts. Ironically, the drop in Venezuelan oil output was a factor in the increase in the global price of oil. [69]

China is a major investor in Venezuelan petroleum and China remains one of the few friends and financiers that Nicolas Maduro's government can reach out to. Over the past ten years, China has dumped over US$50 billion in loans-for-oil in Venezuela. [70] Western observers speculate that should Maduro's government – already on a weak foundation – collapse, this could spell the end of close economic ties between the two countries. [71] Over the past three years, however, the loans have slowed down and Venezuela has been working toward strengthening ties with Beijing. [72]

Overdependence on China

Panama is the site of competition between private American companies and Chinese SOEs hoping to construct a Pacific Ocean port. US Secretary of State Mike Pompeo stated that, while the US welcomed competition from transparent foreign investment in other countries, investment from China, in addition by creating severe debt, often has political aims attached. One example of the political nature of Chinese investment is that shortly after signing on to the BRI, Panama rescinded its recognition of Taiwan. Other criticisms of BRI financing in Latin America include increased corruption, lack of transparency, and the use of Chinese, rather than local labor. [73]

Chinese state media said Pompeo was ignorant and malicious, because he warned of the Latin America death trap. In a speech in Mexico City, Pompeo said "When they show up with deals that seem to be too good to be true, it's often the case that they, in fact, are." [74] Pompeo's warnings seem to be justified when one considers the massive debts faced by many Latin American economies. Even Brazil, which is not specifically plagued by debt to China, is also hurting from overdependence on China. Brazil's economic relations with the PRC are based on soy, oil, and infrastructure construction. All three sectors have been riddled with corruption, resulting in a massive economic downturn. [75] These two examples highlight the dangers of excessive dependence on commodities trade with China.

Chapter 11: Europe

While some countries in Africa are embracing the BRI, most European nations seem to be resisting it. Originally, China seemed to be courting the EU as a whole, but as this strategy has failed, Beijing has switched to one of divide and conquer. To say that Europe has a unified opinion on the BRI would be wrong. Europe contains 50 countries, while the EU will contain 27 after the UK exits the union. Straight away, even a unified EU policy does not denote a unified European strategy. Recently, China's European efforts have been focused on the "16+1" summit which includes 16 Central and Eastern European (CEE) countries, of which 11 are EU member states.

Beyond the 16+1 group, many European leaders see the BRI as a kind of Trojan horse, which could undermine the EU, "disadvantage Western investors, and spread corrupt development practices amongst vulnerable democracies." [1] Those opposed to the 16+1 interpret it as "the grouping together of bilateral partnerships through which China can more easily field competition for Chinese bank loans." [2] While the EU is a transnational organization dedicated to working together, the 16+1 is a loose collection of countries vying for a finite amount of Chinese investment.

As in other BRI countries, the IMF warns that CEE countries receiving BRI loans are in danger of falling into a debt trap. Meanwhile, Chinese financing lacks transparency; this violates EU norms and often results in increased corruption. One place where China has found a willing partner is Montenegro. The country is already prone to corruption, with a Corruption Perception Index ranking of 64th of 180 countries, and an overall score of 46 out of 100. [3] Opaque Chinese infrastructure financing is expected to increase opportunities for corruption. [4]

The host of the 2018 CEE conference was Bulgaria, a country where China National Nuclear Corporation has expressed interest in working on the Belene nuclear power plant, a project which has been underway since 2012, and which is known to be riddled with corruption. Corruption in the project is so extreme that Bulgarian Prime Minister Boyko Borissov dubbed it "the corruption scheme of the century." More recently, however, both the prime minister and Bulgaria's president, Rumen Radev, have expressed their support for the project, because while EU loans come with strict transparency rules, loans from China do not. Beijing's easier investment policies have set back the development of rule of law, as regards investment, in Eastern European countries. A lack of progress in the development of rule of law may scare off Western investors, leaving China as the major or possibly only significant source of financing. To make matters worse, not only does Beijing fail to encourage countries to meet Western standards of transparency, but it also includes terms favorable to Chinese interests, such as granting contracts to Chinese companies. Consequently, *The Diplomat* reports that " the vast majority of BRI projects in the CEE region remain firmly in the hands of Chinese lenders and companies." [5]

Ray Washburne, president and CEO of the Overseas Private Investment Corporation, an intergovernmental agency that channels US private capital into overseas development projects, stated that China "is not in it to help countries out, they're in it to grab their assets." [6] He went on to charge Beijing with intentionally driving recipient countries into debt. Negative feelings about the BRI caused Greenland to accept a Danish, rather than a PRC, company to expand its airport. Officials in Greenland justified the decision by explaining that Greenland's economy is so small that even a modest Chinese investment would represent a significant percentage of the GDP, and give Beijing undue influence. [7]

In July 2018, leading up to the China-EU BRI summit, a report was submitted and signed by 27 of the 28 EU ambassadors to China, denouncing the initiative as an attempt by Beijing to hinder free-trade and grant advantages to PRC companies. The report claimed that the BRI "runs counter to the EU agenda for liberalizing trade and pushes the balance of power in favor of subsidized Chinese companies." [8] The report accused China of using the BRI to shape globalization in China's favor while addressing domestic economic problems such as the reduction of excess capacity, increased export markets, and securing access to raw materials. They were bothered by the lack of adherence to such European principles as transparency, as well as environmental and social standards. [9]

A report released by the GTAI foreign trade and investment marketing agency and the Association of German Chambers of Commerce and Industry found that "80% of projects funded by Chinese state banks had gone to Chinese companies in the past." [10]

Other voices in Europe, while not keen on the current BRI situation, seemed open to participating if some changes are made. Dutch Prime Minister Mark Rutte told *South China Morning Post* , that Dutch firms would like to participate in these projects, "if China was willing to open up the tendering process for its projects to foreign companies." [11] A high-ranking EU ambassador told the press that he did not want the

Europeans to reject the BRI outright, but instead to state the terms under which participation should take place. A German economics ministry official said that the BRI had to consider the needs of all parties. [12] European Commission Vice President Jyrki Katainen said in a speech in Beijing that projects connecting Europe and Asia should adhere market rules and international standards. [13]

When EU leaders attend meetings in China they are often pressured to endorse the BRI. When EU leaders were asked to sign a sign a joint declaration, however, they refused, until certain amendments had been made. To date, China has refused to make any changes. [14] Meanwhile, EU leaders have many of the same grievances with China as US President Donald J. Trump, namely, restricted access to Chinese markets and forced technology transfer. [15] Additional Trump-style resistance comes from French President Emmanuel Macron. He has been encouraging the EU to tighten up on anti-dumping rules against Chinese steel imports, as well as tightening the vetting process for the screening of strategic sector takeovers by Chinese firms. [16]

China's European investments
Chinese investment in Eastern Europe has financed the construction of an airport in Bulgaria, two nuclear reactors in Romania, and a railway line between Serbia and Hungary. [17] A Chinese SOE is also building a high-speed railway between Belgrade and Budapest. Hungary is currently under investigation for violating EU transparency requirements related to public tenders. [18] Seen as a gateway to Europe, Poland is a member of the PRC-led Asian Infrastructure Investment Bank. [19] Poland runs a large trade deficit with China. To support Chinese companies in Poland, the PRC's three largest banks (Industrial and Commercial Bank of China, China Construction Bank, and Bank of China) have all opened offices in Warsaw. [20]

The only Western nation which seems to have fully embraced the BRI is Greece. The UK, France, and Germany have all expressed skepticism. [21] In spite of this skepticism, Chinese projects are being carried out in Europe. [22] A weekly goods train follows an 11,000-km path, taking 16 days, passing through Mongolia and Russia, linking Yiwu outside Shanghai to the Amerikahaven Container Terminal in Amsterdam. [23] Chongqing Municipal Government is subsidizing another cargo train to

Europe. [24] After talks in Beijing, PRC President Xi Jinping and Austrian President Alexander Van der Bellen issued a joint statement establishing a strategic Sino-Austrian partnership, to foster multilateral trade and an open economy. [25]

China and Italy are cooperating on the Five Ports Alliance in the northern Adriatic. "The project, managed by the Northern Adriatic Port Association, involves the three Italian ports of Venice, Trieste, and Ravenna, as well as the Slovenian port of Capodistria, and Fiume in Croatia. Once completed, it will create a docking system for large container ships using an offshore platform at the port of Malamocco near Venice that will allow Chinese cargo ships that go through the Suez Canal to unload products for rail connections throughout Europe." [26]

Since 2016, Athens's Port of Piraeus has been controlled by China Ocean Shipping Company. The company already owns 51% of the port authority and will be able to acquire a further 16% by 2021. The port will become part of the "Maritime Silk Road," granting China access to the Suez Canal and the Mediterranean Sea. China's plan is for Piraeus to become one of Europe's largest container ports. [27]

Dutch Prime Minister Mark Rutte and German Chancellor Angela Merkel have called for greater transparency in Chinese investment in the Balkans, and to keep those investments free from political demands. [28] PRC investment is often conditional on recipient countries supporting Beijing's political aims, such as the isolation of Taiwan. Consequently, Chinese investment has brought Greece and Hungary into the Chinese political sphere. Greece voted against a joint EU human rights statement on China. Greece and Hungary also refused to criticize China in a joint statement on the South China Sea. [29]

EU-China trade grievances

"China is now the EU's second-biggest trading partner behind the United States and the EU is China's biggest trading partner." [30] And yet, when China applied to be granted "market economy status" under WTO rules, EU lawmakers blocked the petition. One of the reasons given was the subsidies Beijing uses to keep its steel artificially cheap. [31] Trump went even further, stating that the US should not have supported China's admission to the WTO, because it has been "proven to be ineffective in securing China's embrace of an open, market-oriented trade regime." [32] While sharing similar concerns to Trump, some EU leaders disagree with his hardball approach; Europe has traditionally taken a softer stance on

China. [33] A report by the European Commission notes that when China joined the WTO, it agreed to liberalize its economy, but while it has made some positive changes, areas which remain a problem are a lack of transparency in industrial policies "and non-tariff measures that discriminate against foreign companies, strong government intervention in the economy, resulting in a dominant position of state-owned firms, unequal access to subsidies and cheap financing, poor protection and enforcement of intellectual property rights." [34] Another EU complaint is that foreign companies are treated differently (and worse) than domestic Chinese companies, which violates WTO rules. [35]

The term "promise fatigue" appears in European reports on the status of trade with China. The European Chamber of Commerce in China released a report on market access which examined 15 sectors – including food, automotives, health care, aviation, and insurance – addressing such concerns as barriers to market access, economic protectionism and discriminatory treatment against foreign firms. [36] The report found that in spite of repeated Chinese promises to further open to foreign firms, it appeared that Beijing was selectively closing sectors of the economy. [37]

As the trade war between the US and China heats up, Beijing has reached out to Europe to formulate a unified front against the US, although the EU and the US face many of the same issues with China trade. [38] Zhang Ming, the head of the PRC mission to the EU said that "China and the EU… should take a clear stance against protectionism, jointly preserve the rules-based multilateral trade order, and keep the global economy on a sound and sustainable track." [39] This is ironic since it is China which has repeatedly been accused of breaking the rules.

Michael Every, head of Asia-Pacific financial markets research at Netherlands-based Rabobank, said that both Washington and Beijing have been attempting to build a coalition of support, but that Beijing is finding it difficult to win allies amid complaints of restricted market access. He went on to say that the PRC runs "the risk of losing support in Europe because of its restrictive trade practices." [40] Brussels has been calling for EU companies to have greater access to Chinese markets. But after years of negotiations, no bilateral investment treaty has been reached. Each year the EU Chamber of Commerce in China has complained about the difficulties European companies encounter when doing business in the PRC. Many of these concerns echo those expressed by the American Chamber of Commerce in China. [41]

The US and the EU almost wound up in a trade war when Trump originally raised tariffs, but at the last minute, the American leader exempted Europe. Some European leaders, such as Macron, expressed anger about US threats and allegations, but nearly all EU leaders agree they are displeased with China for its intellectual property rights violations and non-transparent financing arrangements which run contrary to EU rules. The non-reciprocal nature of access to Chinese markets is another sticking point. "Many Europeans also rail against cash-flush Chinese tycoons who have snapped up European companies, sports clubs and airports, while foreigners are barred from investing in equivalent industries in China." [42]

"New York-based Rhodium Group, a research consultancy, in April showed that Chinese restrictions on foreign investment are higher in every single sector save real estate, compared to the European Union, while many of the big Chinese takeovers in the bloc would not have been possible for EU companies in China." [43] China ranked 78 among 190 economies on the World Bank's Ease of Doing Business report. [44] The OECD ranked China second to last on restrictiveness towards foreign investment. [45] In trade openness, the World Bank ranked China number 148 of 160. [46]

A European report on Chinese intellectual property violations lists complaints of not only counterfeiting of merchandise but also pharmaceuticals, as well as copyrighted materials. The report claims that China is the origin of 80% of pirated and counterfeit goods in Europe. [47] To address these and other concerns along the BRI, rather than using the WTO, China has established its own courts. [48] Ignoring these Chinese courts, in June 2018 the EU launched legal proceedings in the WTO against China regarding intellectual property rights. The EU complaint centers on China's policy of forced technology transfers, [49] and is similar to an investigation into Chinese intellectual property violations which Trump ordered under section 301 of the 1974 US trade law. US complaints address such areas as trade-secret theft, online piracy and forced technology transfer. [50]

Senior PRC officials have proposed forming an alliance with the EU and launching a joint WTO action against the US. The proposal was rejected, however, amid Europe's own complaints about China trade. A European diplomat went so far as to say: "We agree with almost all the complaints the US has against China, it's just we don't agree with how the United States is handling it." [51]

Political observers feel that the US exiting the Paris climate accords and the Iran nuclear deal, plus its trade disputes with Canada and the EU, may be perceived by China as the breakup of the Western block. By reaching out to the EU and other Western nations, China is hoping to capitalize on what it sees as cracks in Western relations. [52] But Europe does not seem to be moving toward the Chinese side. *The Diplomat* reported that several European countries, particularly Germany, France, and the UK, are increasing restrictions on Chinese investment. "At the root of European scrutiny of Chinese investments is a concern that these are not guided solely by business imperatives but are rather part of a concerted state-driven strategy." [53]

PRC companies have been buying up engineering companies in Europe, particularly in Germany. The Berlin-based Mercator Institute for China Studies issued a paper warning of the potential threat posed by China controlling so much of Europe's engineering capacity, and urging that the EU should make rules blocking takeovers which do not comply with EU regulations. [54] In 2016, Berlin blocked the acquisition of semiconductor equipment maker Aixtron by China's Fujian Grand Chip, on grounds of national security. [55] After the 2016 acquisition of German robotics manufacturer KUKA by a Chinese conglomerate, Germany began tightening regulations. [56]

In 2017, Berlin blocked a Chinese company, Yantai Taihai Group, from acquiring Leifeld Metal Spinning, which produces high-specification metals for aerospace, nuclear, and other applications. [57] This was the first time Germany had halted a deal under new laws giving Berlin veto powers in acquisitions related to defense or "critical infrastructure," including electricity supply. Merkel has pushed for the EU to adopt similar rules. [58]

The French government blocked a move by Casil Europe, a holding company created by China's state-owned Shandong Hi-Speed Group and the Hong Kong-based Friedmann Pacific Asset Management, to purchase a controlling interest in the Toulouse airport in southern France. The Chinese firm already owned 49.9% which they had purchased in 2015. [59] Allowing a foreign company to gain a controlling interest was seen as unacceptable.

The Macron government has proposed strengthening the government's ability to block foreign acquisitions, or to levy hefty fines, in

114

cases of national interest, in areas related to artificial intelligence, microchips, space technology and data storage. [60]

Under David Cameron, the UK had been one of the nations most welcoming Chinese investment. Under his successor, Theresa May, there has been a dramatic change of attitude. [61] In 2018, the UK government expanded its powers to assess and reject foreign investment deals in the fields of technology, land, or intellectual property. [62] Under the new scrutiny, flags were raised regarding the involvement of Huawei in a telecommunications deal. The investment rules would apply to foreign purchases of assets and intellectual property. [63] One of the first actions taken under the new law was a ban on UK government agencies doing business with Chinese company ZTE, which was also banned by the US government. [64]

Chapter 12: The United States

"The BRI 'is a made in China, made for China' initiative," said Brian Hook, senior policy advisor to the US Secretary of State and the Department of State's director of policy planning. [1]

Many countries across Asia, Africa, and Latin America have eagerly joined the Belt and Road Initiative, as have some Eastern European countries. Western Europe seems to be taking a more wait-and-see approach, while the US has officially stated that it would not be joining the BRI. In fact, Washington's main interaction with the BRI has been criticism of both China's intent and its practice with regard to the BRI. The US has also issued warnings for some of the debt-ridden countries which have signed on to the initiative.

Testifying about geostrategic drivers and implications of the BRI before the US-China Economic and Security Review Commission, Ely Ratner, vice president and director of studies at the Center for a New American Security, recommended that the US response be set within its overall China policy, and that US policy should be to reassert American leadership in economics, military, politics, and information in the region. [2]

In addition to its economic impact, the BRI figures in China's recent militarization.

Military implications

The People's Liberation Army (PLA) does not answer to the Chinese government, but rather to the Chinese Communist Party. [3] In the past, this meant that the political body which drove the army could outlive a sitting government. Since the abolishing of presidential term limits, however, it is unclear what this now means. What is clear is that, under President Xi Jinping, Beijing has been building up its military. Chinese military spending more than doubled between 2001 and 2011. [4] It has increased each year since then, with growth of more than 7% in 2016 and 8% in 2018. [5]

Historically, the stated purpose of the PLA has been to defend China's borders. It appears China is now building a military capable of waging a foreign war. The PLA Navy launched its second aircraft carrier in 2018, making it the only country apart from the US to have more than one aircraft carrier. [6] China has also established its first official overseas base at Djibouti, with planned installations in several Chinese-invested ports in foreign countries. China has admitted to having militarized the Spratly Islands, and has discussed the possibility of building a base in Afghanistan. [7]

The overland and sea routes of the BRI work in cooperation with its military expansion. Both the BRI and the PLA have helped to increase China's influence throughout Central Asia. In the South China Sea, the PLA Navy is driving Beijing's claims to disputed territories. China's increased emphasis on its navy, particularly in this region, is a direct response to the American military presence. Some experts speculate that, by steering clear of international wars and peacekeeping missions, China may be playing a long game, using the US military to secure stable access to Middle Eastern energy, while slowly building up its own military to take over once US power and influence declines. [8]

Countries such as the Philippines have a legitimate claim to parts of the South China Sea, but find it impossible to stand up to Beijing because they need China's money, and because they lack the military power to refuse too aggressively. Additionally, the US has not made it clear if the "1951 Mutual Defense Treaty with Manila would apply to an attack on Philippine troops or vessels in the South China Sea." [9] Japan, on the other hand, has been given reassurances by President Donald J. Trump that "Article 5 of the US-Japan Treaty of Mutual Cooperation and Security covers the Senkaku Islands," which are disputed by Beijing and Tokyo. Meanwhile, China continues to develop its military assets in the South China Sea. [10]

US alternatives

On October 5, 2018, Trump signed into law the Better Utilization of Investment Leading to Development (BUILD) Act, which will form a new American agency, similar to China's BRI. There will also be a new US

International Development Finance Corp. (IDFC) to provide loans to developing countries for infrastructure and other projects. The total market cap is expected to be around US$60 billion, or roughly one-twentieth the size of the BRI, but BUILD is not exactly meant to compete with the BRI in terms of magnitude. [11] One of the ancillary benefits of developmental aid loans is that they often attract investment from other countries. BRI projects tend not to attract foreign investment to recipient countries for a variety of reasons, including unfair advantages given to PRC companies and the fact that China almost never allows BRI projects to be implemented by non-Chinese companies. US loans, on the other hand, are expected to attract foreign investment which could amplify the volume and impact of any US loans.

In July 2018, US Secretary of State Mike Pompeo announced that aid to the Indo-Pacific region through the IDFC would include US$113 million in direct government investment, as well as an additional US$60 million in loans available to private companies with overseas projects. The Trump administration also agreed to expand US technology exports to the region by US$25 million. The US has also stated that it would be investing US$350 million in Mongolia. Through the Millennium Challenge Corp., a bilateral foreign-aid agency established by the US Congress in 2004, hundreds of millions of US dollars will be invested in transportation in Sri Lanka. Pompeo said Washington wants to help develop local wealth and local economic growth by bringing private money "off the sidelines and into markets." [12] Pompeo went on to say that the US model of development was the healthiest, and that it would help nations to retain their sovereignty. "It is high quality, it is transparent, and it is financially sustainable." [13]

Many believe that Washington's withdrawal from the Trans-Pacific Partnership was a signal that the US was disengaging with the Indo-Pacific region. This is not the case, the US having long preferred bilateral to multilateral trade agreements. In the case of the Indo-Pacific, Washington is planning to step up investment in the region through the Overseas Private Investment Corporation (OPIC).

OPIC bills itself as "a modern US development agency." "The Overseas Private Investment Corporation (OPIC) is a self-sustaining US government agency that helps American businesses invest in emerging markets. Established in 1971, OPIC provides businesses with the tools to manage the risks associated with foreign direct investment, fosters economic development in emerging market countries, and advances US foreign policy and national security priorities. OPIC helps American businesses gain footholds in new markets, catalyzes new revenues and contributes to jobs and growth opportunities both at home and abroad. OPIC fulfills its mission by providing businesses with financing, political risk insurance, advocacy and by partnering with private equity investment fund managers." [14]

OPIC's work is led by private-sector development, resulting in high-quality projects viable over the long term. "But unlike with the Chinese model, contracts are transparent, governments aren't loaded with debt they cannot pay and local workers are hired." [15] As well as helping recipient countries avoid debt traps, BUILD should "help more American businesses invest in emerging markets, including many places that are of key strategic importance to the United States." [16]

American investment will still be small compared to the amount of Chinese investment, but the US – as a major energy exporter – may be able to help countries in the region meet their energy needs. With its various initiatives around the globe, the US appears to be offering countries alternatives to the BRI. As James Mattis said during his stint as US defense secretary, "There's more than one belt and more than one road. There are many belts and many roads to the Indo-Pacific." [17]

A spokesperson for the American Enterprise Institute said Washington should pursue programs of investment in countries such as Vietnam, Indonesia, and the Philippines, "as well as programs to help strengthen the rule of law in these countries so that they are not as susceptible to outright Chinese bribery." [18] Similarly, "US Vice President Mike Pence told an APEC audience... that his country offered 'a better option' that wouldn't imperil small nations' sovereignty by saddling them with unmanageable debt. He went so far as to say, "'We don't offer a constricting belt or one-way road.'" [19]

Another alternative to the BRI is the joint regional infrastructure scheme that was mapped out by Australia, the United States, India, and Japan ("the Quad"). Japan also presents several BRI alternatives, such as official development assistance to promote a broader "Free and Open Indo-Pacific Strategy" including "high-quality infrastructure." [20] The four governments are promoting the Indo-Pacific as an alternative concept to the Asia Pacific, the former stressing the importance of Indian involvement while suggesting that China will not be a leader in these initiatives. [21] Japan and India are also working together to create the Asia Africa Growth Corridor, which they began promoting in May 2017 as an alternative to the BRI's Maritime Silk Road. [22]

While bolstering India's role may seem like a good idea, creating organizations and initiatives which intentionally marginalize China may not be. Many warn against starting a new Cold War. Formulating a comprehensive China strategy has proven difficult for these nations because they are coming from very different internal situations and differing relationships with China. Another issue is Washington's preference for bilateral, rather than multilateral, agreements; the Trump administration is even more so inclined. And unlike the Washington-Moscow relationship during the Cold War, the Washington-Beijing relationship is not one of complete enmity. The Trump administration, and most American political leaders, hope to have constructive economic relations with China, rather than simply containing China. [23]

Australia and Japan likely prefer US leadership to Chinese leadership in the Indo-Pacific. For India, however, this creates other contradictions of foreign policy as India has historically avoided making very specific commitments to other countries or organizations, but rather maintain good relations with as many countries as possible. [24]

Indo-Pacific countries such as Papua New Guinea (PNG) find themselves caught between the quad and Chinese aid and investment. PNG Foreign Minister Rimbink Pato said the country welcomes investment from both the US and China. "Mr Pato said China as a new donor country would present 'challenges' and said that Australia remained a 'partner of choice' for PNG, both on security and infrastructure." [25]

While many countries are willing to accept Chinese money, few – with the exception of Djibouti – seem willing to host PRC military bases, even where US or Australian bases are seen as acceptable.

In the end, India announced it would not be joining the Quad, a decision which was in keeping with its general policy of "multipolarity in the Indo-Pacific region and non-bloc security architecture." [26] India will, however continue to participate in other initiatives and cooperate with the India-Japan-Australia trilateral, as well as the Indo-US 2+2 dialogue. India is also in separate talks with Russia on the Indo-Pacific region. [27]

The trade war

For years, economists have been saying that the Chinese economy has cracks in it. Historically, whenever Beijing saw its economy beginning to slow, they used government spending and massive infrastructure projects, including the BRI, to bolster the economy. Now, public debt stands at 250% of GDP, raising the question: How much more public spending can China manage before the economy crashes? [28] The PRC is greatly dependent on trade, specifically with the US, a source of income now threatened by the trade war. Some believe the effects of a slowing economy are already present. In August 2018, infrastructure investment – which had accounted for 44% of China's GDP in 2017 – hit a record low. Whether the trade war will cause a further economic slowdown remains to be seen, but the IMF has already warned Beijing not to continue using credit to stimulate its economy. This raises another question: Without using credit, will China be able to make good on its US$1 trillion of promised BRI investment?

NOTES

Foreword

1. *South China Morning Post* , "Beijing's 'Belt and Road Initiative' will benefit the world," February 12, 2018, http://www.scmp.com/comment/insight-opinion/article/2132943/beijings-belt-and-road-initiative-will-benefit-world

2. Ibid

3. Tang, F., "Beijing eyes Hong Kong and London for fresh Belt and Road funds," April 12, 2018, *South China Morning Post* , http://www.scmp.com/news/china/economy/article/2141487/beijing-eyes-hong-kong-and-london-fresh-belt-and-road-funds

4. Watts, G., "President Xi charts out his promised land in idyllic Hainan," April 10, 2018, *Asia Times* , http://www.atimes.com/article/president-xi-charts-promised-land-idyllic-hainan/?utm_source=The+Daily+Report&utm_campaign=5b6dfb3b85-EMAIL_CAMPAIGN_2018_04_10&utm_medium=email&utm_term=0_1f8bca137f-5b6dfb3b85-31520157

5. Hillman, J., "China's Belt and Road Initiative: Five Years Later," January 25, 2018, Center for Strategic and International Studies, https://www.csis.org/analysis/chinas-belt-and-road-initiative-five-years-later-0

6. GB Times, "China to cover Belt and Road countries with Beidou navigation system by 2018," September 13, 2017, https://gbtimes.com/china-to-cover-belt-and-road-countries-with-beidou-navigation-system-by-2018

7. Ma, A., "Inside 'Belt and Road,' China's mega-project that is linking 70 countries across Asia, Europe, and Africa," January 31, 2018, Business Insider, http://www.businessinsider.com/what-is-belt-and-road-china-infrastructure-project-2018-1

8. Lee, Y., "Xi's One Belt One Road: A Plan Too Big to Fail?" December 8, 2017, *The Diplomat* , https://thediplomat.com/2017/12/xis-one-belt-one-road-a-plan-too-big-to-fail/

9. Gabuev, A., "Belt and Road to Where?" December 11, 2017, Global Affairs, http://eng.globalaffairs.ru/book/Belt-and-Road-to-Where-19214

10. Ibid.

11. Yamada, G. and S. Palma, "Is China's Belt and Road working? A progress report from eight countries," March 29, 2018, *Nikkei Asian Review* , https://asia.nikkei.com/Print-Edition/Issue-2018-03-29?n_cid=NARAN185&utm_source=facebook&utm_medium=infeed&utm_campaign=IC%20V2min&utm_content=March%2029%20BELT%20AND%20ROADBLOCKS

12. Gabuev, A., "Belt and Road to Where?"

13. Ibid.

Chapter 1

1. Bishop, B., "China wants to reshape the global order," January 19, 2018, Axios, https://www.axios.com/chinas-growing-global-aspirations-in-the-xi-jinping-era-1516305566-aa5be206-c156-4313-8229-cfa88af9b75a.html

2. Bader, L., "China's 6 Magical Economic Corridors," August 20, 2015, Market Mogul, https://themarketmogul.com/chinas-6-magical-economic-corridors/

3. Shah, A., "How Does China–Pakistan Economic Corridor Show the Limitations of China's 'One Belt One Road' Model," May 2018, *Asia & The Pacific Policy Studies* Volume 5, Issue 2, pages 378–385, https://onlinelibrary.wiley.com/doi/full/10.1002/app5.224

4. Meyers, J., "China's Belt and Road Forum lays groundwork for a new global order," May 15, 2017, *Los Angeles Times* , http://www.latimes.com/world/asia/la-fg-china-belt-road-20170515-story.html

5. Ibid.

6. Lee, Y., "Xi's One Belt One Road: A Plan Too Big to Fail?" December 8, 2017, *The Diplomat* , https://thediplomat.com/2017/12/xis-one-belt-one-road-a-plan-too-big-to-fail/

7. Reuters, "China launches propaganda push for Xi Jinping after social media backlash," 26 Feb 2018, https://www.cnbc.com/2018/02/25/china-presidential-term-limits-propaganda-push-for-xi-jinping-after-social-media-backlash.html

8. Lee, Y., "Xi's One Belt One Road: A Plan Too Big to Fail?"

9. BBC, "Xi Jinping 'most powerful Chinese leader since Mao Zedong'," October 24, 2017, https://www.youtube.com/watch?v=E_Y9yQaE89E

10. Reuters, "China launches propaganda push for Xi Jinping after social media backlash."

11. *The Economist*, 2017, cited in Shah, A. R., "How Does China–Pakistan Economic Corridor Show the Limitations of China's 'One Belt One Road' Model."

12. Lee, Y., "Xi's One Belt One Road: A Plan Too Big to Fail?"

13. Scissors, D., "Private Data, Not Private Firms: The Real Issues in Chinese Investment," January 10, 2018, American Enterprise Institute, http://www.aei.org/publication/private-data-not-private-firms-the-real-issues-in-chinese-investment/

14. Retka, J., "China Funded 70% of Cambodian Roads, Bridges: Minister, July 24, 2017, *The Cambodia Daily*, https://www.cambodiadaily.com/business/china-funded-70-of-cambodian-roads-bridges-minister-132826/

15. Meyers, J., "China's Belt and Road Forum lays groundwork for a new global order."

16. Ma, A., "Inside 'Belt and Road,' China's mega-project that is linking 70 countries across Asia, Europe, and Africa," January 31, 2018, Business Insider, http://www.businessinsider.com/what-is-belt-and-road-china-infrastructure-project-2018-1

17. Yamada, G. and S. Palma, "Is China's Belt and Road working? A progress report from eight countries."

18. Hillman, J., "China's Belt and Road Initiative: Five Years Later," January 25, 2018, Center for Strategic and International Studies, https://www.csis.org/analysis/chinas-belt-and-road-initiative-five-years-later-0

19. Eva, J. Q. Lin and J. Tunningley, "China's Belt and Road Initiative: Regional Outlooks for 2018," Global Risk Insights, https://globalriskinsights.com/2018/01/chinas-belt-and-road-initiative-regional-outlooks-for-2018/

20. Ibid.

21. Hillman, J., "China's Belt and Road Initiative: Five Years Later."

22. Ibid.

23. Ibid.

24. Heide, D. et al., "EU ambassadors band together against Silk Road," April 17, 2018, *Handelsblatt*, https://global.handelsblatt.com/politics/eu-ambassadors-beijing-china-silk-road-912258

25. Lo, K., "Netherlands keen on Chinese investment but wants belt and road to benefit foreign companies," April 12, 2018, *South China Morning Post* , http://www.scmp.com/news/china/diplomacy-defence/article/2141261/netherlands-keen-chinese-investment-wants-belt-and-road

26. Liu, Z., "Xi Jinping fails to get formal backing from Theresa May on belt and road plan," February 1, 2018, *South China Morning Post* , http://www.scmp.com/news/china/diplomacy-defence/article/2131649/xi-jinping-fails-get-formal-backing-theresa-may-belt

27. Erlanger, S., "Europe Once Saw Xi Jinping as a Hedge Against Trump. Not Anymore," March 4, 2018, *New York Times* , https://www.nytimes.com/2018/03/04/world/europe/europe-china-xi-trump-trade.html

28. Ibid.

29. Ibid.

30. Scissors, D., "Private Data, Not Private Firms: The Real Issues in Chinese Investment."

31. Gong, X., "Why some in Southeast Asia still have reservations about China's Belt and Road Initiative," March 21, 2018, Today Online, https://www.todayonline.com/commentary/why-some-south-east-asia-still-have-reservations-about-chinas-belt-and-road-initiative

32. Yamada, G. and S. Palma, "Is China's Belt and Road working? A progress report from eight countries."

33. Ibid.

34. Ibid.

35. Shah, A. R., "How Does China–Pakistan Economic Corridor Show the Limitations of China's 'One Belt One Road' Model."

36. Beechmarch, H., "Embracing China, Facebook and Himself, Cambodia's Ruler Digs In," March 17, 2018, *New York Times* , https://www.nytimes.com/2018/03/17/world/asia/hun-sen-cambodia-china.html

37. Tang, F., "Beijing eyes Hong Kong and London for fresh Belt and Road funds."

38. Lee, Y., "Xi's One Belt One Road: A Plan Too Big to Fail?"

39. Eva, J. Q. Lin and J. Tunningley, "China's Belt and Road Initiative: Regional Outlooks for 2018."

40. Scissors, D., "Private Data, Not Private Firms: The Real Issues in Chinese Investment."

41. He, H., "Is China's belt and road infrastructure development plan about to run out of money?" April, 14, 2018, *South China Morning*

Press ,
http://www.scmp.com/news/china/economy/article/2141739/chinas-belt-and-road-infrastructure-development-plan-about-run
42. Ibid.
43. Ibid.
44. Yamada, G. and S. Palma, "Is China's Belt and Road working? A progress report from eight countries."

Chapter 2

1. Booth, A., "ASEAN and China," September 12, 2017, Asia Dialogue (China Policy Institute),
https://cpianalysis.org/2017/09/12/asean-and-china/
2. Xinhua, "China, ASEAN to advance trade, investment with upgraded FTA," September 14, 2017,
http://www.ecns.cn/business/2017/09-14/273480.shtml
3. Tan, J., "Why is China leaving Singapore out in the cold?" June 3, 2017, Asean Today,
https://www.aseantoday.com/2017/06/why-is-china-leaving-singapore-out-in-the-cold/
4. Eva, J. Q. Lin and J. Tunningley, "China's Belt and Road Initiative: Regional Outlooks for 2018."
5. Li, X. and Z. Cheng, "China's Window of Opportunity in the South China Sea," July 26, 2017, *The Diplomat* ,
http://thediplomat.com/2017/07/chinas-window-of-opportunity-in-the-south-china-sea/
6. Eva, J. Q. Lin and J. Tunningley, "China's Belt and Road Initiative: Regional Outlooks for 2018."
7. UNCTAD, "ASEAN Investment Report 2016: Foreign Direct Investment and MSME Linkages,"
https://unctad.org/en/PublicationsLibrary/unctad_asean_air2016d1.pdf
8. Abbate, F. and S. Rosina, "ASEAN-China trade growth: facts, factors and prospects," June 14, 2016, New Mandala,
http://www.newmandala.org/asean-china-trade-growth-facts-factors-and-prospects/
9. Suherdjoko, "China, ASEAN celebrate 'diamond decade' of relations," June 6, 2016, *Jakarta Post* ,
https://www.thejakartapost.com/seasia/2016/06/06/china-asean-celebrate-diamond-decade-of-relations.html
10. Bello, W., "China and Southeast Asia: Emerging Problems in an Economic Relationship," December 15, 2006, El Transnational Institute, https://www.tni.org/es/node/8577

11. Cordenillo, R., "The Economic Benefits to ASEAN of the ASEAN-China Free Trade Area (ACFTA)," January 18, 2005, ASEAN, https://asean.org/?static_post=the-economic-benefits-to-asean-of-the-asean-china-free-trade-area-acfta-by-raul-l-cordenillo

12. ASEAN Up, "ASEAN infographics: population, market, economy," March 26, 2018, http://aseanup.com/asean-infographics-population-market-economy/

13. Statistics Times, "List of Asian countries by GDP per capita," June 5, 2018, http://statisticstimes.com/economy/asian-countries-by-gdp-per-capita.php

14. Abbate, F. and S. Rosina, "ASEAN-China trade growth: facts, factors and prospects."

15. Ibid.

16. Ibid.

17. UNCTAD, "ASEAN Investment Report 2016: Foreign Direct Investment and MSME Linkages."

18. Abbate, F. and S. Rosina, "ASEAN-China trade growth: facts, factors and prospects."

19. Salidjanova, N. and I. Koch-Weser, "China's Economic Ties with ASEAN: A Country-by-Country Analysis," March 17, 2015, US-China Economic and Security Review Commission, https://www.uscc.gov/sites/default/files/Research/China%27s%20Economic%20Ties%20with%20ASEAN.pdf

20. Ibid.

21. UNCTAD, "ASEAN Investment Report 2016: Foreign Direct Investment and MSME Linkages."

22. Salidjanova, N. and I. Koch-Weser, "China's Economic Ties with ASEAN: A Country-by-Country Analysis."

23. Ibid.

24. Asia Regional Integration Center, "Free Trade Agreements," https://aric.adb.org/fta-country

25. Heydrian, R., "Singapore-led Asean favors China over US," April 30, 2018, Asia Times .

26. Ibid.

27. Ibid.

28. World Bank, "GDP per capita (current US$)," https://data.worldbank.org/indicator/NY.GDP.PCAP.CD

29. Heritage Foundation, "China 2018, Index of Economic Freedom," https://www.heritage.org/index/country/china

30. Transparency International, "China Corruption Perceptions Index 2018," https://www.transparency.org/country/CHN

31. Economist Intelligence Unit, "Democracy Index 2017: Free speech under attack," https://www.eiu.com/public/topical_report.aspx?campaignid=DemocracyIndex2017

32. World Bank, "GDP per capita (current US$)."

33. Heritage Foundation, "United States of America 2018, Index of Economic Freedom," https://www.heritage.org/index/country/unitedstates

34. Transparency International, "United States of America Corruption Perceptions Index 2018," https://www.transparency.org/country/USA

35. Economist Intelligence Unit, "Democracy Index 2017: Free speech under attack."

36. World Bank, "The World Bank in Singapore: Overview," October 10, 2018, https://www.worldbank.org/en/country/singapore/overview

37. Heritage Foundation, "Singapore 2018, Index of Economic Freedom," http://www.heritage.org/index/country/singapore

38. Transparency International, "Singapore Corruption Perceptions Index 2018," https://www.transparency.org/country/SGP

39. Economist Intelligence Unit, "Democracy Index 2017: Free speech under attack."

40. Low, A., "Why Singapore's Economic Slowdown May be Coming to an End," July 7, 2017, *South China Morning Post* , http://www.scmp.com/week-asia/business/article/2067919/why-singapores-economic-slowdown-may-be-coming-end

41. Ibid.

42. Nathan, S., "Financial Institutions: 3 Ways the Singapore Government Is Intensifying Anti Money Laundering Efforts," March 24, 2017, Asia Law Network, http://learn.asialawnetwork.com/2017/03/24/financial-institutions-3-ways-the-singapore-government-is-intensifying-anti-money-laundering-efforts/

43. Low, A., "Why Singapore's Economic Slowdown May be Coming to an End."

44. Foon, H., "China projects to hit Singapore," January 15, 2017, *The Star* ,

http://www.thestar.com.my/news/nation/2017/01/15/china-projects-to-hit-singapore-the-giant-republics-aggressive-investments-in-ports-and-rail-links-i/#gYzOgFP0CmddKGLP.99

45. Raj, K., "Singapore face two major challenges in 2017 – with China and tightening capital outflow," December 22, 2016, *The Independent* , http://www.theindependent.sg/singapore-face-two-major-challenges-in-2017-with-china-and-tightening-capital-outflow/

46. Erickson, A., "Malaysia cancels two big Chinese projects, fearing they will bankrupt the country," August 21, 2018, *Washington Post* , https://www.washingtonpost.com/world/asia_pacific/malaysia-cancels-two-massive-chinese-projects-fearing-they-will-bankrupt-the-country/2018/08/21/2bd150e0-a515-11e8-b76b-d513a40042f6_story.html?noredirect=on&utm_term=.cc3c39dbfcf7

47. Channel News Asia, "How Singapore's port helped change the country's economy," April 21, 2015, https://www.sqfeed.com/2015/04/21/the-port-of-singapore-has-played-a-significant-role-in-the-development-of-singapore-helping-the-republic-become-a-first-world-economy-in-one-generation-the-maritime-industry-currently-contributes-ab/

48. Raj, K., "Singapore face two major challenges in 2017 – with China and tightening capital outflow."

49. Aggarwal, N., "S'pore is China's largest investor," November 6, 2015, Business Times, http://www.businesstimes.com.sg/hub/business-china-special/spore-is-chinas-largest-investor

50. Bloomberg, "Temasek: The Model for China's Sovereign Wealth Fund?" July 31, 2008, https://www.bloomberg.com/news/articles/2008-07-30/temasek-the-model-for-chinas-sovereign-wealth-fund-businessweek-business-news-stock-market-and-financial-advice

51. Williams, A., "Singapore and China central banks renew bilateral currency swap arrangement," March 15, 2016, *Straits Times* , http://www.straitstimes.com/business/banking/singapore-and-china-central-banks-renew-bilateral-currency-swap-arrangement

52. Chang, R., "Success of Guangzhou Knowledge City raises bar in Sino-Singapore projects: PM Lee," September 12, 2014, *Straits Times* , http://www.straitstimes.com/asia/east-asia/success-of-guangzhou-knowledge-city-raises-bar-in-sino-singapore-projects-pm-lee

53. Sino-Singapore Guangzhou Knowledge City, "Company Profile," http://www.ssgkc.com/P01_01.asp

54. Cheong, D., "Singapore and China sign deal to boost cooperation on Belt and Road Initiative," April 12, 2018, *Straits Times* , https://www.straitstimes.com/asia/east-asia/singapore-and-china-sign-deal-to-boost-cooperation-on-belt-and-road-initiative

55. World Bank, "GDP per capita (current US$)," https://data.worldbank.org/indicator/NY.GDP.PCAP.CD?locations=TH

56. World Bank, "Thailand Overview," September 2018, http://www.worldbank.org/en/country/thailand/overview

57. Transparency International, "Thailand Corruption Perceptions Index 2018," https://www.transparency.org/country/THA

58. Economist Intelligence Unit, "Democracy Index 2017: Free speech under attack."

59. Heritage Foundation, "Thailand 2018, Index of Economic Freedom," http://www.heritage.org/index/country/Thailand

60. Handley, H., "Thailand in 2017: a Changing Investment Landscape, February 17, 2017, ASEAN Briefing, http://www.aseanbriefing.com/news/2017/02/17/thailand-2017-changing-investment-landscape.html

61. Workman, D., "Thailand's Top Trading Partners," February 1, 2019, WTEx, http://www.worldstopexports.com/thailands-top-import-partners

62. Bilaterals.org, "China-Thailand," May 2012, http://www.bilaterals.org/?-China-Thailand

63. China Investment Overseas, "Chinese Investment in Thailand Gains Speed," September 2, 2016, http://www.china-invests.net/20160902/41620.aspx

64. The American Interest, "Thailand's Pivot to China Continues," February 18, 2016, http://www.the-american-interest.com/2016/02/17/thailands-pivot-to-china-continues/

65. Reuters, "Thailand approves US$1.47 bln budget to join China-led AIIB," January 26, 2016, http://www.reuters.com/article/thailand-aiib-idUSL3N15A3O3

66. Reuters, "Thailand pins growth hopes on big infrastructure projects, but outlays tiny so far," July 20, 2018, *South China Morning Post* , http://www.scmp.com/news/asia/southeast-asia/article/2017530/thailand-pins-growth-hopes-big-infrastructure-projects

67. Potkin, F., "Thailand bets on China-led AIIB to finance massive infrastructure needs, February 16, 2016, East By Southeast,

http://www.eastbysoutheast.com/thailand-bets-on-china-led-aiib-to-finance-massive-infrastructure-needs/

68. Sriring, O. and S. Staporncharnchai, "From car parts to condos, faltering Thailand lures Chinese money," May 17, 2016, Reuters, http://www.reuters.com/article/us-thailand-china-investment-idUSKCN0Y72D5

69. Xinhua, "More Chinese investment welcomed in Thailand's high-tech sector: Minister," January 22, 2016, *China Daily* , http://www.chinadaily.com.cn/business/2016-01/22/content_23206795.htm

70. Chayutworakan, S., "10 millionth Chinese tourist this year arrives in Thailand," December 19, 2018, *Bangkok Post* , https://www.bangkokpost.com/business/tourism-and-transport/1597194/10-millionth-chinese-tourist-this-year-arrives-in-thailand

71. Sriring, O. and S. Staporncharnchai, "From car parts to condos, faltering Thailand lures Chinese money."

72. Shi, J., "Chinese investors upbeat on prospects in Thailand despite uncertainty after king's death," July 20, 2018, *South China Morning Post* , http://www.scmp.com/news/china/economy/article/2028986/chinese-remain-upbeat-investment-prospects-thailand-despite

73. Ehrlich, R., "Thai junta deftly rebalances its US-China relations," April 18, 2018, *Asia Times* , https://www.asiatimes.com/2018/04/article/thai-junta-deftly-rebalances-us-china-relations/

74. Ibid.

75. World Factbook, "Burma," 2018, CIA, https://www.cia.gov/library/publications/the-world-factbook/geos/bm.html

76. Heritage Foundation, "2018 Index of Economic Freedom, Burma," https://www.heritage.org/index/country/burma

77. Transparency International, "Myanmar, 2018 Corruption Perception Index," https://www.transparency.org/country/MMR

78. Economist Intelligence Unit, "Democracy Index 2017: Free speech under attack."

79. Observatory of Economic Complexity, "Burma," https://atlas.media.mit.edu/en/profile/country/mmr/

80. Consult-Myanmar, "China First in Overall Foreign Investment List," June 22, 2017, https://consult-myanmar.com/2017/06/22/china-first-in-overall-foreign-investment-list/

81. Lintner, B., "How China gets what it wants in Myanmar," April 24, 2018, *Asia Times*, http://www.atimes.com/article/how-china-gets-what-it-wants-in-myanmar/

82. Ibid.

83. Ibid.

84. Ibid.

85. Ibid.

86. Heritage Foundation, "2018 Index of Economic Freedom, Cambodia," http://www.heritage.org/index/country/cambodia

87. Transparency International, "Cambodia, 2018 Corruption Perception Index," https://www.transparency.org/country/KHM

88. Economist Intelligence Unit, "Democracy Index 2017: Free speech under attack."

89. *The Economist*, "The giant's client: Why Cambodia has cosied up to China," January 21, 2017, https://www.economist.com/asia/2017/01/21/why-cambodia-has-cosied-up-to-china

90. UNCTAD, "ASEAN Investment Report 2016: Foreign Direct Investment and MSME Linkages."

91. Trading Economics, "Cambodia Balance of Trade," http://www.tradingeconomics.com/cambodia/balance-of-trade

92. Observatory of Economic Complexity, "Cambodia," http://atlas.media.mit.edu/en/profile/country/khm/

93. UNCTAD, "ASEAN Investment Report 2016: Foreign Direct Investment and MSME Linkages."

94. Ibid.

95. Ibid.

96. Salidjanova, N. and I. Koch-Weser, "China's Economic Ties with ASEAN: A Country-by-Country Analysis."

97. Sovan, N. and P. Mao, "Spotlight: Chinese investors, tourists contribute to Cambodia's socio-economic development: business leaders," January 12, 2018, Xinhua, http://www.xinhuanet.com/english/2018-01/12/c_136891499.htm

98. Xinhua, "Cambodia, China's Shaanxi province sign deal to boost trade, investment," March 27, 2017, http://www.xinhuanet.com//english/2017-03/27/c_136161689.htm

99. Beechmarch, H., "Embracing China, Facebook and Himself, Cambodia's Ruler Digs In," March 17, 2018, *New York Times*, https://www.nytimes.com/2018/03/17/world/asia/hun-sen-cambodia-china.html

100. Ibid.
101. Ibid.
102. Ibid.
103. Janssen, P., "Misaligned rails keep SEAsia delinked from China," May 4, 2018, Eurasia News Online, https://eurasia-news-online.com/2018/05/13/misaligned-rails-keep-se-asia-de-linked-from-china/
104. Minority Rights, "Cambodia Chinese," http://minorityrights.org/minorities/chinese-2/
105. Filippi, J., "A history of the Chinese in Cambodia," February 8, 2013, *Phnom Penh Post* , http://www.phnompenhpost.com/post-plus/history-chinese-cambodia
106. Chen, S., "The Key of Chinese Identity: A Historical Survey of Languages Usage in Chinese Cambodian Community," Department of Anthropology, University of Hawaii at Manoa, https://www.academia.edu/5579670/The_Key_of_Chinese_Identity_A_Historical_Survey_of_Languages_Usage_in_Chinese_Cambodian_Community
107. Kyne, P., "Chinese schools: back from the brink," June 25, 1999, *Phnom Penh Post* , http://www.phnompenhpost.com/national/chinese-schools-back-brink
108. Ibid.
109. Ibid.
110. Ibid.
111. Ibid.
112. Minority Rights, "Cambodia Chinese."
113. Kyne, P., "Chinese schools: back from the brink."
114. Ibid.
115. Verver, M., "Templates of 'Chineseness' and Trajectories of Cambodian Chinese Entrepreneurship in Phnom Penh," Cross-Currents e-Journal No. 4, https://cross-currents.berkeley.edu/e-journal/issue-4/Verver
116. Ibid.
117. Ibid.
118. Loy, I., "Learning Chinese on the Rise in Cambodia," May 22, 2013, *The Diplomat* , http://thediplomat.com/2013/05/learning-chinese-on-the-rise-in-cambodia/
119. Kyne, P., "Chinese schools: back from the brink."

120. Vannarin, N., "In Cambodia, English Classes More Popular Than Chinese," VOA, June 9, 2015, http://www.voanews.com/a/in-cambodia-english-classes-more-popular-than-chinese/2813254.html

121. Verver, M., "Templates of 'Chineseness' and Trajectories of Cambodian Chinese Entrepreneurship in Phnom Penh."

122. Ibid.

123. Nhean, M., "Chinese New Year: family, food and prosperity for the year ahead," January 29, 2014, *Phnom Penh Post* , http://www.phnompenhpost.com/post-plus/chinese-new-year-family-food-and-prosperity-year-ahead

124. Xinhua, "Cambodia Gearing up for Chinese New Year Celebrations," February 7, 2016, *Khmer Times* , https://www.khmertimeskh.com/35467/cambodia-gearing-up-for-chinese-new-year-celebrations/

125. Xinhua, "Chinese language schools mushrooming in Cambodia," October 10, 2011, China.org, http://www.china.org.cn/learning_chinese/news/2011-10/10/content_23581580.htm

126. Zhang, Z., Y. Xie and Y. Li, "Who knew learning Chinese could be so valuable?" May 29, 2016, Hanban News, http://english.hanban.org/article/2016-05/29/content_644716.htm

127. Minority Rights, "Cambodia Chinese."

128. Zhang R., and B. Lei, "Confucius Institute opens Chinese-language class in Cambodia," January 21, 2010, *China Daily* , http://www.chinadaily.com.cn/china/2010-01/21/content_9358625.htm

129. Royal University of Phnom Penh, Department of Chinese, "Background," http://www.rupp.edu.kh/ifl/chinese/?page=Background

130. Xinhua, "More Cambodian students seek degree in Chinese language," June 24, 2014, ECNS, http://www.ecns.cn/2014/06-24/120599.shtml

131. Chen, L., "It Pays to Learn Chinese, In Cambodia," January 24, 2015, WorldCrunch, http://www.worldcrunch.com/culture-society/it-pays-to-learn-chinese-in-cambodia

132. Abundance of Life International School, "Welcome to ALIS," http://www.aliscambodia.com/

133. Khemara, S., "China Gives US$600m to Cambodia in Exchange for International Support," July 15, 2016, VOA, http://www.voacambodia.com/a/china-gives-600-million-to-cambodia-in-exchange-for-international-support/3419875.html

134. Associated Press, "China forgives US$90 million debt owned by Cambodia," October 14, 2016, Taiwan News, https://www.taiwannews.com.tw/en/news/2995967

135. Wu, W., "It pays to be friends with Beijing, but why is big China wooing small Cambodia?" October 14, 2016, *South China Morning Post* , http://www.scmp.com/news/china/diplomacy-defence/article/2027840/why-big-china-wooing-small-cambodia

136. Ibid.

137. Loy, I., "Learning Chinese on the Rise in Cambodia."

138. Vannarin, N., "In Cambodia, English Classes More Popular Than Chinese."

139. Ibid.

140. Sokhorng, C., "Tourism gears for China rising," October 21, 2016, *Phnom Penh Post* , http://www.phnompenhpost.com/business/tourism-gears-china-rising

141. Serey, S. and K. Mondul, "Chinese Schools a Hit in Cambodia," April 25, 2012, Radio Free Asia, http://www.rfa.org/english/news/cambodia/chinese-schools-04252012161714.html

142. Zhang, Z., Y. Xie and Y. Li, "Who knew learning Chinese could be so valuable?"

143. Reilly, J., "The role of China as an education aid donor," 2015, UNESCO, https://unesdoc.unesco.org/ark:/48223/pf0000232475

144. Ibid.

145. Kawashima, S., "Cambodian Views on the US, China and Japan," March 12, 2018, *The Diplomat* , https://thediplomat.com/2018/03/cambodian-views-on-the-u-s-china-and-japan/

146. Thul, P., "Defiant Hun Sen tells US to cut all aid to Cambodia," November 19, 2017, Reuters, https://www.reuters.com/article/us-cambodia-usa/defiant-hun-sen-tells-u-s-to-cut-all-aid-to-cambodia-idUSKBN1DJ049

147. Ibid.

148. Karbaum, M., "Cambodia Breaks With the West," December 22, 2017, *The Diplomat* , https://thediplomat.com/2017/12/cambodia-breaks-with-the-west/

149. Heritage Foundation, "2018 Index of Economic Freedom, Laos," http://www.heritage.org/index/country/Laos

150. Transparency International, "Laos, 2018 Corruption Perception Index," https://www.transparency.org/country/LAO

151. Economist Intelligence Unit, "Democracy Index 2017: Free speech under attack."

152. Observatory of Economic Complexity, "Laos," http://atlas.media.mit.edu/en/profile/country/lao/

153. Corben, R., "Slowing China Economy Ripples Into Laos," July 13, 2016, VOA, http://www.voanews.com/a/slowing-china-economy-ripples-into-laos/3416226.html

154. *Vientiane Times* , "Laos, China boost trade and investment cooperation," June 21, 2016, http://annx.asianews.network/content/laos-china-boost-trade-and-investment-cooperation-20338

155. Vietstock Lao, "China banks join forces to boost trade," November 25, 2016, http://en.vietstock.com.vn/2016/11/lao-china-banks-join-forces-to-boost-trade-71-247641.htm

156. Corben, R., "Slowing China Economy Ripples Into Laos."

157. Corben, R., "Laos Looks to Balance China's Growing Economic Influence," April 23, 2015, VOA, https://www.voanews.com/a/laos-looks-to-balance-china-growing-economic-influence/2731417.html

158. Yamada, G. and S. Palma, "Is China's Belt and Road working? A progress report from eight countries."

159. Trading Economics, "Vietnam - Economic Indicators," https://tradingeconomics.com/vietnam/indicators

160. Heritage Foundation, "2018 Index of Economic Freedom, Vietnam," http://www.heritage.org/index/country/Vietnam

161. Ibid.

162. Vietnam Breaking News, "Eximbank has highest NPL ratio," November 4, 2016, https://www.vietnambreakingnews.com/2016/11/eximbank-has-highest-npl-ratio/

163. Economist Intelligence Unit, "Vietnam: Banking sector risk," March 9 2016, http://www.eiu.com/industry/article/764045660/vietnam-banking-sector-risk/2016-03-24

164. Global Edge, "Vietnam: Trade Statistics, 2016," https://globaledge.msu.edu/countries/vietnam/tradestats

165. Xinhua, China top trade partner of Vietnam: Vietnamese official, March 8, 2016 http://europe.chinadaily.com.cn/business/2016-03/08/content_23781703.htm

166. Vietnam Net, "Chinese investment into Vietnam on the sharp rise," February 10, 2017, http://english.vietnamnet.vn/fms/business/172454/chinese-investment-into-vietnam-on-the-sharp-rise.html

167. Bach, D., "Top FDI source China pours over US$56 billion into Vietnam with nearly 5,000 projects," May 4, 2016, http://e.vnexpress.net/news/news/top-fdi-source-china-pours-over-56-billion-into-vietnam-with-nearly-5-000-projects-3397081.html

168. Ibid.

169. Vietnam Net, "Chinese investment into Vietnam on the sharp rise."

170. Bach, D., "Top FDI source China pours over US$56 billion into Vietnam with nearly 5,000 projects."

171. Pham, M., "China firms eye 'Made in Vietnam' windfall - if Obama's TPP survives," Reuters, November 6, 2016, http://www.reuters.com/article/vietnam-china-trade-idUSL4N19Y2XQ

172. Masutomo, T. and J. Teng Jing Xuan, "Indonesia's China-Financed High-Speed Rail Project Off Track," October 11, 2018, Caixin Global, https://www.caixinglobal.com/2018-10-11/indonesias-china-financed-high-speed-rail-project-off-track-101333896.html

173. Ibid.

174. Eva, J. Q. Lin and J. Tunningley, "China's Belt and Road Initiative: Regional Outlooks for 2018."

175. Aguinaldo, C., "What lies ahead for the Philippines on China's Belt and Road Initiative?" January 20, 2019, BusinessWorld, https://www.bworldonline.com/what-lies-ahead-for-the-philippines-on-chinas-belt-and-road-initiative/

176. Ibid.

Chapter 3

1. World Factbook, "Micronesia, Federated States of," 2018, CIA, https://www.cia.gov/library/publications/the-world-factbook/geos/fm.html

2. Pale, S., "Is the Pacific Ocean big enough for both China and the US?" November 21, 2015, New Eastern Outlook, http://journal-neo.org/2015/11/21/is-the-pacific-ocean-big-enough-for-both-china-and-the-us/

3. Theodora.com, "Guam Economy 2018," February 18, 2018, https://theodora.com/wfbcurrent/guam/guam_economy.html

4. Pale, S., "Is the Pacific Ocean big enough for both China and the US?"

5. World Factbook, "Micronesia, Federated States of."

6. Ibid.

7. Zhang, J. "China's Role in the Pacific Islands Region," chapter in *Regionalism, Security & Cooperation in Oceania* (ed by R. Azizian and C. Cramer; APCSS; 2015), http://apcss.org/wp-content/uploads/2015/08/C3-China-Pacific-Zhang.pdf

8. Ibid.

9. Bozzato, F., "Gifts that Bind: China's Aid to the Pacific Island Nations," *Asia Japan Journal* 12 (2017), https://www.a-jrc.jp/pdf/20171025174804.pdf

10. Zhang, J. "China's Role in the Pacific Islands Region."

11. Ibid.

12. Xinhua, "China Cultural Center in Fiji inaugurated," December 15, 2015, http://news.xinhuanet.com/english/2015-12/15/c_134918742.htm

13. Zhang, J. "China's Role in the Pacific Islands Region."

14. Cheng, D., "Countering Chinese Inroads into Micronesia," October 27, 2016, Heritage Foundation, http://www.heritage.org/research/reports/2016/10/countering-chinese-inroads-into-micronesia

15. Ibid, and Matelski, T. "America's Micronesia Problem," February 19, 2016, *The Diplomat* , http://thediplomat.com/2016/02/americas-micronesia-problem/

16. Matelski, T. "America's Micronesia Problem."

17. Ibid.

18. Ibid.

19. Feizkhah, E. "How to win friends... Beijing is courting tiny Pacific nations," June 4, 2001, *Time* , http://content.time.com/time/world/article/0,8599,2056147,00.html

20. Cheng, D., "Countering Chinese Inroads into Micronesia."

21. Feizkhah, E., "How to win friends... Beijing is courting tiny Pacific nations."

22. PTI, "Indians leaving Fiji due to economic, political woes," September 21, 2013, *Business Standard* , http://www.business-standard.com/article/pti-stories/indians-leaving-fiji-due-to-economic-political-woes-expert-113092100286_1.html

23. Zhang, J. "China's Role in the Pacific Islands Region."

24. Ibid.

25. Feizkhah, E. "How to win friends... Beijing is courting tiny Pacific nations."

26. Ibid.

27. Deutsche Welle, "China has become a 'major donor' in the Pacific Islands region," March 3, 2015, http://www.dw.com/en/china-

has-become-a-major-donor-in-the-pacific-islands-region/a-18290737

28. Ibid.

29. Feizkhah, E. "How to win friends... Beijing is courting tiny Pacific nations."

30. Yu, C., "China's Economic Relations with Pacific Island Countries," August 12, 2014, National Center for Oceania Studies, Sun Yatsen University (China), https://www.victoria.ac.nz/chinaresearchcentre/publications/papers/YU-Changsen-Chinas-Economic-Relations-with-Pacific-Island-Countries.pdf

31. World Factbook, "Micronesia, Federated States of," and Pale, S. "Is the Pacific Ocean big enough for both China and the US?"

32. World Bank, "GDP per capita (current US$)," 2018, https://data.worldbank.org/country/Palau

33. Daleno, G., "China impacts Guam, Saipan, Palau economies," October 16, 2015, Pacific Daily News, http://www.guampdn.com/story/news/2015/10/16/china-impacts-guam-saipan-palau-economies/74036548/

34. Farry, W., "Palau reaction shows not everyone craves China's outbound tourism," April 13, 2015, Global Times, http://gbtimes.com/travel/palau-reaction-shows-outbound-tourism-has-negatives-well-positives

35. World Factbook, "Micronesia, Federated States of."

36. Lyons, K., "'Palau against China!': the tiny island standing up to a giant," September 8, 2018, The Guardian, https://www.theguardian.com/global-development/2018/sep/08/palau-against-china-the-tiny-island-defying-the-worlds-biggest-country

37. Agence France-Presse, "Chinese tourist invasion transforms remote Palau... and not everyone is happy," March 16, 2015, South China Morning Post, http://www.scmp.com/news/china/foreign-relations/article/1738288/chinese-descend-remote-palau-wanderlust-deepens

38. Ibid.

39. Pale, S. "Is the Pacific Ocean big enough for both China and the US?"

40. Agence France-Presse, "Chinese tourist invasion transforms remote Palau... and not everyone is happy," and Farry, W., "Palau reaction shows not everyone craves China's outbound tourism."

41. Lyons, K., "'Palau against China!': the tiny island standing up to a giant."

42. Daleno, G., "China impacts Guam, Saipan, Palau economies."
43. Island Times, "Chinese Investors Plan Large Resort In Palau," September 5, 2014, http://micronesiaforum.org/index.php?p=/discussion/12501/chinese-investors-plan-large-resort-in-palau
44. Pale, S. "Is the Pacific Ocean big enough for both China and the US?"
45. Sheikh, S. "In Micronesia, China Upsets Obama's Asia Tilt," November 27, 2015, Asia Sentinel, http://www.asiasentinel.com/econ-business/in-micronesia-china-upsets-obama-asia-tilt/
46. Matelski, T. "America's Micronesia Problem."
47. Pale, S. "Is the Pacific Ocean big enough for both China and the US?"
48. Matelski, T. "America's Micronesia Problem."
49. Leis, S., "Micronesia's future between China and the US," June 16, 2012, East Asia Forum, http://www.eastasiaforum.org/2012/06/16/micronesia-s-future-between-china-and-the-us/
50. Ibid.
51. Raatior, V., "Chuuk State Government Negotiating for Chinese Casino," February 14, 2015, Chuuk Reform Coalition, http://www.chuukstate.org/chuuk-state-government-negotiating-for-chinese-casino/
52. Daleno, G., "China impacts Guam, Saipan, Palau economies."
53. Ibid.
54. Pale, S. "Is the Pacific Ocean big enough for both China and the US?"
55. Daleno, G., "China impacts Guam, Saipan, Palau economies."
56. Pale, S. "Is the Pacific Ocean big enough for both China and the US?"
57. Yu, C., "China's Economic Relations with Pacific Island   Countries."
58. Ibid.
59. Ibid.
60. Hodge, A., "China loanees face 'debt distress'," March 28, 2018, *The Australian* , https://www.theaustralian.com.au/news/world/one-in-three-lined-up-for-chinas-bri-loans-face-debt-distress/news-story/b26c2ce383eac0198b1948625f7a2aee
61. Ibid.
62. Zhang, J. "China's Role in the Pacific Islands Region."

63. Morris, D., 'A Remote Pacific Island Faces up to China," June 26, 2017, *The Diplomat* , https://thediplomat.com/2017/06/a-remote-pacific-island-faces-up-to-china/

64. Boyd, A., "'Five Eyes' seek to counter China's Pacific influence," April 25, 2018, *Asia Times* , http://www.atimes.com/article/five-eyes-seek-to-counter-chinas-pacific-influence/

65. PMC Editor, "Chinese banks provide 40 percent of Fiji's foreign loans," May 24, 2017, Asia Pacific Report, https://asiapacificreport.nz/2017/05/24/chinese-banks-provide-40-percent-of-fijis-foreign-loans/

66. Klan, A., "Pacific nations drowning in Chinese debt," January 29, 2018, *The Australian* , https://www.theaustralian.com.au/national-affairs/pacific-nations-drowning-in-chinese-debt/news-story/082de1ecc957c9c4380bb9cb8555fa95

67. Ibid.

68. Ibid.

69. ABC, "China puts intermediate range 'Guam killer' DF-26 missile into service," April 27, 2018, http://www.abc.net.au/news/2018-04-27/china-flexes-muscles-with-guam-killer-missile/9704306

70. Reuters, "China is reportedly proposing a permanent military base in the South Pacific," April 9, 2018, CNBC, https://www.cnbc.com/2018/04/09/china-is-reportedly-proposing-a-military-base-in-the-south-pacific.html

71. Hillman, J., "Clouds gathering around China's Belt and Road," May 16, 2018, *Nikkei Asian Review* , https://asia.nikkei.com/Opinion/The-clouds-gathering-around-China-s-Belt-and-Road2

72. *Vanuatu Independent* , "Vanuatu signs up to One Belt, One Road initiative," November 20, 2018, https://vanuatuindependent.com/2018/11/20/vanuatu-signs-one-belt-one-road-initiative/

Chapter 4

1. Trading Economics, "Russia GDP per capita 1989-2018," https://tradingeconomics.com/russia/gdp-per-capita

2. Heritage Foundation, "2018 Index of Economic Freedom, Russia," https://www.heritage.org/index/country/russia

3. Trading Economics, "Russia GDP Annual Growth Rate 1996-2018," https://tradingeconomics.com/russia/gdp-growth-annual

4. Transparency International, "Russia Corruption Perception Index," https://www.transparency.org/country/RUS

5. Economist Intelligence Unit, "Democracy Index Russia 2017," http://pages.eiu.com/rs/753-RIQ-438/images/Democracy_Index_2017.pdf

6. Tang, F., "Moscow and Beijing's joint investment fund to grow to US$2 billion, paving way for 'dozens of deals'," November, 1, 2017, *South China Morning Post*, http://www.scmp.com/news/china/economy/article/2117857/moscow-and-beijings-joint-investment-fund-grow-us2-billion-paving

7. Yuan, J., "What the Belt and Road means for Sino-Russian relations, March 16, 2018, University of Nottingham Asia Research Institute, http://theasiadialogue.com/2018/03/16/what-the-belt-and-road-means-for-sino-russian-relations/

8. *South China Morning Post*, "Chinese in the Russian Far East: A Geopolitical Time Bomb," July 8, 2017, http://www.scmp.com/week-asia/geopolitics/article/2100228/chinese-russian-far-east-geopolitical-time-bomb

9. Ibid.

10. Ibid.

11. China Briefing, "The Far Reaching Chinese-Russian Silk Belt & Road JV," July 13, 2017 http://www.china-briefing.com/news/2017/07/13/far-reaching-chinese-russian-silk-belt-road-jv.html

12. Daly, R. and M. Rojansky, "China's Global Dreams Give Its Neighbors Nightmares," March 12, 2018, *Foreign Policy*, http://foreignpolicy.com/2018/03/12/chinas-global-dreams-are-giving-its-neighbors-nightmares/

13. Yuan, J., "What the Belt and Road means for Sino-Russian relations."

14. Ibid.

15. Lukin, A., "Putin's Silk Road gamble," February 8, 2018, *Washington Post*, https://www.washingtonpost.com/news/theworldpost/wp/2018/02/08/putin-china/?utm_term=.54ddf1fb610d

16. Ibid.

17. Ibid.

18. Observatory of Economic Complexity, "Russia," https://atlas.media.mit.edu/en/profile/country/rus/

19. Workman, D., "Russia's Top Trading Partners," November 4, 2018, WTEx, http://www.worldstopexports.com/russias-top-import-partners/

20. Trading Economics, "Russia Foreign Direct Investment - Net Flows 1994-2018," https://tradingeconomics.com/russia/foreign-direct-investment

21. Lukin, A., "Putin's Silk Road gamble."

22. SteelGuru, "Commercial Port of Vladivostok, Tianjin Port Group sign agency agreement in Tianjin," June 16, 2018, https://steelguru.com/logistic/commercial-port-of-vladivostok-tianjin-port-group-sign-agency-agreement-in-tianjin/483058

23. Hu Y., " Sino-Russian Cooperation, Exchange Increase Under Belt and Road Initiative," March 16, 2018, Sputnik News, https://sputniknews.com/analysis/201803161062581637-china-russia-cooperation-increase-belt-and-road/

24. China Briefing, "The Far Reaching Chinese-Russian Silk Belt & Road JV."

25. Tang, F., "Moscow and Beijing's joint investment fund."

26. China Briefing, "The Far Reaching Chinese-Russian Silk Belt & Road JV."

27. Ibid.

28. Tang, F., "Moscow and Beijing's joint investment fund."

29. Ibid.

30. *South China Morning Post* , "Chinese in the Russian Far East."

31. Ibid.

32. Lukin, A., "Putin's Silk Road gamble."

33. Daly, R. and M. Rojansky, "China's Global Dreams Give Its Neighbors Nightmares."

34. Yuan, J., "What the Belt and Road means for Sino-Russian relations."

35. Lukin, A., "Putin's Silk Road gamble."

36. Daly, R. and M. Rojansky, "China's Global Dreams Give Its Neighbors Nightmares."

37. Ibid.

38. Ibid.

39. Bisenov, N. and S. Lindhardt, "Linking China to the EU's 'gateway' for exporters," March 28, 2018, *Nikkei Asian Review* , https://asia.nikkei.com/Politics/International-Relations/Linking-China-to-the-EU-s-gateway-for-exporters

40. Ibid.

41. Daly, R. and M. Rojansky, "China's Global Dreams Give Its Neighbors Nightmares."

42. Overland, I. and R. Vakulchuk, "China's Belt and Road Gets a Central Asian Boost," May 3, 2018, *The Diplomat* ,

https://thediplomat.com/2018/05/chinas-belt-and-road-gets-a-central-asian-boost/

43. Hussain, T., "In Afghanistan, Putin Courts China in Search of 'Another Syria'," January 8, 2017, *South China Morning Post* , http://www.scmp.com/week-asia/geopolitics/article/2060032/afghanistan-putin-courts-china-search-another-syria

44. White, J. B., "Trump says US troops will remain in Afghanistan as rapid exit would leave 'vacuum' for terrorists," August 22, 2017, *The Independent* , https://www.independent.co.uk/news/world/americas/us-politics/trump-afghanistan-announce-war-us-army-escalation-pakistan-a7905821.html

45. Jennings, R., "China Needs A Win In Afghanistan To Keep Its Edge In Asian Trade," February 27, 2018, *Forbes* , https://www.forbes.com/sites/ralphjennings/2018/02/27/china-needs-a-win-in-afghanistan-to-keep-its-edge-in-asian-trade/#3356a1561d5c

46. Overland, I. and R. Vakulchuk, "China's Belt and Road Gets a Central Asian Boost."

47. Jennings, R., "China Needs A Win In Afghanistan To Keep Its Edge In Asian Trade."

48. Laruelle, M. (editor), *China's Belt and Road Initiative and Its Impact in Central Asia* , page 9. Washington, D.C.:The George Washington University, Central Asia Program, 2018, https://centralasiaprogram.org/wp-content/uploads/2017/12/OBOR_Book_.pdf

49. Voices on Central Asia, "China's Belt and Road Initiative and its Impact in Central Asia," January 19, 2018, http://voicesoncentralasia.org/chinas-belt-and-road-initiative-and-its-impact-in-central-asia/

50. *China's Belt and Road Initiative and Its Impact in Central Asia* , page 11

51. Ibid, page 33.

52. Voices on Central Asia, "China's Belt and Road Initiative and its Impact in Central Asia."

53. Ibid.

54. Ibid.

55. *China's Belt and Road Initiative and Its Impact in Central Asia* , page 11

56. Voices on Central Asia, "China's Belt and Road Initiative and its Impact in Central Asia."

57. *China's Belt and Road Initiative and Its Impact in Central Asia,* page 3

58. Voices on Central Asia, "China's Belt and Road Initiative and its Impact in Central Asia."

59. Ibid.

60. *China's Belt and Road Initiative and Its Impact in Central Asia* , page 31

61. Ibid, page 30.

62. *China's Belt and Road Initiative and Its Impact in Central Asia* , page 5

63. Ibid, page 6.

64. Ibid, page 33.

65. Ibid, page 27.

66. Aneja, U., "Pakistan-China Relations Recent Developments," IPCS Special Report, June 26, 2006

67. Parashar, S., "Russia throws its weight behind China-Pakistan corridor, keeps India on tenterhooks," December 19, 2016, *Times of India* , http://timesofindia.indiatimes.com/india/russia-throws-its-weight-behind-china-pakistan-corridor-keeps-india-on-tenterhooks/articleshow/56053869.cms

68. *Pakistan Today* , "Russia's joining of CPEC to enhance China, Russia and Pakistan cooperation," January 7, 2017, https://www.pakistantoday.com.pk/2017/01/07/russias-joining-of-cpec-to-enhance-china-russia-and-pakistan-cooperation/

Chapter 5

1. Albert, E., "China's Big Bet on Soft Power," February 9, 2018, Council on Foreign Relations, https://www.cfr.org/backgrounder/chinas-big-bet-soft-power

2. Westcott, B., "Socialism with Chinese characteristics?" March 10, 2018, CNN, https://www.cnn.com/2018/03/10/asia/china-npc-communist-party-phrases-intl/index.html

3. Albert, E., "China's Big Bet on Soft Power."

4. Hillman, J., "China's Belt and Road Initiative: Five Years Late."

5. Albert, E., "China's Big Bet on Soft Power."

6. Ibid.

7. Ibid.

8. Voices on Central Asia, "China's Belt and Road Initiative and its Impact in Central Asia."

9. Ibid.

10. Albert, E., "China's Big Bet on Soft Power."

11. Ibid.

12. Ibid.

13. Zhai, K., "China Approves Giant Propaganda Machine to Improve Global Image," March 20, 2018, Bloomberg, https://www.bloomberg.com/news/articles/2018-03-20/xi-creates-voice-of-china-broadcaster-to-improve-global-image
14. Albert, E., "China's Big Bet on Soft Power."
15. Ibid.
16. Brzeski, P., "Disney's Marvel to Co-Produce 'Iron Man 3' in China," April 16, 2012, *Hollywood Reporter* , https://www.hollywoodreporter.com/news/disney-marvel-iron-man-3-china-co-production-dmg-312323
17. Chan, E., "Chinese animation studio behind Kung Fu Panda 3 dreams of global box office success," February 10, 2018, *South China Morning Post* , https://www.scmp.com/business/companies/article/2132773/chinese-animation-studio-behind-kung-fu-panda-3-dreams-global-box
18. Brzeski, P., "Kung Fu Panda 3' Becomes China's Biggest Animated Film Ever," February 28, 2016, Hollywood Reporter, https://www.hollywoodreporter.com/news/kung-fu-panda-3-becomes-871149
19. Albert, E., "China's Big Bet on Soft Power."
20. Hu H., "Shaolin kung fu diplomacy," October 12, 2013, *China Daily* , http://www.chinadaily.com.cn/culture/art/2013-10/12/content_17026585.htm
21. Albert, E., "China's Big Bet on Soft Power."
22. Liu, X., "Remember these things when serving Chinese guests," presentation prepared for "Arktis Uudest potkua elintarvikevientiin – seminaari," May 5, 2017, Luke Natural Resource Institute Finland
23. Trading Economics, "China GDP per capita 1960-2017," https://tradingeconomics.com/china/gdp-per-capita
24. World Tourism Cities Federation, "'One Belt , One Road' A New Driving Force Of International Tourism," July 2015, http://en.wtcf.org.cn/pdf/World%20Tourism%20Cities%20201507.pdf
25. World Tourism Cities Federation, "Join Hands in the New Development of the Belt and Road Tourism," March 2017, http://www.wtcf.org.cn/uploadfile/2017/0502/20170502012439306.pdf
26. World Tourism Cities Federation, "'One Belt , One Road' A New Driving Force Of International Tourism."
27. Li, R., "Dancing with the Dragon: The Trans-Asia Railway and its Impact on Thailand," March 4, 2016, Yusof Ishak Institute,

https://www.iseas.edu.sg/images/pdf/ISEAS_Perspective_2016_9.pdf

28. DBS Asian Insights, "ASEAN Travel & Hospitality," July 2016.

29. HSBC (media release), "Belt and Road Initiatives to Further Bolster Indonesia and China Economic Cooperation," May 22, 2017.

30. New China TV (YouTube channel), "Thirteenth Five-Year Plan," October 26, 2015, https://www.youtube.com/watch?v=m91zBt94LI0

31. Timmons, H. and G. Yang, "A mysterious video attempts to explain the Chinese Dream to the world," January 2, 2014, Quartz, https://qz.com/162694/this-mysterious-video-attempts-to-explain-the-chinese-dream-to-the-world/

32. Huang, Z., "China's craziest English-language propaganda videos are made by one mysterious studio, October 27, 2015 https://qz.com/533850/chinas-craziest-english-language-propaganda-videos-are-made-by-one-mysterious-studio/

33. Huang, Z., "Working for a Chinese boss is great, ordinary Americans explain in this slick new pro-China video," September 22, 2015, Quartz, https://qz.com/506651/working-for-a-chinese-boss-is-great-ordinary-americans-explain-in-this-slick-new-pro-china-video/

34. Ibid.

35. Huang, Z., "Can you get through all five minutes of this sickly sweet video about the UK-China friendship?" October 19, 2015, Quartz, https://qz.com/527237/can-you-get-through-all-five-minutes-of-this-sickly-sweet-video-about-the-uk-china-friendship/

36. China Daily (YouTube channel), "Children from Belt and Road countries sing out their gratitude," May 9, 2017, https://www.youtube.com/watch?v=H6Adz_arAYE

37. Ibid.

38. Goodman, P., "In Era of Trump, China's President Champions Economic Globalization," January 17, 2017, New York Times, https://www.nytimes.com/2017/01/17/business/dealbook/world-economic-forum-davos-china-xi-globalization.html?_r=0

39. Gracie, C., "China's big push for its global trade narrative," BBC, May 12, 2017, http://www.bbc.com/news/world-asia-china-39880163

40. China Daily (YouTube channel), "What's the Belt and Road Initiative? Belt and Road Bedtime Stories Episode 1," https://www.youtube.com/watch?v=uKhYFFLBaeQ

41. Ibid.

42. Ibid.

43. China Daily, "'Belt and Road Bedtime Stories' Episode 5," May 13, 2017,

http://www.chinadaily.com.cn/beltandroadinitiative/2017-05/13/content_29333251.htm

44. Ibid.

45. Albert, E., "China's Big Bet on Soft Power."

46. Zhai, K., "China Approves Giant Propaganda Machine to Improve Global Image."

47. McCormick, A., "The Stumbling Block to China's Soft Power," April 17, 2018, *The Diplomat* , https://thediplomat.com/2018/04/racism-the-stumbling-block-to-chinas-soft-power/

48. Chengdu Revolution, "This Is China," 2016, https://genius.com/Chengdu-revolution-this-is-china-lyrics

49. Chen, A., "China's Confucius Institute faces backlash at prestigious US school," May 15, 2014, *South China Morning Post* , https://www.scmp.com/news/china-insider/article/1511268/chinas-confucius-institute-faces-backlash-prestigious-us-school

50. Lim, L. and A. Furze, "Confucius Institute in NSW education department 'unacceptable' – analyst," December 7, 2017, *The Guardian* , https://www.theguardian.com/world/2017/dec/08/confucious-institute-in-nsw-education-department-unacceptable-analyst

51. Lo, A., "Confucius Institutes: China's benign outreach or something more sinister?" July 14, 2018, *South China Morning Post* , https://www.scmp.com/week-asia/geopolitics/article/2154444/confucius-institutes-chinas-benign-outreach-or-something-more

Chapter 6

1. Focus Economics, "Pakistan Economic Outlook," February 19, 2019, https://www.focus-economics.com/countries/pakistan

2. Xinhua, "CPEC is the biggest flagship project of BRI: Ahsan," February 15, 2018, China-Pakistan Economic Corridor, http://www.cpecinfo.com/news/cpec-is-the-biggest-flagship-project-of-bri-ahsan/NDg3NA==

3. Schwemlein, J., "Pakistan's Economic Turmoil Threatens China's Ambitions," August 16, 2018, *Foreign Policy* , https://foreignpolicy.com/2018/08/16/pakistans-economic-turmoil-threatens-chinas-ambitions-cpec/

4. Shah, A. R., "How Does China–Pakistan Economic Corridor Show the Limitations of China's 'One Belt One Road' Model."

5. Crabtree, J., "China is pumping cash into Pakistan, but that might not convince other foreign investors," February 19, 2018, CNBC, https://www.cnbc.com/2018/02/19/china-and-pakistans-belt-and-road-plan-might-not-convince-other-investors.html

6. Focus Economics, "Pakistan Economic Outlook."

7. Crabtree, J., "China is pumping cash into Pakistan, but that might not convince other foreign investors."

8. Desai, R., "Pakistan and China's debt trap diplomacy," January 19, 2018, *Straits Times* , http://www.straitstimes.com/opinion/pakistan-and-chinas-debt-trap-diplomacy

9. Ibid.

10. Patranobis, S., "China against UN intervention in the Maldives," February 8, 2018, *Hindustan Times* , https://www.hindustantimes.com/world-news/china-against-un-intervention-in-the-maldives/story-jLFi3lqkEyj3adbpdsoaML.html

11. Yamada, G. and S. Palma, "Is China's Belt and Road working? A progress report from eight countries."

12. Patranobis, S., "China against UN intervention in the Maldives."

13. Kuronuma, Y., "Maldives faces Chinese 'land grab' over unpayable debts, ex-leader warns," February 13, 2018, *Nikkei Asian Review* , https://asia.nikkei.com/Politics/International-Relations/Maldives-faces-Chinese-land-grab-over-unpayable-debts-ex-leader-warns

14. Yamada, G. and S. Palma, "Is China's Belt and Road working? A progress report from eight countries."

15. Miglani, S. and S. Aneez, "Asian giants China and India flex muscles over tiny Maldives," March 7, 2018, Reuters, https://www.reuters.com/article/us-maldives-politics/asian-giants-china-and-india-flex-muscles-over-tiny-maldives-idUSKCN1GJ12X

16. Agence France-Presse, "Sri Lanka to base navy's Southern Command at Chinese-run Hambantota port Colombo," June 30, 2018, *South China Morning Post* , https://www.scmp.com/news/china/diplomacy-defence/article/2153246/sri-lanka-base-navys-southern-command-chinese-run

17. PTI, "Chinese Naval ship arrives in Lanka on goodwill visit," August 9, 2018, *The Economic Times* , http://economictimes.indiatimes.com/articleshow/65334401.cms?utm_source=contentofinterest&utm_medium=text&utm_campaign=cppst

18. Desai, R., "Pakistan and China's debt trap diplomacy."

19. PTI, "China's strict conditions force Pakistan not to include Diamer-Bhasha Dam in CPEC: Officials," July 13, 2018, *The Economic Times* , http://economictimes.indiatimes.com/articleshow/61660935.cms?ut m_source=contentofinterest&utm_medium=text&utm_campaign=cp pst

20. Shah, A. R., "How Does China–Pakistan Economic Corridor Show the Limitations of China's 'One Belt One Road' Model."

21. PTI, "Pak may not seek IMF bailout, asking China, Saudi for financial help: PM," October 18, 2018, *Business Standard* , https://www.business-standard.com/article/international/pak-may-not-seek-imf-bailout-asking-china-saudi-for-financial-help-pm-118101800657_1.html

22. Shah, A. R., "How Does China–Pakistan Economic Corridor Show the Limitations of China's 'One Belt One Road' Model."

23. Ibid.

24. Ibid.

25. Shakil, F.M., "Pakistan's duty concessions to China threaten local industry," March 30, 2018, *Asia Times* , https://www.bilaterals.org/?pakistan-s-duty-concessions-to&lang=en

26. Ibid.

27. Ibid.

28. Duchâtel, M., "Terror overseas: understanding China's evolving counter-terror strategy," October 26, 2016, European Council on Foreign Relations, http://www.ecfr.eu/publications/summary/terror_overseas_understan ding_chinas_evolving_counter_terror_strategy7160

29. Shah, A. R., "How Does China–Pakistan Economic Corridor Show the Limitations of China's 'One Belt One Road' Model."

30. Iyengar, R., "Pakistan cozies up to China on trade after Trump tweet," January 3, 2018, CNN Money, http://money.cnn.com/2018/01/03/news/economy/pakistan-china-trump-trade-yuan-dollar/index.html

31. Crabtree, J., "China is pumping cash into Pakistan, but that might not convince other foreign investors."

32. Iyengar, R., "Pakistan cozies up to China on trade after Trump tweet."

33. Agence France-Presse, "Pakistan allows use of Chinese yuan for trade, investment," January 3, 2018, *Straits Times* , http://www.straitstimes.com/asia/south-asia/pakistan-allows-use-of-chinese-yuan-for-trade-investment

34. Bhutta, Z., "Tajikistan to join Pakistan road link bypassing Afghanistan," February 24, 2017, *Express Tribune* , https://tribune.com.pk/story/1337274/tajikistan-join-pakistan-road-link-bypassing-afghanistan/
35. Johnson, K., "China's Bid to Upend the Global Oil Market," January 18, 2018, *Foreign Policy* , http://foreignpolicy.com/2018/01/18/chinas-bid-upend-global-oil-market-petroyuan-shanghai/
36. Gao, C., "Why Is China Holding the China-Pakistan-Afghanistan Dialogue Now?" December 27, 2017, *The Diplomat* , https://thediplomat.com/2017/12/why-is-china-holding-the-china-pakistan-afghanistan-dialogue-now/
37. Hussain, T., "Is China Turning Up Heat On India Through Pakistan Flank And Doklam Standoff?" July 21, 2017, *South China Morning Post* , http://www.scmp.com/week-asia/geopolitics/article/2103646/china-turning-heat-india-through-pakistan-flank-amid-doklam
38. Reuters, "Pentagon report singles out Pakistan as home of future Chinese military base," June 7, 2017, Dawn, https://www.dawn.com/news/1337991
39. *Financial Tribune* , "Iran-China Traders Agree to Sideline US Dollar," December 5, 2017, https://financialtribune.com/articles/economy-business-and-markets/77359/iran-china-traders-agree-to-sideline-us-dollar
40. Shah, A. R., "How Does China–Pakistan Economic Corridor Show the Limitations of China's 'One Belt One Road' Model."
41. Ibid.
42. Ibid.
43. Ibid.
44. Escobar, P., "It's BRI against Indo-Pacific all over again," April 27, 2018, The Saker, https://thesaker.is/its-bri-against-indo-pacific-all-over-again/
45. Panda, A., "If India Won't Put Up With the Belt and Road, Why Is It the Largest Recipient of AIIB Funds?" March 19, 2018, *The Diplomat* , https://thediplomat.com/2018/03/if-india-wont-put-up-with-the-belt-and-road-why-is-it-the-largest-recipient-of-aiib-funds/
46. Siddiqui, S., "Shanghai Co-operation Organization is aiming high," May 3, 2018, *Asia Times*
47. Ibid.
48. Ghani, M.J., "Pakistan and the web of international economic corridors," March 12, 2018, *Dawn* , https://www.dawn.com/news/1394620

Chapter 7

1. Clark, S, M. Lamar and B. Hope, "The Trouble With Sovereign-Wealth Funds," December 22, 2015, *Wall Street Journal* , http://www.wsj.com/articles/the-trouble-with-sovereign-wealth-funds-1450836278

2. Wilson, R. "An Introduction To Sovereign Wealth Funds," October 5, 2018, Investopedia, http://www.investopedia.com/articles/economics/08/sovereign-wealth-fund.asp#ixzz3wulJRE28

3. Clark, S, M. Lamar and B. Hope, "The Trouble With Sovereign-Wealth Funds."

4. CNBC, "The world's biggest sovereign wealth funds in 2017," September 20, 2017, http://www.cnbc.com/2015/07/17/the-worlds-biggest-sovereign-wealth-funds.html

5. Ibid.

6. Koch-Weser, I. and Haacke, O. "China Investment Corporation: Recent Developments in Performance, Strategy, and Governance," June 25, 2013, US-China Economic and Security Review Commission, https://www.uscc.gov/Research/china-investment-corporation-recent-developments-performance-strategy-and-governance

7. Zhu, R. "Report on the Outline of the Tenth Five-Year Plan for National Economic and Social Development," 2001, Official Publication; and Nash, P., "China's 'Going Out' Strategy," May 10, 2012, Diplomatic Courier, http://www.diplomaticourier.com/china-s-going-out-strategy/

8. Freeman, C. and J. Wen,"China's Investment in the United States - National Initiatives, Corporate Goals, and Public Opinion," November 2011, Center for Strategic and International Studies, http://thealamedan.org/sites/default/files/111107_freeman_briefing_china_investment_in_us_0.pdf

9. Ibid.

10. Ibid.

11. Koch-Weser, I. and Haacke, O. "China Investment Corporation: Recent Developments in Performance, Strategy, and Governance."

12. Pei, M. "The coming deluge: Should the US fear Chinese investment?" October 28, 2014, *Fortune* , http://fortune.com/2014/10/28/us-china-foreign-investment/

13. Rocha, E., "China's sovereign wealth fund to open first US office," December 15, 2015, Reuters, http://www.reuters.com/article/us-cn-invst-new-york-idUSKBN0TX22120151214

14. Anderlini, J., "China's sovereign wealth fund shifts focus to agriculture," June 14, 2014, *Financial Times* , https://www.ft.com/content/64362b08-f61a-11e3-a038-00144feabdc0

15. Scott, M. "Chinese Sovereign Wealth Fund to Buy Stake in Heathrow Airport," November 1, 2012, *New York Times* , http://dealbook.nytimes.com/2012/11/01/chinese-sovereign-wealth-fund-to-buy-stake-in-heathrow-airport/?ref=topics&_r=0

16. Sputnik News, "China Officially Joins European Bank for Reconstruction and Development," January 15, 2016, https://sputniknews.com/asia/201601151033219133-china-officially-joins-ebrd/

17. Cao, B., "CIC buys stake in New York tower in US property push," January 5, 2011, *China Daily* , http://www.chinadaily.com.cn/bizchina/2011-01/05/content_11798373.htm

18. Wei, L. and J. Dean, "CIC Looks to Pile Cash Into US Real Estate," September 9, 2009, *Wall Street Journal* , http://www.wsj.com/articles/SB125243309793493085

19. Koch-Weser, I. and Haacke, O. "China Investment Corporation: Recent Developments in Performance, Strategy, and Governance."

20. McMahon, D., "CIC Offers a Glimpse Into US Holdings," February 9, 2010, Wall Street Journal, http://www.wsj.com/articles/SB10001424052748703427704575052303975503216

21. Bloomberg, "China Wealth Fund CIC Posts 10.6% Return as Equity Rally," July 27, 2013, http://www.bloomberg.com/news/articles/2013-07-26/china-wealth-fund-reports-10-6-return-amid-global-equity-rally

22. Reuters, "China to Move Wealth Fund HQ to NY, Signaling Increased Focus on US," December 15, 2015, http://www.nbcnews.com/business/business-news/china-move-wealth-fund-hq-n-y-signaling-increased-focus-n479906

23. Anderlini, J., "Chinese fund CIC under fire over overseas losses," June 18, 2014, CNBC, http://www.cnbc.com/2014/06/18/chinese-fund-cic-under-fire-over-overseas-losses.html

24. Pei, M. "The coming deluge: Should the US fear Chinese investment?"

25. Koven, P. and C. Cattaneo, "Fortune Lost: The short, brutal and costly ride of China Investment Corp. in Canada," June 1, 2015,

Financial Post ,
http://business.financialpost.com/news/energy/fortune-lost-the-short-brutal-and-costly-ride-of-china-investment-corp-in-canada?__lsa=d577-6925
26. Freeman, C. and J. Wen,"China's Investment in the United States - National Initiatives, Corporate Goals, and Public Opinion."
27. Rocha, E., "China's sovereign wealth fund to open first US office."
28. Ibid.
29. Koch-Weser, I. and Haacke, O. "China Investment Corporation: Recent Developments in Performance, Strategy, and Governance."
30. McMahon, D., "CIC Offers a Glimpse Into US Holdings."
31. Wei, L. and J. Dean, "CIC Looks to Pile Cash Into US Real Estate."
32. Koven, P. and C. Cattaneo, "Fortune Lost: The short, brutal and costly ride of China Investment Corp. in Canada."
33. Koch-Weser, I. and Haacke, O. "China Investment Corporation: Recent Developments in Performance, Strategy, and Governance."
34. International Forum of Sovereign Wealth Funds, "Santiago Principles," https://www.ifswf.org/santiago-principles-landing/santiago-principles
35. McMahon, D., "CIC Offers a Glimpse Into US Holdings."
36. Koch-Weser, I. and Haacke, O. "China Investment Corporation: Recent Developments in Performance, Strategy, and Governance."
37. Ibid.
38. Cao, B., "CIC buys stake in New York tower in US property push."
39. Ibid.
40. Koch-Weser, I. and Haacke, O. "China Investment Corporation: Recent Developments in Performance, Strategy, and Governance."
41. White, G. "The 7 Strategic Industries The Chinese Government Loves And Why You Should Too," February 3, 2011, Business Insider, http://www.businessinsider.com/the-7-strategic-industries-the-chinese-government-loves-2011-2
42. Yu, X., "China-led bank spreads its wings to Africa, South America to bankroll infrastructure projects," January 16, 2018, *South China Morning Post* , http://www.scmp.com/business/banking-finance/article/2128343/china-led-bank-spreads-its-yuan-africa-south-america
43. Tang, F., "Beijing eyes Hong Kong and London for fresh Belt and Road funds," April 12, 2018, *South China Morning Post* ,

http://www.scmp.com/news/china/economy/article/2141487/beijing-eyes-hong-kong-and-london-fresh-belt-and-road-funds

44. Ibid.

45. Ibid.

46. International Monetary Fund, "IMF and the People's Bank of China Establish a New Center for Modernizing Economic Policies and Institutions," May 14, 2017, https://www.imf.org/en/News/Articles/2017/05/14/pr17167-imf-and-china-establish-a-new-center-for-modernizing-economic-policies-and-institutions

47. Mangi, F. and D. Murtaught, "China seen slowing spending on Belt and Road energy projects," March 12, 2018, *The Economic Times* , https://economictimes.indiatimes.com/news/international/world-news/china-seen-slowing-spending-on-belt-and-road-energy-projects/articleshow/63269102.cms

48. Hussain, A., "Relevant to ACCA Qualification Paper F9 Introduction to Islamic finance," 2011, https://www.academia.edu/9438054/RELEVANT_TO_ACCA_QUAL IFICATION_PAPER_F9_Introduction_to_Islamic_finance?auto=dow nload

49. Garrett, K., "Introduction to Islamic finance," ACCA Think Ahead, https://www.accaglobal.com/ca/en/student/exam-support-resources/fundamentals-exams-study-resources/f9/technical-articles/introduction-to-islamic-finance.html

50. Ibid.

51. Mohammed, R., "Hot trend in 2017: Rise of Islamic banks on Main St. USA," December 2, 2016, CNBC, https://www.cnbc.com/2016/12/02/under-the-radar-islamic-banks-rise-in-th.html

52. Asian Development Bank, "ADB, Islamic Finance in Key Asian Countries," January 24, 2017, https://www.adb.org/news/infographics/islamic-finance-key-asian-countries

53. Islamic Corporation for the Development of the Private Sector, "China: Forging the Next Phase of Growth," March 2017, page 37, https://icd-ps.org/uploads/files/China%20-%20Forging%20the%20Next%20Phase%20of%20Growth%20-%20March%2020171528184711_6882.pdf

54. Dubai Islamic Bank, "Overview of the Global Islamic Finance Industry," Global Islamic Finance Report, 2007 and 2017, http://www.gifr.net/publications/gifr2017/intro.pdf

55. Ibid.

56. Islamic Corporation for the Development of the Private Sector, "China: Forging the Next Phase of Growth," March 2017, page 50-51.

57. Islamic Corporation for the Development of the Private Sector, "China: The Time is Now, March 2016," page 58.

58. Islamic Corporation for the Development of the Private Sector, "China: Forging the Next Phase of Growth," March 2017, page 50-51.

59. Ibid, page 43.

60. Ibid.

61. Ibid, page 44.

62. Islamic Banking Department, State Bank of Pakistan, "Islamic Banking Bulletin," October-December 2016

63. Islamic Corporation for the Development of the Private Sector, "China: Forging the Next Phase of Growth," March 2017, page 46.

64. Thng Y.R., "Islamic Finance as a Tool of Chinese Financial Diplomacy," October 3, 2016, Islamic Finance, https://www.islamicfinance.com/2016/10/islamic-finance-tool-chinese-financial-diplomacy/

65. Islamic Corporation for the Development of the Private Sector, "China: The Time is Now, March 2016," page 58.

66. Islamic Corporation for the Development of the Private Sector, "China: Forging the Next Phase of Growth," March 2017, page 23.

67. Ibid.

68. EY, "World Islamic Banking Competitiveness Report 2016," page 36, https://www.ey.com/Publication/vwLUAssets/ey-world-islamic-banking-competitiveness-report-2016/%24FILE/ey-world-islamic-banking-competitiveness-report-2016.pdf

69. IFN Forum Pakistan 2016, "Post Forum Analysis Report," September 26, 2016, https://redmoneyevents.com/main/framework/assets/2016/reports/Pakistan2016_postreport.pdf

70. Islamic Banking Department, State Bank of Pakistan, "Islamic Banking Bulletin."

71. EY, "World Islamic Banking Competitiveness Report 2016," page 6.

72. IFN Forum Pakistan 2016, "Post Forum Analysis Report."

73. Ibid.

Chapter 8

1. Downs, E., "China-Middle East Energy Relations," June 6, 2013, Brookings Institute, https://www.brookings.edu/testimonies/china-middle-east-energy-relations/

2. Lin, C., "The Belt and Road and China's Long-term Visions in the Middle East," October 2017, ISPSW Strategy Series: Focus on Defense and International Security, Issue 512, http://www.css.ethz.ch/content/dam/ethz/special-interest/gess/cis/center-for-securities-studies/resources/docs/ISPSW-512%20Lin.pdf

3. Yao, K., "China-Arab States Cooperation Forum in the Last Decade," July 17, 2018, *Journal of Middle Eastern and Islamic Studies (in Asia)* Vol. 8, No. 4, https://www.tandfonline.com/doi/abs/10.1080/19370679.2014.12023253

4. Ibid.

5. Ibid.

6. Alterman, J. "China's Balancing Act in the Gulf," August 21, 2013, Center for Strategic and International Studies, https://www.csis.org/analysis/chinas-balancing-act-gulf

7. Yao, K., "China-Arab States Cooperation Forum in the Last Decade."

8. State Council (PRC), "China's Arab Policy Paper," January 2016, http://english.gov.cn/archive/publications/2016/01/13/content_281475271412746.htm

9. Yao, K., "China-Arab States Cooperation Forum in the Last Decade."

10. Alterman, J. "China's Balancing Act in the Gulf."

11. Karoui, H., "Sino-Arab Cooperation: on the right way?" August 10, 2015, CCTV.com.

12. Mackenzie, P. "A Closer Look at China-Iran Relations - Roundtable Report," September 2010, CNA Analysis and Solutions, https://www.cna.org/CNA_files/PDF/D0023622.A3.pdf

13. Alterman, J. "China's Balancing Act in the Gulf."

14. Xinhua, "Interview: Arab-China ties "ideal", Xi's visit to Arab League "very important event": AL chief," January 19, 2016, *Global Times* , http://www.globaltimes.cn/content/964362.shtml

15. Gurtovs, M., "China Model Hits the Road: Xi Jinping's Middle East Trip in Context," February 5, 2016, China-US Focus, http://www.chinausfocus.com/foreign-policy/the-china-model-hits-the-road-xi-jinpings-middle-east-trip-in-context/

16. Ibid.

17. Xinhua, "Interview: Arab-China ties "ideal", Xi's visit to Arab League "very important event": AL chief."

18. Gurtovs, M., "China Model Hits the Road: Xi Jinping's Middle East Trip in Context."

19. State Council (PRC), "China's Arab Policy Paper," January 2016.

20. Ibid.

21. Aronson, G., "China's vision of the Middle East," January 21, 2016, Al Jazeera, http://www.aljazeera.com/indepth/opinion/2016/01/china-vision-middle-east-160121052018955.html

22. Pember-Finn, T., "China and the Middle East: The Emerging Security Nexus," Summer 2011, *Greater China* 11, no. 1

23. Ibid.

24. Center for Strategic and International Studies, "China and the Gulf," April 26, 2013, https://csis-prod.s3.amazonaws.com/s3fs-public/legacy_files/files/attachments/130426_Summary_JohnsonAlterman.pdf

25. Wang, Z., "Why China Has Not Sent Troops to Strike the Islamic State," March 15, 2016, China-US Focus, https://www.chinausfocus.com/peace-security/why-china-has-not-sent-troops-to-strike-the-islamic-state/

26. Ibid.

27. Aronson, G., "China's vision of the Middle East."

28. Liu, T., "China's economic engagement in the Middle East and North Africa," January 2014, FRIDE Policy Brief, http://fride.org/descarga/PB_173_China_economic_engagement_in_MENA.pdf

29. Ibid.

30. State Council (PRC), "China's Arab Policy Paper."

31. Ibid.

32. Yao, K., "China-Arab States Cooperation Forum in the Last Decade."

33. Sun, D. and Z. Yahia, "China's Economic Diplomacy towards the Arab Countries: challenges ahead?" March 20, 2015, Journal of Contemporary China 24(95):1-19

34. Zhao, M., "China's Middle East Opportunity," February 3, 2016, China-US Focus, http://www.chinausfocus.com/foreign-policy/chinas-middle-east-opportunity

35. Zheng, S., "China and Saudi Arabia to team up on US$20 billion investment fund," July 20, 2018, *South China Morning Post* , http://www.scmp.com/news/china/diplomacy-

defence/article/2108175/china-and-saudi-arabia-team-us20-billion-investment

36. Feng, C., "Embracing Interdependence: The Dynamics of China and the Middle East," April 28, 2015, Brookings Institute, https://www.brookings.edu/research/embracing-interdependence-the-dynamics-of-china-and-the-middle-east/

37. Shahzad, A., "Pakistan invites Saudi Arabia to join China's Belt and Road corridor," September 20, 2018, Reuters, https://www.reuters.com/article/us-pakistan-saudi-silkroad/pakistan-invites-saudi-arabia-to-join-chinas-belt-and-road-corridor-idUSKCN1M02DA

38. Liu, T., "China's economic engagement in the Middle East and North Africa."

39. Zha, D. and M. Meidan, "China and the Middle East in a New Energy Landscape," October 2015, Chatham House, https://www.chathamhouse.org/sites/default/files/publications/research/20151021ChinaMiddleEastEnergyDaojiongMeidan.pdf

40. Albawaba Business, "Bank of China opens Bahrain branch," July 19, 2004, https://www.albawaba.com/business/bank-china-opens-bahrain-branch

41. Workman, D., "Top 15 Crude Oil Suppliers to China," February 25, 2019, WTEx, http://www.worldstopexports.com/top-15-crude-oil-suppliers-to-china/

42. Liu, T., "China's economic engagement in the Middle East and North Africa."

43. Tiezzi, S., "China's Balancing Act in Iran," January 26, 2016, The Diplomat , http://thediplomat.com/2016/01/chinas-balancing-act-in-iran/

44. Pember-Finn, T., "China and the Middle East: The Emerging Security Nexus."

45. Tiezzi, S., "China's Balancing Act in Iran" and: Alterman, J. "China's Balancing Act in the Gulf."

46. Agence France-Presse, "Iran seeks economic ties worth US$600 billion with China," January 24, 2016, The National, http://www.thenational.ae/iran-seeks-economic-ties-worth-us600-billion-with-china

47. Tiezzi, S., "China's Balancing Act in Iran."

48. Zambelis, C. and B. Gentry, "China through Arab Eyes: American Influence in the Middle East," Spring 2008, Parameters, https://ssi.armywarcollege.edu/pubs/parameters/articles/08spring/zambelis.pdf

49. Ibid.

50. Ibid.

51. Review of *China Considers the Middle East* (L. Harris, 1995) by W.B. Quandt, March/April 1995, Foreign Affairs, https://www.foreignaffairs.com/reviews/capsule-review/1995-03-01/china-considers-middle-east

52. Feng, C., "Embracing Interdependence: The Dynamics of China and the Middle East."

53. Luft, G. "China's New Grand Strategy for the Middle East," January 26, 2016, Foreign Policy, http://foreignpolicy.com/2016/01/26/chinas-new-middle-east-grand-strategy-iran-saudi-arabia-oil-xi-jinping/

54. Alterman, J., Statement to "China and the Middle East" Hearing, June 6, 2013, US-China Economic and Security Review Commission, https://www.uscc.gov/sites/default/files/transcripts/USCC%20Hearing%20Transcript%20-%20June%206%202013.pdf

55. Ibid.

56. Goodman, P., "China Invests Heavily In Sudan's Oil Industry," December 23, 2004, *Washington Post* , http://www.genocidewatch.org/images/Sudan-23-Dec-04-China_Invests_Heavily_In_Sudan_s_Oil_Industry.pdf

57. Ibid.

58. Schenker, D., "China-Middle East Relations: A Change in Policy?" March 18, 2013, Carnegie Endowment for International Peace, http://carnegieendowment.org/2013/03/18/china-middle-east-relations-change-in-policy/g0uq

59. Alterman, J., Statement to "China and the Middle East" Hearing.

60. Yao, K., "Development of Sino-Arab Relations and the Evolution of China's Middle East Policy in the New Era," 2007, *Journal of Middle Eastern and Islamic Studies 6 (in Asia)* Vol. 1, No. 1, http://mideast.shisu.edu.cn/_upload/article/95/18/6200c4ab4c0f9dd480c085468452/3f6d50ec-3ef9-4e97-8e8f-8f9f81d878f6.pdf

61. Lewis, S., "China's Oil Diplomacy and Relations with the Middle East," September 2002, James A. Baker III Institute for Public Policy, https://www.bakerinstitute.org/files/713/

62. Alterman, J., "Middle East Notes and Comment: Beyond the Silk Road," November 27, 2007, Center for Strategic and International Studies, https://www.csis.org/analysis/middle-east-notes-and-comment-november-2007-beyond-silk-road

63. Ibid.

64. He W., "China-Egypt relations taking on a new lease of life," June 13, 2016, China.org.cn, http://www.china.org.cn/opinion/2016-06/13/content_38654643.htm

65. Eva, J. Q. Lin and J. Tunningley, "China's Belt and Road Initiative: Regional Outlooks for 2018."

66. He W., "China-Egypt relations taking on a new lease of life."

67. Eva, J. Q. Lin and J. Tunningley, "China's Belt and Road Initiative: Regional Outlooks for 2018."

68. Alterman, J., "Middle East Notes and Comment: Beyond the Silk Road."

69. Mackenzie, P. "A Closer Look at China-Iran Relations - Roundtable Report."

70. Eva, J. Q. Lin and J. Tunningley, "China's Belt and Road Initiative: Regional Outlooks for 2018."

71. Mackenzie, P. "A Closer Look at China-Iran Relations - Roundtable Report."

72. Alterman, J., "Middle East Notes and Comment: Beyond the Silk Road."

73. Singh, M., "China's Middle East Tour," January 24, 2016, *Foreign Affairs*, https://www.foreignaffairs.com/articles/china/2016-01-24/chinas-middle-east-tour

74. Gady, F., "China, Iran to Deepen Military Ties," December 14, 2017, *The Diplomat*, https://thediplomat.com/2017/12/china-iran-to-deepen-military-ties/

75. Mackenzie, P. "A Closer Look at China-Iran Relations - Roundtable Report."

76. Ibid.

77. Alterman, J., Statement to "China and the Middle East" Hearing.

78. Eva, J. Q. Lin and J. Tunningley, "China's Belt and Road Initiative: Regional Outlooks for 2018."

Chapter 9

1. Huang, K., "Xi Jinping signs up Senegal for belt and road plan, pledges closer Africa ties, Sunday," 22 July, 2018, *South China Morning Post*, https://www.scmp.com/news/china/diplomacy-defence/article/2156327/president-xi-jinping-pledges-closer-africa-ties-during

2. Sun, Y., "The political significance of China's latest commitments to Africa," September 12, 2018, Brookings Institute, https://www.brookings.edu/blog/africa-in-focus/2018/09/12/the-political-significance-of-chinas-latest-commitments-to-africa/

3. Pigato, M. and W. Tang, "China and Africa: Expanding Economic Ties in an Evolving Global Context," March 2015, World Bank, https://www.worldbank.org/content/dam/Worldbank/Event/Africa/Inv esting%20in%20Africa%20Forum/2015/investing-in-africa-forum-china-and-africa-expanding-economic-ties-in-an-evolving-global-context.pdf

4. Robertson, W. and L. Benabdallah, "China pledged to invest US$60 billion in Africa. Here's what that means," January 7, 2016, *Washington Post* , https://www.washingtonpost.com/news/monkey-cage/wp/2016/01/07/china-pledged-to-invest-60-billion-in-africa-heres-what-that-means/?utm_term=.5fa9e2a379b2 ; and: Knowledge@Wharton, "China's Investments in Africa: What's the Real Story?" January 19, 2016, Wharton School of the University of Pennsylvania, http://knowledge.wharton.upenn.edu/article/chinas-investments-in-africa-whats-the-real-story/

5. Eva, J. Q. Lin and J. Tunningley, "China's Belt and Road Initiative: Regional Outlooks for 2018."

6. South African Institute of International Affairs, "The China-Africa Toolkit," September 2009, https://saiia.org.za/wp-content/uploads/2018/10/China-Africa_toolkit_200909.pdf

7. Chen, W., D. Dollar and H. Tang, "China's direct investment in Africa: Reality versus myth," September 3, 2015, Brookings Institute, https://www.brookings.edu/blog/africa-in-focus/2015/09/03/chinas-direct-investment-in-africa-reality-versus-myth/

8. Institute of Developing Economies, "China's Mining Footprint in Africa," 2009, Japan External Trade Organization, https://www.ide.go.jp/English/Data/Africa_file/Manualreport/cia_08.h tml

9. Eva, J. Q. Lin and J. Tunningley, "China's Belt and Road Initiative: Regional Outlooks for 2018."

10. Ibid.

11. Sun, Y., "The political significance of China's latest commitments to Africa."

12. Shen, X., "Private Chinese investment in Africa : myths and realities," January 1, 2013, World Bank, http://documents.worldbank.org/curated/en/488211468216585858/P rivate-Chinese-investment-in-Africa-myths-and-realities

13. Chen, W., D. Dollar and H. Tang, "China's direct investment in Africa: Reality versus myth."

14. Maverick, J., "The 3 Reasons Why Chinese Invest in Africa," October 14, 2018, Investopedia,

http://www.investopedia.com/articles/active-trading/081315/3-reasons-why-chinese-invest-africa.asp

15. Chen, W., D. Dollar and H. Tang, "China's direct investment in Africa: Reality versus myth."

16. Shinn, D., "Lessons From The Field: China's Investments in Africa," November 20, 2012, Wilson Center, https://africaupclose.wilsoncenter.org/chinas-investments-in-africa/

17. Knowledge@Wharton, "China's Investments in Africa: What's the Real Story?"; and Dollar, D., H. Tang and W. Chen, "Why is China investing in Africa? Evidence from the firm level," August 12, 2015, Brookings Institute, https://www.brookings.edu/research/why-is-china-investing-in-africa-evidence-from-the-firm-level/

18. Robertson, W. and L. Benabdallah, "China pledged to invest US$60 billion in Africa. Here's what that means."

19. *The Economist* , "Not as easy as it looks," November 21, 2015, http://www.economist.com/news/middle-east-and-africa/21678777-western-worries-about-chinas-burgeoning-influence-africa-may-be-overblown-not

20. Knowledge@Wharton, "China's Investments in Africa: What's the Real Story?"

21. Robertson, W. and L. Benabdallah, "China pledged to invest US$60 billion in Africa. Here's what that means."

22. Chen, W., D. Dollar and H. Tang, "China's direct investment in Africa: Reality versus myth."

23. Dollar, D., H. Tang and W. Chen, "Why is China investing in Africa? Evidence from the firm level."

24. Meyer, R. and C. Alden, "Banking on Africa: Chinese Financial Institutions and Africa," December 2008, South African Institute of International Affairs, https://saiia.org.za/wp-content/uploads/2008/10/saia_sop_14_meyer_alden_20081201.pdf

25. Ibid.

26. Brautigam, D., "5 Myths About Chinese Investment in Africa," December 4, 2015, *Foreign Policy* , http://foreignpolicy.com/2015/12/04/5-myths-about-chinese-investment-in-africa/

27. Knowledge@Wharton, "China's Investments in Africa: What's the Real Story?"

28. Middlehurst, C., "Chinese loans to Africa could trigger another debt crisis," December 15, 2015, China Dialogue, https://www.chinadialogue.net/article/show/single/en/8470-Chinese-loans-to-Africa-could-trigger-another-debt-crisis

29. Dollar, D., H. Tang and W. Chen, "Why is China investing in Africa? Evidence from the firm level."

30. Meyer, R. and C. Alden, "Banking on Africa: Chinese Financial Institutions and Africa."

31. Pigato, M. and W. Tang, "China and Africa: Expanding Economic Ties in an Evolving Global Context"; and Brautigam, D., "5 Myths About Chinese Investment in Africa."

32. Meyer, R. and C. Alden, "Banking on Africa: Chinese Financial Institutions and Africa."

33. Knowledge@Wharton, "China's Investments in Africa: What's the Real Story?"

34. Ibid.

35. Meyer, R. and C. Alden, "Banking on Africa: Chinese Financial Institutions and Africa."

36. Xinhua, "Interview: Zimbabwe seeks deeper economic ties with China to boost economy, says President Mnangagwa," April 1, 2018, http://www.xinhuanet.com/english/2018-04/01/c_137080600.htm

37. Crabtree, J., "Zimbabwe opposition leader reportedly wants to give Chinese investors the boot," May 3, 2018, CNBC, https://www.cnbc.com/2018/05/03/zimbabwe-opposition-leader-wants-to-give-china-investors-the-boot.html

38. Eva, J. Q. Lin and J. Tunningley, "China's Belt and Road Initiative: Regional Outlooks for 2018."

39. Ibid.

40. Week in China, "Digging a hole," April 13, 2018, https://www.weekinchina.com/2018/04/digging-a-hole-3/

41. *The Australian* , "One in Three Lined up for China's BRI Loans Faces Debt Distress," March 28, 2018, https://www.theaustralian.com.au/news/world/one-in-three-lined-up-for-chinas-bri-loans-face-debt-distress/news-story/b26c2ce383eac0198b1948625f7a2aee

42. Trading Economics, "Guinea GDP per capita," https://tradingeconomics.com/guinea/gdp-per-capita ; and Huang, K., "Xi Jinping signs up Senegal for belt and road plan, pledges closer Africa ties."

43. Huang, K., "Xi Jinping signs up Senegal for belt and road plan, pledges closer Africa ties."

44. Chutel, L., "No, China is not taking over Zambia's national electricity supplier. Not yet, anyway," September 18, 2018, Quartz, https://qz.com/africa/1391111/zambia-china-debt-crisis-tests-china-in-africa-relationship/

45. Meyer, R. and C. Alden, "Banking on Africa: Chinese Financial Institutions and Africa."

46. Ibid.

47. Zadek, S., "How China is rewriting the rules of investment in Africa," December 4, 2013, China Dialogue, https://www.chinadialogue.net/article/show/single/en/5896-How-China-is-rewriting-the-rules-of-investment-in-Africa

48. Middlehurst, C., "Chinese loans to Africa could trigger another debt crisis."

49. Bosshard, P. "Chinese loans could fuel regional conflict in East Africa," January 14, 2013, China Dialogue, https://www.chinadialogue.net/article/show/single/en/5601-Chinese-loans-could-fuel-regional-conflict-in-East-Africa

50. Meyer, R. and C. Alden, "Banking on Africa: Chinese Financial Institutions and Africa."

51. China-Africa Development Fund, "Investment Philosophy," http://www.cadfund.com/en/NewsInfo.aspx?NId=400

52. Meyer, R. and C. Alden, "Banking on Africa: Chinese Financial Institutions and Africa."

53. Ibid.

54. Ibid.

55. Ibid.

56. Kuo, S., "China's Investment In Africa - The African Perspective," July 8, 2015, Forbes , http://www.forbes.com/sites/riskmap/2015/07/08/chinas-investment-in-africa-the-african-perspective/#168f6d7a16e2

57. Ibid.

58. Ibid.

59. Cui, S., "Special report: China's image crisis in Ghana," March 13, 2013, China Dialogue, https://www.chinadialogue.net/article/show/single/en/6005-Special-report-China-s-image-crisis-in-Ghana

60. Ibid.

61. Monde, N., "Growing Chinese influence creates mixed feelings in Cameroon," July 15, 2014, China Dialogue, https://www.chinadialogue.net/article/show/single/en/7139-Growing-Chinese-influence-creates-mixed-feelings-in-Cameroon

62. Hu, J., "China's firms battle each other in Africa," September 15, 2014, China Dialogue, https://www.chinadialogue.net/article/show/single/en/7309-China-s-firms-battle-each-other-in-Africa

63. Levitt, T., "China's elitist approach to overseas investments," February 25, 2013, China Dialogue, https://www.chinadialogue.net/article/show/single/en/5736-China-s-elitist-approach-to-overseas-investments

64. Sun, Y., "The political significance of China's latest commitments to Africa."

65. *The Economist* , "Not as easy as it looks."

66. Ibid.

67. Ibid.

68. Ibid.

69. Dasgupta, S., "Chinese Investment in Africa Falls by 40%," November 25, 2015, VOA, http://www.voanews.com/content/chinese-investment-to-africa-falls-by-40-percent/3072974.html

70. Hu, J., "China's firms battle each other in Africa."

71. Bosshard, P. "Chinese loans could fuel regional conflict in East Africa."

Chapter 10

1. Brînză, A., "Redefining the Belt and Road Initiative," March 20, 2018, *The Diplomat* , https://thediplomat.com/2018/03/redefining-the-belt-and-road-initiative/

2. Wang X., "Mahathir's Pushback Against Chinese Deals Shows Belt and Road Plan Needs Review," August 26, 2018, *South China Morning Post* , https://www.scmp.com/week-asia/opinion/article/2161069/mahathirs-pushback-against-chinese-deals-shows-belt-and-road-plan

3. Peters, E., "China's Evolving Role in Latin America: Can It Be a Win-Win?" 2015, Atlantic Council, http://publications.atlanticcouncil.org/chinalatam//

4. Gillespie, P., "China's big bet on Latin America is going bust," February 16, 2016, CNN, http://money.cnn.com/2016/02/16/news/economy/china-latin-america-projects-fail/

5. Peters, E., "China's Evolving Role in Latin America: Can It Be a Win-Win?"

6. Gillespie, P., "Latin America: China's power play right under the US," CNN, http://money.cnn.com/2016/02/11/news/economy/china-latin-america-billions-of-dollars-loans-investments/

7. Pineo, R. "China and Latin America: What You Need To Know," July 25, 2015, Council on Hemispheric Affairs,

http://www.coha.org/china-and-latin-america-what-you-need-to-know/

8. Weich, R, "China Looks to Expand Investment in Latin America, Eyes Raw Materials," February 12, 2016, Latin Post, http://www.latinpost.com/articles/114867/20160212/china-looks-to-expand-investment-in-latin-america-eyes-raw-materials.htm

9. Gillespie, P., "Latin America: China's power play right under the US."

10. Ibid.

11. Peters, E., "China's Evolving Role in Latin America: Can It Be a Win-Win?"

12. Gillespie, P., "China's big bet on Latin America is going bust."

13. Kaplan, S., "Why China is investing US$250 billion in Latin America," February 4, 2015, *Washington Post* , https://www.washingtonpost.com/blogs/monkey-cage/wp/2015/02/04/why-china-is-investing-250-billion-in-latin-america/

14. Pacific Basin Research Center, "The Opportunities and Challenges of Growing East Asian-Latin American Economic Relations," August 19, 2015, http://www.pbrc.soka.edu/pacific_basin_news/2015/08/taskforce-report.pdf

15. Ibid.

16. Ibid.

17. Ibid.

18. Ibid.

19. Peters, E., "China's Evolving Role in Latin America: Can It Be a Win-Win?"

20. Pacific Basin Research Center, "The Opportunities and Challenges of Growing East Asian-Latin American Economic Relations."

21. Peters, E., "China's Evolving Role in Latin America: Can It Be a Win-Win?"

22. Xinhua, "China, CELAC to map out cooperation plan over next five years: Xi," January 8, 2015, http://news.xinhuanet.com/english/china/2015-01/08/c_133905137.htm

23. Peters, E., "China's Evolving Role in Latin America: Can It Be a Win-Win?"

24. Myers, M., "China & LAC: Doing the Math," July 20, 2015, The Dialogue, http://www.thedialogue.org/blogs/2015/07/china-lac-doing-the-math/

25. Xinhua, "China, CELAC to map out cooperation plan over next five years: Xi."

26. Myers, M., "China & LAC: Doing the Math."

27. Ibid.

28. Peters, E., "China's Evolving Role in Latin America: Can It Be a Win-Win?"

29. Ray, R. et. al, "China in Latin America: Lessons for South-South Cooperation and Sustainable Development," 2015, Boston University Global Economic Governance Initiative, https://www.bu.edu/gdp/files/2015/04/China-in-Latin-America-Lessons-for-South-South-Cooperation-Sustainable-Development.pdf

30. O'Neil, S. K., "Foreign Direct Investment in Latin America," June 4, 2015, Council on Foreign Relations, http://blogs.cfr.org/oneil/2015/06/04/foreign-direct-investment-in-latin-america/

31. Pacific Basin Research Center, "The Opportunities and Challenges of Growing East Asian-Latin American Economic Relations."

32. Coyer, P. "Undermining America While Washington Sleeps: China In Latin America," January 31, 2016, *Forbes* , http://www.forbes.com/sites/paulcoyer/2016/01/31/undermining-america-while-washington-sleeps-china-in-latin-america/#1153b8446694

33. Gillespie, P., "Latin America: China's power play right under the US."

34. Dollar, D., "China's Investment in Latin America," January 2017, Geoeconomics and Global Issues (Paper 4), Brookings Institute, https://www.brookings.edu/wp-content/uploads/2017/01/fp_201701_china_investment_lat_am.pdf

35. Wolf, C. et. al., "China's Foreign Aid and Government-Sponsored Investment Activities," 2013, Rand Corporation, https://www.rand.org/content/dam/rand/pubs/research_reports/RR100/RR118/RAND_RR118.pdf

36. Ibid.

37. Peters, E., "China's Evolving Role in Latin America: Can It Be a Win-Win?"

38. Bloomberg, "China's Pivot to Latin America," May 26, 2015, https://www.bloomberg.com/view/articles/2015-05-25/china-s-pivot-to-latin-america

and: Gustafson, I. "The Dubious Impact of Chinese Investment in Latin America," June 1, 2016, Council on Hemispheric Affairs,

http://www.coha.org/the-dubious-impact-of-chinese-investment-in-latin-america/
39. Peters, E., "China's Evolving Role in Latin America: Can It Be a Win-Win?"
40. Ibid.
41. Ibid.
42. Myers, M., "China & LAC: Lessons from Bahamar," July 30, 2015, The Dialogue,
http://www.thedialogue.org/blogs/2015/07/china-lac-lessons-from-bahamar/
43. Peters, E., "China's Evolving Role in Latin America: Can It Be a Win-Win?"
44. Kaplan, S., "Why China is investing US$250 billion in Latin America."
45. Peters, E., "China's Evolving Role in Latin America: Can It Be a Win-Win?"
46. Gustafson, I., "The Dubious Impact of Chinese Investment in Latin America."
47. Sanchez, C., "Mexico halts Chinese mega-mall project after damage to environment," January 28, 2015, *Los Angeles Times* ,
http://www.latimes.com/world/mexico-americas/la-fg-mexico-closing-chinese-megamall-20150128-story.html
48. Gustafson, I., "The Dubious Impact of Chinese Investment in Latin America."
49. Gillespie, P., "China's big bet on Latin America is going bust."
50. Ibid.
51. Ibid.
52. Myers, M., "China & LAC: Lessons from Bahamar."
and: Lippert, J. and D. McCarty, "The Ghosts of Baha Mar: How a US$3.5 Billion Paradise Went Bust," January 4, 2016, Bloomberg,
http://www.bloomberg.com/news/articles/2016-01-04/the-ghosts-of-baha-mar-how-a-3-5-billion-paradise-went-bust
53. House, R. and L. McLeod-Roberts, "China takes long view on Latin American infrastructure investment," May 26, 2016, *Financial Times* , http://www.ft.com/cms/s/3/c33c6854-2351-11e6-aa98-db1e01fabc0c.html#axzz4FxELgVAF
54. Magnier, M., "China Dials Back Its Lending to Wobbly Venezuela," February 24, 2017, *Wall Street Journal* ,
https://blogs.wsj.com/chinarealtime/2017/02/24/china-dials-back-its-lending-to-wobbly-venezuela/
55. Gustafson, I., "The Dubious Impact of Chinese Investment in Latin America."

56. Peters, E., "China's Evolving Role in Latin America: Can It Be a Win-Win?"

57. Watson, K., "What will China's investment do for Latin America?" July 7, 2015, BBC, http://www.bbc.com/news/world-33424532

58. Peters, E., "China's Evolving Role in Latin America: Can It Be a Win-Win?"

59. Ibid.

60. Bloomberg, "China's Pivot to Latin America."

61. Pacific Basin Research Center, "The Opportunities and Challenges of Growing East Asian-Latin American Economic Relations."

62. Gustafson, I., "The Dubious Impact of Chinese Investment in Latin America."

63. Peters, E., "China's Evolving Role in Latin America: Can It Be a Win-Win?"

64. Pacific Basin Research Center, "The Opportunities and Challenges of Growing East Asian-Latin American Economic Relations."

65. Coyer, P. "Undermining America While Washington Sleeps: China In Latin America."

66. Ibid.

67. Coyer, P., "Venezuela's Future - Mortgaged By Chavismo In Cooperation With China," January 26, 2016, *Forbes*, http://www.forbes.com/sites/paulcoyer/2016/01/16/venezuelas-future-mortgaged-by-both-chavismo-and-china/#602d262577bb

68. Ibid.

69. Ibid.

70. Ferchen, M., "China and Latin America: A Complex Reality," June 26, 2018, Brink News, https://www.brinknews.com/china-and-latin-america-a-complex-reality/

71. Wang X., "Mahathir's Pushback Against Chinese Deals Shows Belt and Road Plan Needs Review."

72. Pons, C. and C. Shepherd, "Venezuela's Maduro travels to China in search of fresh funds," September 13, 2018, Reuters, https://www.reuters.com/article/us-venezuela-china/venezuelas-maduro-travels-to-china-in-search-of-fresh-funds-idUSKCN1LS2UL

73. Churchill, O. "Mike Pompeo warns Panama and other nations about accepting China's 'belt and road' loans," October 20, 2018, *South China Morning Post*, https://www.scmp.com/news/china/diplomacy/article/2169449/mike-pompeo-warns-panama-and-other-nations-about-accepting

74. Reuters, "Chinese state media hits out at 'ignorant and malicious' Mike Pompeo for Latin America debt warning," October 22, 2018, *South China Morning Post* , https://www.scmp.com/news/china/diplomacy/article/2169576/chinese-state-media-hits-out-ignorant-and-malicious-mike-pompeo

75. Ferchen, M., "China and Latin America: A Complex Reality."

Chapter 11

1. Witthoeft, A., "What Is China's Objective With the 2018 16+1 Summit?" June 8, 2018, *The Diplomat* , https://thediplomat.com/2018/06/what-is-chinas-objective-with-the-2018-161-summit/

2. Ibid.

3. Transparency International, "Montenegro, 2018 Corruption Perception Index," https://www.transparency.org/country/MNE

4. Weidenfeld, J., "China's Europe Policy Poses a Challenge to EU Cohesion,"
August 16, 2018, *The Diplomat* , https://thediplomat.com/2018/08/chinas-europe-policy-poses-a-challenge-to-eu-cohesion/

5. Witthoeft, A., "What Is China's Objective With the 2018 16+1 Summit?"

6. Dorsey, J., "China Struggles With Belt And Road Pushback," September 17, 2018, Lobelog, https://lobelog.com/china-struggles-with-belt-and-road-pushback/

7. Ibid.

8. Heide, D. et al., "EU ambassadors band together against Silk Road."

9. Ibid.

10. Ibid.

11. Lo, K., "Netherlands keen on Chinese investment but wants belt and road to benefit foreign companies."

12. Heide, D. et al., "EU ambassadors band together against Silk Road."

13. Le Corre, P., "Europe's mixed views on China's One Belt, One Road initiative," May 23, 2017, Brookings Institute, https://www.brookings.edu/blog/order-from-chaos/2017/05/23/europes-mixed-views-on-chinas-one-belt-one-road-initiative/

14. Heide, D. et al., "EU ambassadors band together against Silk Road."

15. Ibid.

16. Escobar, P., "Why Europe is afraid of the New Silk Roads," April 25, 2018, *Asia Times* , http://www.atimes.com/article/why-europe-is-afraid-of-the-new-silk-roads/

17. Lo, K., "Netherlands keen on Chinese investment but wants belt and road to benefit foreign companies."

18. Le Corre, P., "Europe's mixed views on China's One Belt, One Road initiative."

19. Bisenov, N. and S. Lindhardt, "Linking China to the EU's 'gateway' for exporters," March 28, 2018, *Nikkei Asian Review* , https://asia.nikkei.com/Politics/International-Relations/Linking-China-to-the-EU-s-gateway-for-exporters

20. Ibid.

21. Lo, K., "Netherlands keen on Chinese investment but wants belt and road to benefit foreign companies."

22. Gabuev, A., "Belt and Road to Where?"

23. Lo, K., "Netherlands keen on Chinese investment but wants belt and road to benefit foreign companies."

24. Gabuev, A., "Belt and Road to Where?"

25. Zheng, S., "Can China play the globalisation card to win 'trade war' allies in Europe?" April, 9, 2018, *South China Morning Post* , http://www.scmp.com/news/china/diplomacy-defence/article/2140914/can-china-use-globalisation-card-win-trade-war-allies

26. Quartz, "The five port project creates float all boats scenario for the BRI in Europe," October 9, 2017, https://www.business.hsbc.com/china-growth/the-european-five-port-project

27. Le Corre, P., "Europe's mixed views on China's One Belt, One Road initiative."

28. Lo, K., "Netherlands keen on Chinese investment but wants belt and road to benefit foreign companies."

29. Bohman, V., J. Mardell and T. Romig, "Responding to China's Belt and Road Initiative: Two steps for a European strategy," June 26, 2018, Mercator Institute of China Studies, https://www.merics.org/en/blog/responding-chinas-belt-and-road-initiative-two-steps-european-strategy

30. European Commission, "Trade Policy. Countries and regions, China," April 16, 2018, http://ec.europa.eu/trade/policy/countries-and-regions/countries/china/

31. Le Corre, P., "Europe's mixed views on China's One Belt, One Road initiative."

32. Bloomberg, "EU to join Trump in criticising China's role in global trade," July 11, 2018, *Straits Times* , https://www.straitstimes.com/world/europe/eu-to-join-trump-in-criticising-chinas-role-in-global-trade

33. Agence France-Presse, "As China reaches out for help in trade war, European Union finds itself caught in the crossfire," April 7, 2018, *South China Morning Post* , https://www.scmp.com/news/world/europe/article/2140674/eu-feels-heat-china-us-trade-row

34. European Commission, "Trade Policy. Countries and regions, China."

35. Deutsche Welle, "The EU's other trade dispute: China," https://www.dw.com/en/the-eus-other-trade-dispute-china/a-44047566

36. Wu, W., "Action not words needed on foreign access to China markets, says chamber," September 19, 2017, *South China Morning Post* , https://www.scmp.com/news/china/economy/article/2111777/action-not-words-needed-foreign-access-china-markets-says-chamber

37. Ibid.

38. Agence France-Presse, "As China reaches out for help in trade war, European Union finds itself caught in the crossfire."

39. Ibid.

40. Zheng, S., "Can China play the globalisation card to win 'trade war' allies in Europe?"

41. Le Corre, P., "Europe's mixed views on China's One Belt, One Road initiative."

42. Agence France-Presse, "As China reaches out for help in trade war, European Union finds itself caught in the crossfire."

43. Reuters, "China pressures EU to issue statement against Donald Trump's trade policies," July 4, 2018, *Global News* , https://globalnews.ca/news/4311326/china-eu-trade-war-donald-trump/

44. Trading Economics, "Ease of Doing Business in China 2008-2018," https://tradingeconomics.com/china/ease-of-doing-business

45. Agence France-Presse, "As China reaches out for help in trade war, European Union finds itself caught in the crossfire."

46. TheGlobalEconomy.com, "Trade openness - country rankings," 2015, https://www.theglobaleconomy.com/rankings/trade_openness/

47. European Commission, "China remains chief concern in latest EU report on the protection and enforcement of intellectual property

rights," March 12, 2018, http://trade.ec.europa.eu/doclib/press/index.cfm?id=1813

48. Lo, K., "Netherlands keen on Chinese investment but wants belt and road to benefit foreign companies."

49. European Commission, "EU launches WTO case against China's unfair technology transfers," June 1, 2018, http://trade.ec.europa.eu/doclib/press/index.cfm?id=1852

50. Stearns, J., "EU Takes China to the WTO Over Technology-Transfer Practices," June 1, 2018, Bloomberg, https://www.bloomberg.com/news/articles/2018-06-01/europe-takes-china-to-the-wto-over-technology-transfer-practices

51. Reuters, "China pressures EU to issue statement against Donald Trump's trade policies."

52. Ibid.

53. Brattberg, E. and E. Soula, "Is Europe Finally Pushing Back On Chinese Investments?" September 14, 2018, *The Diplomat* , https://thediplomat.com/2018/09/is-europe-finally-pushing-back-on-chinese-investments/

54. Zhang, D., "Exit the Dragon? Chinese investment in Germany," February 5, 2018, Deutsche Welle, https://www.dw.com/en/exit-the-dragon-chinese-investment-in-germany/a-42457712

55. Kastner, J., "Germany toughens stance on Chinese investment," August 2, 2018, *Nikkei Asian Review* , https://asia.nikkei.com/Business/Business-Deals/Germany-toughens-stance-on-Chinese-investment

56. Zhang, D., "Exit the Dragon? Chinese investment in Germany."

57. Kastner, J., "Germany toughens stance on Chinese investment."

58. Ibid.

59. Agence France-Presse, "France to block Chinese group taking control of Toulouse airport: source," February 27, 2018, ABS-CBN News, https://news.abs-cbn.com/business/02/27/18/france-to-block-chinese-group-taking-control-of-toulouse-airport-source

60. Rosemain, M. et al., "France to bolster anti-takeover measures amid foreign investment boom," July 19, 2018, Reuters, https://www.reuters.com/article/us-france-investment/france-to-bolster-anti-takeover-measures-amid-foreign-investment-boom-idUSKBN1K922D

61. Klein, J., "It's not just the US: around the world, doors are shutting on Chinese investment," September 15, 2018, *South China Morning Post* , https://www.scmp.com/business/banking-finance/article/2163974/its-not-just-us-around-world-doors-are-shutting-chinese

62. MacAskill, A. and B. Martin, "Britain to tighten foreign takeover rules amid China worries," July 24, 2018, Reuters, https://uk.reuters.com/article/uk-britain-m-a-rules/britain-to-tighten-foreign-takeover-rules-amid-china-worries-idUKKBN1KD2DL

63. Kottasová, I., "UK cracks down on foreign investment to protect national security,
July 24, 2018, CNN,
https://money.cnn.com/2018/07/24/investing/foreign-investment-rules-uk/index.html

64. Klein, J., "It's not just the US: around the world, doors are shutting on Chinese investment."

Chapter 12

1. Press Trust of India, "BRI a made in China, made for China initiative: US official," July 30, 2018, *The Economic Times* , https://economictimes.indiatimes.com/news/international/world-news/bri-a-made-in-china-made-for-china-initiative-us-official/articleshow/65195619.cms

2. Ratner, E. (Testimony), "Geostrategic and Military Drivers and Implications of the Belt and Road Initiative," January 25, 2018, Council on Foreign Relations,
https://www.cfr.org/report/geostrategic-and-military-drivers-and-implications-belt-and-road-initiative

3. Lavin, F., "China is expanding its navy, and we need to consider why," September 27, 2018, *Dallas News* ,
https://www.dallasnews.com/opinion/commentary/2018/09/27/china-is-expanding-its-navy-and-we-need-to-consider-why

4. Military Education, "Show of Force: The Growth of The Chinese Military," 2018, http://www.militaryeducation.org/chinese-military-growth/

5. Xinhua, "China to increase 2018 defense budget by 8.1%," May 3, 2018,
http://www.xinhuanet.com/english/2018-03/05/c_137018039.htm

6. Lavin, F., "China is expanding its navy, and we need to consider why."

7. Connars, J., "A sleeping dragon rises: China's military buildup, September 10, 2018, *Asia Times* , http://www.atimes.com/a-sleeping-dragon-rises-chinas-military-buildup/

8. Cavanna, T., "What Does China's Belt and Road Initiative Mean for US Grand Strategy?" June 5, 2018, *The Diplomat* , https://thediplomat.com/2018/06/what-does-chinas-belt-and-road-initiative-mean-for-us-grand-strategy/

9. Chellaney, B., "China expands its control in South China Sea," September 17, 2018, *Japan Times* , https://www.japantimes.co.jp/opinion/2018/09/17/commentary/world-commentary/china-expands-control-south-china-sea/#.XAd6w2gzblU

10. Ibid.

11. Jaipragas, B., "Trump Strikes a Blow in US-China Struggle With BUILD Act to Contain Xi's Belt and Road," October 20, 2018, *South China Morning Post* , https://www.scmp.com/week-asia/geopolitics/article/2169441/trump-strikes-blow-us-china-struggle-build-act-contain-xis

12. Shi, J., "US competes with China's 'Belt and Road Initiative' with US$113 million Asian investment programme," August 2, 2018, *South China Morning Post* , https://www.scmp.com/news/china/economy/article/2157381/us-competes-chinas-belt-and-road-initiative-new-asian-investment

13. Ibid.

14. Overseas Private Investment Corporation, "Who We Are," https://www.opic.gov/

15. Washburne, R., "The US can counter China's 'Belt and Road Initiative'," September 4, 2018, *Washington Post* , https://www.washingtonpost.com/opinions/the-us-can-counter-chinas-belt-and-road-initiative/2018/09/04/533661d0-ad57-11e8-9a7d-cd30504ff902_story.html?utm_term=.165ff7816dfa

16. Ibid.

17. Shi, J., "US competes with China's 'Belt and Road Initiative' with US$113 million Asian investment programme."

18. Ibid.

19. Wroe, D., "Papua New Guinea rejects US criticisms of Chinese 'Belt and Road'," November 20, 2018, *Sydney Morning Herald* , https://www.smh.com.au/politics/federal/papua-new-guinea-rejects-us-criticisms-of-chinese-belt-and-road-20181120-p50h5o.html

20. Reuters, "Australia, US, India and Japan in talks to establish Belt and Road alternative: report," February 18, 2018, https://www.reuters.com/article/us-china-beltandroad-quad/australia-u-s-india-and-japan-in-talks-to-establish-belt-and-road-alternative-report-idUSKCN1G20WG

21. Zhu, Z., "Can the Quad Counter China's Belt and Road Initiative?, March 14, 2018, *The Diplomat* , https://thediplomat.com/2018/03/can-the-quad-counter-chinas-belt-and-road-initiative/

22. Ibid.

23. Ibid.
24. Csenger, A., "The Quadrilateral Security Dialogue (Quad)," October 11, 2018, Pageo, http://www.geopolitika.hu/en/2018/10/11/the-quadrilateral-security-dialogue-quad/
25. Wroe, D., "Papua New Guinea rejects US criticisms of Chinese 'Belt and Road'."
26. Chaudhury, D., "India not to join US-led counter to China's BRI," August 7, 2018, *The Economic Times* , https://economictimes.indiatimes.com/news/politics-and-nation/india-not-to-join-us-led-counter-to-chinas-bri/articleshow/65300729.cms
27. Ibid.
28. Lee, X., "Trump's tariffs threaten China's economy. It already has cracks," September 24, 2018, CNBC, https://www.cnbc.com/2018/09/24/trumps-trade-war-threatens-chinese-economy-china-already-has-cracks.html

About the author

Antonio Graceffo PhD China-MBA, works as an economics researcher and university professor in China. He holds a PhD from Shanghai University of Sport Wushu Department, where he wrote his dissertation "A Cross Cultural Comparison of Chinese and Western Wrestling," in Chinese. He is the author of 11 books, including *A Deeper Look at the Chinese Economy* , *The Wrestler's Dissertation* , and *Warrior Odyssey* . He has completed post-doctoral coursework in economics at Shanghai University, specializing in US-China trade, China's Belt and Road Initiative, and Trump-China economics. His China economic reports are featured regularly in *The Foreign Policy Journal* and published in Chinese by the Shanghai Institute of American Studies, a Chinese government think tank.

A Deeper Look at the Chinese Economy

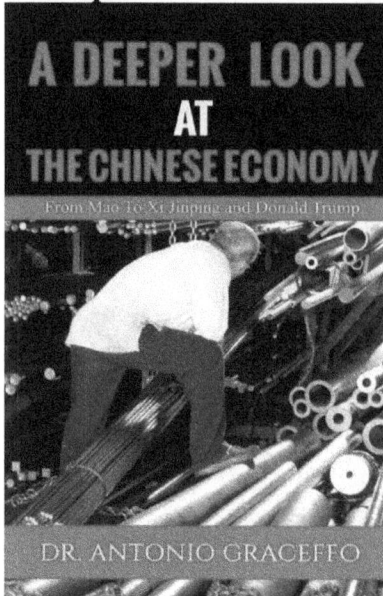

For the first three quarters of the last century, the People's Republic of China was one of the poorest countries in the world. Since the beginning of reforms in 1978, however, the economy has grown at an incredible pace. During the 21st century, the Chinese economy has emerged as the second largest and one of the most influential in the world. This book provides a very brief history of the pre-1978 Chinese economy, then focuses more deeply on China's engagement with and impact on the world, covering everything from China's rising middle class – which is now larger than the entire population of the US – to China's thirst for high-end consumer products. The Belt and Road Initiative, China's ambitious plan to go global, is closely examined, as are financial factors such as the internationalization of the currency, China's growing debt, and its shadow banking system. Finally, the dynamic between Chinese leader Xi Jinping and US President Donald Trump will be looked at in great detail, as Sino-US trade relations could change the course of the world economy.

Read more in *A Deeper Look at the Chinese Economy* by Dr. Antonio Graceffo, available in paperback and Kindle from Amazon.

The Wrestler's Dissertation: Chinese and Western Wrestling

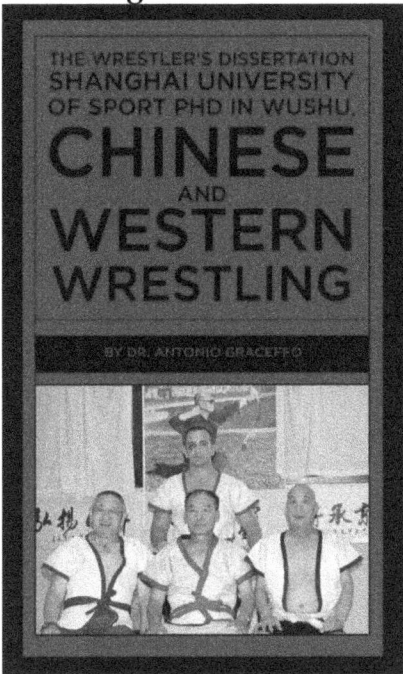

Pankration, Gladiators, Mongolia, Shaolin kung fu, Catch Wrestling, the Olympics, Wushu, Pro Wrestling, Sanda, and MMA...

The Wrestler's Dissertation traces the history and evolution of Western wrestling, from Ancient Greece, to catch wrestling champion Frank Gotch, and on to Gorgeous George, Hulkamania, and UFC champion Daniel Cormier. During the same period, across the Pacific, China was transforming itself from a loose collection of warring kingdoms to a modern nation state. Behind the Great Wall, Chinese *shuai jiao* wrestling was growing out of countless regional and ethnic wrestling styles from Mongolia, Manchuria, and Korea. Shaolin Temple was also incorporating Chinese wrestling techniques into wushu forms, and eventually sanda (kickboxing). In the last twenty years, Chinese wrestling has collided with Western wrestling in the Olympics, MMA, and now pro wrestling. This book explores the similarities and differences between Western and Chinese wrestling from a cultural, historical, and technical standpoint – and seeks to understand why Western wrestling is so much more aggressive, competitive, and violent.

In 2013, martial arts author and traveler Antonio Graceffo was awarded a PhD scholarship to Shanghai University of Sport (SUS). His major was Chinese wushu and his dissertation title was "A Cross Cultural

Comparison of Chinese and Western Wrestling." The entire three-year course was taught in Chinese, during which time Antonio conducted both academic and field research, training with the wrestling team, learning Chinese traditional *shuai jiao* wrestling, as well as Greco Roman and freestyle wrestling. At SUS, he cross-trained in Chinese sanda and Japanese judo. He also trained freestyle in Cambodia, sanda in Vietnam, catch wrestling in Singapore, and professional wrestling in New York. After graduating in 2016, he set about translating his dissertation into English. In Antonio's own words: "A standard PhD dissertation is a dry, academic affair with all of the life sucked out of it." This book, however, is not the actual dissertation; it is an English language version with all of the interesting bits put back in.

Read more in *The Wrestler's Dissertation* by Dr. Antonio Graceffo, available in paperback and Kindle from Amazon.

www.ingramcontent.com/pod-product-compliance
Lightning Source LLC
Chambersburg PA
CBHW031958190326
41520CB00007B/295